GW00541603

The Left and Israel

The Left and Israel

Party-Policy Change and Internal Democracy

June Edmunds

First published in Great Britain 2000 by
MACMILLAN PRESS LTD
Houndmills, Basingstoke, Hampshire RG21 6XS and London
Companies and representatives throughout the world

A catalogue record for this book is available from the British Library.

ISBN 0–333–73863–2

 First published in the United States of America 2000 by
ST. MARTIN'S PRESS, INC.,
Scholarly and Reference Division,
175 Fifth Avenue, New York, N.Y. 10010

ISBN 0–312–22605–5

Library of Congress Cataloging-in-Publication Data
Edmunds, June, 1961–
The left and Israel : party-policy change and internal
democracy / June Edmunds.
    p.   cm.
Includes bibliographical references and index.
ISBN 0–312–22605–5 (cloth)
1. Great Britain—Politics and government—1945–   2. Right and
left (Political science)   3. Great Britain—Foreign
relations—Israel.   4. Zionism.   5. Arab–Israeli conflict.   I. Title.
JN231 .E36   1999
327.4105694—dc21   99–38451
                                                                CIP

This book is printed on paper suitable for recycling and made from fully managed and sustained forest sources.

10   9   8   7   6   5   4   3   2   1
09   08   07   06   05   04   03   02   01   00

Printed and bound in Great Britain by
Antony Rowe Ltd, Chippenham, Wiltshire

Contents

Part II The CPGB, the French Left and Conclusion

6 **The British Communist Party and Israel: from the Establishment of the Jewish State to the Invasion of Lebanon**   **111**
    Changing Attitudes towards Israel   112
    Explaining the Evolution of the CPGB's Attitudes   119
    Conclusion: Comparing the CPGB and Labour   125

7 **The French Left and Israel: from the Creation of the Jewish State to the Invasion of Lebanon**   **134**
    The French Socialist Party   134
    The French Communist Party   147
    Conclusion: Comparing the British and French Left   154

8 **Conclusion**   **158**
    Policy Change: Internal and External Factors   158
    Intra-Party Democracy   166

Appendix 1: Sources   172
Appendix 2: Pro-Israel Labour MPs, 1956   175
Appendix 3: Pro-Israel Labour MPs, 1967   177
Appendix 4: Pro-Arab Labour MPs, 1967   180
Appendix 5: Pro-Palestinian Labour MPs, 1982   181
Appendix 6: Pro-Palestinian Labour Activists, 1982   183

Notes and References   184

Bibliography   196

Index   210

List of Tables

vii

Preface and Acknowledgements

This book is based on my doctoral thesis which was motivated by the debates in the late 1980s over the left's attitude towards Israel and the question of whether contemporary left-wing anti-Zionism was a new form of anti-semitism. As a student of race relations, I naively thought that it was impossible for the left to be racist in any way and I wanted to explore the issue further. Had I known how difficult this project was going to be, I certainly would have thought about doing something else. However, I did continue and, as the project evolved, I moved partially away from the initial question to the matter of how and why the left's attitudes towards Israel changed during the postwar period and the general question of policy change in political parties. On the premise that Israel's wars with the Arab countries and its treatment of Palestinian nationalism increasingly challenged the left's view of the state as progressive, I organised the study around major crises in Middle East history. Aware of the sensitivity of the topic, I have tried to avoid assessing Israeli policy, restricting myself as far as possible to describing Israel's rationale for engaging in the conflicts. Based on an inductive method, this study provides a simple account of Labour's, in particular, but also the British Communist Party's and the French left's attitudes, towards these various turning-points in Israel's history. Despite its narrative style and chronological structure, the project is not a history, partly because the requisite sources are unavailable and partly because I am not a historian. Nor is it a study of foreign policy or international relations. I carried out the research because of its intrinsic interest and in order to shed light on the theoretical question of political parties and policy change.

I could not have completed this study without the help of a number of organisations and people and I should like the opportunity to thank them.

Professional acknowledgements

The ESRC, the University of London Central Research Fund (Irwin Fund) and the LSE provided me with funding during various stages of this research project. This enabled me not only to carry out research in the UK but also in Paris, an experience that I greatly enjoyed. During the course of my work I used a number of libraries and archives and am grateful to all those who helped me with my research. However, I should like to single out Stephen Bird from the Labour Party archives at the Museum of Labour Party History in Manchester for being particularly helpful. At the LSE a number of academics provided an extremely stimulating environment for my studies and I thoroughly enjoyed and learnt a lot from the Sociology Department's Research Seminar. I should like to thank my doctoral supervisor, Dr Christopher Husbands, for his sharp attention to detail and for giving me a healthy respect for facts, something, which I did not really have before becoming his student. I am also indebted to Professor Patrick Dunleavy for his very helpful supervision given in a spirit of complete generosity. I should also like to thank Dr Rodney Barker and Professor Vicky Randall for their very useful comments and advice.

Personal acknowledgements

During my time doing this research I got to know a number of people all of whom, at different points, were good friends. However, there are a few who deserve a special mention. From the LSE I should like to thank Kathryn Dean and Mauricio Domingues for many interesting debates over a whole range of issues. In Canterbury, where I live, I have enjoyed the company of a number of people who were not at all related to my work and who helped me to forget my project for whole days! In particular, I should like to thank Derrie and John for their support and Nick for his patience and encouragement. My family has also always been very encouraging, particularly my parents, Mary and Hugh, who sacrificed such a lot for me to complete my studies. Robert and Asako deserve thanks for their support and for putting me up in London whenever I needed to stay and I should like to thank Alan and Susan, David and Eleanor just for being there. Finally, my most special thanks go to Josephine, who was born during this research, for being the most wonderful distraction and for giving me more pleasure than anything I know.

JUNE EDMUNDS

Abbreviations

ACCT	Association of Cinematograph, Television and Allied Technicians
AEUW, TASS	Amalgamated Union of Engineering Workers, Technical, Administrative and Supervisory Section
AFL	American Federation of Labour
AFP	Association France–Palestine
AUT	Association of University Teachers (not affiliated to Labour)
BOD	Board of Deputies of British Jews
BUF	British Union of Fascists
CAABU	Council for the Promotion of Arab-British Understanding
CERES	Centre d'Études et de Recherche et d'Éducation Socialiste
CGT	Confédération Générale du Travail
CIR	Convention des Institutions Républicains
CLP	Constituency Labour Party
CLPD	Campaign for Labour Party Democracy
CND	Campaign for Nuclear Disarmament
CNFM	Convention Nationale des Français Musulmans
COHSE	Confederation of Health Service Employees
CPGB (CP)	Communist Party of Great Britain
CPSU	Communist Party of the Soviet Union
CRIF	Conseil Réprésentatif des Institutions Juives de France
EDM	Early Day Motion
EEC	European Economic Community
EETPU	Electrical, Electronic, Telecommunication and Plumbing Union
EMU	Ethnic Minorities Unit
FBU	Fire Brigades Union
FGDS	Fédération de la Gauche Démocrate et Socialiste
FLN	Front de la Libération Nationale (Algerian)
GLC	Greater London Council
GMB	General, Municipal, Boilermakers and Allied Trades Union
ILP	Independent Labour Party

JAFC	Jewish Anti-Fascist Committee (CPSU)
JSG	Jewish Socialists' Group
LCC	Labour Co-ordinating Committee
LCC	London County Council
LCP	Labour Committee on Palestine
LFI	Labour Friends of Israel
LMEC	Labour Middle East Council
LPACR	Labour Party Annual Conference Report
LSE	London School of Economics and Political Science
MAP	Medical Aid for Palestine
MCF	Movement for Colonial Freedom
MESC	Middle East Sub-Committee (Labour)
MRAP	Mouvement Contre le Racisme et Pour l'Amitié Entre Les Peuples
MSF	Manufacturing, Science and Finance
NALGO	National and Local Government Officers Association (not affiliated to Labour)
NCLW (A)	National Conference of Labour Women (Agenda)
NEC	National Executive Committee
NGA	National Graphic Association
NGOs	Non-Governmental Organisations
NJC	National Jewish Committee (CPGB)
NLR	New Left Review
NUCPS	National Union of Civil and Public Servants
NUM	National Union of Mineworkers
NUPE	National Union of Public Employees
NUT	National Union of Teachers (not affiliated to Labour)
OMOV	One Member One Vote
PCF	Parti Communiste Français
PFLP	Popular Front for the Liberation of Palestine
PLO	Palestine Liberation Organisation
PLP	Parliamentary Labour Party
PS	Parti Socialiste
PSC	Palestine Solidarity Campaign
PSU	Parti Socialiste Unifié
SFIO	Section Français de l'Internationale Ouvrière
SFP	Scottish Friends of Palestine
SI	Socialist International
SOA	Socialist Organiser Alliance
SOGAT 82	Society of Graphical and Allied Trades (1982)
STUC	Scottish Trades Union Congress

SWP	Socialist Workers' Party
TGWU	Transport and General Workers Union
TUC	Trades Union Congress
TUFP	Trades Union Friends of Palestine
UCATT	Union of Construction, Allied Trades and Technicians
UNESCO	United Nations Educational, Scientific and Cultural Organisation
UNO	United Nations Organisation
UNRWA	United Nations Relief and Works Agency for Palestine Refugees
WCFS	Bundist Workers' Circle Friendly Society
WRP	Workers' Revolutionary Party
WZO	World Zionist Organisation

1
Introduction

Political parties and policy change

Political scientists have paid a lot of attention to political parties. A glance at a leading text on the subject reveals the diversity of their preoccupations. Scholars have looked at issues ranging from the origins of political parties; types of parties, including cadre, mass and catch-all parties; electoral identification with political parties and changing electoral allegiances; changes from class-based to postmaterialist politics; types of party system and the transformations of the party system (Mair, 1990, pp. 1–11). In the literature on parties and policy issues there has been a strong emphasis on how parties influence government policy and coalition formation (Katz and Mair, 1994, p. 1), stemming from the fact that parties are a part of government and can translate electoral opinion into practice (Budge and Keman, 1990, p. 1).

Surprisingly little has been written about how policy making takes place in political parties and internal decision-making processes (Harmel and Janda, 1994, p. 261). Most of the literature has tended to focus on party systems rather than parties' internal lives. It has been suggested that this tendency stems from a number of factors including, first, the particular role parties play in society which has led political scientists to look at their relative strength and the role of elected representatives; second, the inaccessibility of internal party documents and third, researchers' own reasons for studying political parties such as their interest in democracy. However more interest has recently been shown in the internal dynamics of parties (Lawson, 1990, pp. 106–7). The existing literature on parties' internal lives pays considerable attention to the location of power and whether or not the leadership has control over policy-making

1

or the parties' congresses or conferences (ibid., p. 112). That is, it is interested in whether parties are internally democratic. Michels (1959) first raised this question. He was particularly interested in socialist parties because they adhere in principle to internal democratic procedures. However he concluded that whatever the parties' intentions, they tend to move towards leadership control over time (Seyd and Whiteley, 1992, p. 204).

McKenzie's later study addressed this debate in relation to the main British political parties (McKenzie, 1963). Following Michels, he suggested that, despite the ostensible differences between the Conservative and Labour Parties in terms of the distribution of power, they are in fact quite similar. He claimed that in both parties the parliamentary leadership dominates the policy-making process. Furthermore he thought that this enhances parliamentary democracy because to allow activists to determine policy would undermine accountability to the electorate (Seyd and Whiteley, 1992, p. 20).

Some contemporary authors have disputed the notion of the inevitability of leadership dominance, suggesting instead that whether or not there is internal democracy remains an open-ended rather than closed question and that it depends on a whole range of contingent factors (Kavanagh, 1982). Minkin's (1980) examination of Labour's policy-making process lends support to this view. In contrast to McKenzie (1963), he suggested that intra-party democracy does not work in a clear-cut way. Rather it is rooted in the process of bargaining and concessions between the parliamentary leadership and the extra-parliamentary party, and that the leadership's authority depends on this process. Also in contrast to McKenzie, Minkin believed that intra-party democracy is not incompatible with parliamentary democracy (Seyd and Whiteley, 1992, p. 20).

In principle, Labour is committed to activists having a role in policy making. Composed of a direct membership – that is, individual constituency party members – and an indirect membership, including affiliated bodies such as the trade unions, both sections have a say on conference decisions (Seyd, 1987, p. 3). Until recently resolutions that obtained the requisite two-thirds majority at the party's annual conference were supposed to be incorporated into the official policy programme. The recent introduction of one member one vote (OMOV) is thought, at least by its advocates, to have enhanced the party's democratic structure by undermining the power of the unions' block vote.

However in the past the leadership and the Parliamentary Labour

Party (PLP), often with the support of the unions' block vote, tended to control policy outcomes (Seyd, 1987, pp. 4–5). Conference decisions that achieved a two-thirds majority have not always been included in the party's manifesto. Furthermore, measures taken in the early 1980s aimed at advancing internal democracy have not necessarily put a hold on the process of centralisation. Since then the leadership has put in place a number of measures that have empowered the parliamentary front bench and heightened the leader's control over party policy and strategy (Webb, 1994, pp. 109, 122). Similar claims have been made in relation to Labour's counterpart in France. In principle the Parti Socialiste (PS) is pluralistic and committed to the mass membership having a say in policy formulation (Criddle 1987, p. 153). Unlike the Labour Party, the PS does not have formal links with trade unions. Based solely on direct membership organised into sections, section representatives attend the Federal Congress in order to debate the policies that go on to the biennial National Congress. The National Congress elects the Directing Committee, which goes on to elect the Executive Bureau and the National Secretariat (Gaffney 1990, p. 62). It has even been suggested that the PS is the most internally democratic of the French political parties because it operates a system of proportional representation when electing members to its executive bodies (Bell and Criddle, 1988, p. 210). The party's factionalism results from these bodies allowing a diversity of opinion and the leadership's hands-off approach to Congress debates (ibid., p. 134).

Nevertheless, as in the British case, there has been a tendency towards leadership control, a state of affairs that was enhanced after the introduction of presidentialism. Policy debates have tended to reflect the distribution of power between the competing currents (Gaffney, 1990, p. 63). Even Bell and Criddle have qualified their portrayal of the party as the most internally democratic with the proviso that Mitterrand and his entourage were very dominant. They put this situation down to the nature of the political system under the Fifth Republic, where the presidential system and the frequency of elections 'demands leadership control over activists' and argue that the need to elect a president critically affects the party's programme (Bell and Criddle, 1988, p. 236).

There has been a lot less scholarly controversy over the nature of the British and French communist parties' internal structures. Both the Communist Party of Great Britain (CPGB) and the Parti Communiste Français (PCF) have been organised according to the principle of democratic centralism. In the case of the British party, this has entailed a highly centralised organisation with power located principally in the Political Committee (Callaghan, 1988, p. 235). Although the PCF allows internal debates, the higher bodies' decisions take precedence over these of the lower bodies (Raymond, 1990, p. 44).

The PCF's democratic centralism has meant that the political elite has tended to dominate the grass roots and it has been claimed that the elections and debates are perfunctory (Criddle, 1987, p. 154). The politburo's tendency to expell dissidents was not found in the PS under Mitterrand's leadership (Bell and Criddle, 1988, p. 134).

The other important question in the growing literature on political parties' internal lives is whether external or internal pressures are the primary determinants of party programmes. According to the external model, party policy changes in response to outside influences such as public opinion or problems in the economy. Proponents of this model suggest that party elites respond to external influences and alter their policy in an effort to win votes. This conception stems largely from the analysis of parties as vote maximisers. Supporters of this model believe that insofar as parties try to be inclusive, responsive and representative of public opinion, democracy is enhanced (Burns, 1997, pp. 514–16).

One of the difficulties of understanding programmatic change in this way is that it tends to underestimate parties' autonomy in responding to environmental changes (Mulé, 1997, p. 500). In contrast the internal model holds that policy evolves because of changes in the ideas of the party elites, who may modify policy for both political and economic reasons, including a deliberate effort to lead public opinion. In terms of the implications for democracy, supporters of this view feel that democracy depends on parties being able to persuade the public to support their positions (Burns, 1997, pp. 514–6). This model portrays party leaders as active rather than passive insofar as they can actively create and shape identities rather than reproduce them. According to this standpoint, societal divisions are important only to the extent that political parties mobilise the groups affected by them. Political parties act independently and formulate policy packages to create new identities, especially after major electoral defeats (Mulé, 1997, p. 500).

Recent studies of party change have therefore offered theoretical frameworks for understanding how programmatic developments take place. However there have been very few empirical studies of policy evolution through an examination of single issues (Burns, 1997,

p. 514). Although this charge has been made about the study of parties in the United States, the problem is general. Labour Party policy developments in the 1980s have been well documented. However the accounts cover a diverse range of issues such as internal organisational changes, nationalisation, unilateralism, membership of the EEC (Seyd, 1987), macro-economic policy, inflation and incomes policy, the unions, the market, the state and planning, social ownership and industrial democracy (Shaw, 1994, pp. 41–52). Moreover they have not explicitly tried to use these policy issues as a way of shedding light on the question of policy change. Furthermore, especially in the case of the Labour Party, authors have focused far more on aspects of domestic and defence policy than on contemporary international policies.

In this study I explore the issues of how policy change takes place and intra-party democracy through an examination of left-wing parties in Britain and France and developments in their attitude towards a single issue. I have chosen to consider left-wing parties because they are, ostensibly at least, the most committed to internal democratic procedures. Because of the relative lack of studies on Labour's international policy I have also chosen to explore an aspect of international affairs, namely the arguments over Israel. The Israeli–Arab conflict provides a pertinent case study because the history of the Middle East has included a succession of challenges to the left, enabling an examination of how intra-party factors interact with external ones. The issue itself, the Israeli–Arab conflict, is of intrinsic interest because socialists have found the question of nationalism particularly intractable, given the antipathy between the particularist principles of nationalism and the left's universalism. Faced with the need to confront nationalism, socialists have been faced with a further problem: how to reconcile competing nationalist aspirations.

This international problem is also of considerable current significance. Although the heated controversies over Israel in the 1980s have given way to calm and a new consensus based on recognition of the national rights of both the Israelis and the Palestinians, the issue remains a thorny one. The electoral victory of the right-wing Likud party and the Israeli government's subsequent retreat on aspects of the Oslo agreements led Robin Cook, who had previously signalled introducing an ethical element into Labour's foreign policy, openly to criticise Israeli policy. Moreover, despite the recent victory of the Israeli Labour Party under Barak's leadership and its commitment to speeding up the peace process, Israel's electoral system allows parties such as the right-wing Shas party considerable political leverage in key ministries. This could mean that whatever Barak's intentions, he might be forced to make compromises that could result in continuing difficulties in the peace process.

I focus principally on the British Labour Party in order to provide an in-depth empirical analysis. I consider mainly the evolution of the Labour Party's position from the postwar period to the late 1980s. Just one volume considers the Labour Party and Zionism in a methodical and detailed way, looking at Labour's policy in the post-First World War period and through various crises until 1948, that is, Gorny's (1983) account of the views of various strands of the party: the leadership, from Arthur Henderson to Clement Attlee; the Fabians through a consideration of the Webbs; and the Labour left, including the ILP. A critical limitation of this volume is its failure to grapple with the moral and political issues at stake for the Labour Party in its assessment of Zionism and the genuine sense of dilemma within the labour movement over the conflicting claims to Palestine (Lockman, 1984, pp. 135–6).

Using a narrative style, I look at Labour's responses to four critical turning points in the history of the Middle East: the period surrounding the establishment of the Jewish state; the 1956 Suez War; the 1967 Arab–Israeli War; and the invasion of Lebanon in 1982 and its aftermath. I have chosen to organise the book around these events for two reasons. First, they triggered debate within the left. Second, they represent important turning points in the history of the Israeli–Arab conflict and called into question entrenched attitudes, forcing socialists to confront rival national claims. Although the 1973 war was important, I have not included it because the debates centred principally on the oil crisis rather than the rival nationalist claims. This study seeks to shed light on the way Labour's ideology interacted with these developments and the process of policy change.

I consider the leaderships' attitudes and how they compare with other party sections' views, including the PLP and the constituency parties, trade unions and Labour Women. I also spend some time looking at the Labour left's views because of this faction's customary oppositional role. The fact that the study covers a fairly long period creates some difficulties about what is meant by the left. Here I am referring to groups that have defined themselves as being on the party's left, such as Keep Left, activists associated with the *Tribune* newspaper and, later, members linked with the Campaign for Labour Party Democracy in some way. What distinguishes them from other groups is their attempt to try to keep the leadership in line with policies defined as socialist at a given time and their decision to work within the party towards this goal. I describe groups and people such as these as the soft left and contrast them with far left groups such as Militant or Trotskyists, who, despite operating within the party, are committed to revolutionary politics.

For comparative reasons I provide a less detailed examination of the French Parti Socialiste and the communist left in Britain and France. With respect to the British–French comparison, the part played by particular historical and political circumstances needs to be addressed. Did French socialists' experience of Nazism produce a specific effect? Did the fact that France had a different colonial experience from Britain in the Middle East play a part in shaping left attitudes? Unlike in Britain, moreover, the French left has a history of fragmentation and rivalry between two large parties. Did this affect its approach to the Arab–Israeli conflict? The interest also stems from the fact that the French president has considerably more say in foreign policy than the British prime minister.

By extension, and because of the links between the French Communist Party and the PS as well as the PCF's centrality in the international communist movement, the French communists' approach to international affairs has attracted a considerable body of research. In contrast the CPGB, having been a much less significant player in British political life, has only spawned a tiny number of studies, of which the one by Newton (1969) is the most noteworthy. With respect to the communist left, the existing literature on its attitude towards the Middle East conflict assumes that its position has been unchanging and static, determined by ideological heritage and Soviet policy. The question of whether the communist parties' stance has generated internal dissent and whether national political factors have influenced their policy positions needs to be considered. For example, has the British party been less circumscribed than the French party, given the former's marginal position in the political system?

In the following section I shall give a brief overview of the left's traditional attitudes towards Zionism and Israel, followed by an account of the book's structure and some of the methodological difficulties involved in carrying out a study such as this.

The left, Zionism and Israel

Zionism is a Jewish nationalist movement that emerged in the late 1800s in response to widespread anti-Jewish feeling and activities in Eastern and Central Europe. It started as a secular movement and its primary aim was to create a sovereign Jewish state as a way of resolving the difficulties faced by the Jewish diaspora. After a period of growing Jewish settlement in Palestine, the state of Israel was formed in May 1948. Its creation resulted from war with a number of Arab countries, and the conflicts caused by establishing a state during a period of decolonisation in the Middle East have been central to the region's history throughout the postwar period and remain unresolved.

In general, the social democratic left has tended to be less hostile to Zionism and Israel than the Marxist and communist left and has been more sympathetic to the idea of a Jewish national identity. In the period after the First World War in particular, reformist socialists began increasingly to acknowledge Jewish national self-determination. Indeed they thought that Zionism was compatible with democracy and progress. British socialists such as George Lansbury and Ramsay MacDonald and French socialists such as Leon Blum sympathised with Zionist aims for this reason (Wistrich, 1979a, pp. 11–12).

Since its establishment, Israel has generally been able to count on the support of parties such as the Labour Party and the French Socialist Party. Harold Wilson in Britain and Guy Mollet in France expressed a strong attachment to the Jewish state. The social democratic left's identification with Israel rests on three main factors: the influence of nineteenth-century liberalism on social democratic thought – liberalism opposed the religious persecution of the Jews and fought for the removal of legal restrictions on Jewish participation in Western society; the tradition of reformism that enabled social democrats to reject aspects of Marxist doctrine and to view Israel as historically justified; and the historically close association between Western Jews and social democratic parties (Rubinstein, 1982, pp. 103–4). The Israeli Labour Party's dominance from 1948 to 1977 also contributed to this sense of unity. Starting off as Mapai in 1930, the Labour Party was formed in 1965 with the merger of three left-wing groups, including Mapai (Ovendale, 1989, p. 242). Like the British Labour Party, the Israeli one was a member of the Socialist International.

The picture has been quite different within international communism, which has traditionally shown considerable hostility towards Zionism because of its commitment to internationalism. The various national communist parties have tended to mirror the stand taken by the Communist Party of the Soviet Union (CPSU). Despite the sense of mutual identification between British Jews and communism in the 1930s and 1940s as a result of the rise of fascism and the communists' role in anti-fascist activities (Alderman, 1992, p. 293) the CPGB has consistently and mechanically adopted an anti-Zionist stand. The party saw Zionism as the weapon of the bourgeoisie, a reactionary movement that divided the Jewish working class. In the context of the Cold War, British communists viewed Zionism as an agent of American imperialism. Like the British party, the PCF held that Zionism was a bourgeois form of nationalism that divided the working class. Former Jewish members of the party have testified to the PCF's uncompromising line on Zionism (Kriegel, 1984). Faced with criticism, the party regularly persuaded prominent Jewish members such as Maxime Rodinson and Annie Besse (later Kriegel) to defend its view of Zionism (Caute, 1964, p. 202; Cohen and Wall, 1985, p. 93).

In the 1940s, socialists were confronted with two movements for national self-determination: Jewish and Arab. The question of Palestine divided the left in an unprecedented manner and cut across the division between colonialists and anti-colonialists (Howe, 1993, pp. 148–9). As the Israeli–Arab conflict intensified, especially in the post-1967 period, the dilemmas facing the left were sharpened. Sartre succinctly expressed this sense of predicament. As a result of his experience of the war, Sartre strongly identified with the Jews. He reported his horror of anti-Semitism in a short book on the subject (Sartre, 1965). However the Algerian national liberation movement also made him sensitive to the Arab cause. When the 1967 war broke out he felt torn by a sense of conflicting loyalties, and claimed that the conflict had paralysed the left. Despite devoting an entire volume of *Les Temps Modernes* to the hostilities, Sartre still concluded that the two cases were virtually irreconcilable.

As a result of the rise of Palestinian nationalism, a shift to the right in Israel and developments in the United Nations such as the 1976 General Assembly resolution stating that Zionism was a form of racism, the Israeli–Arab conflict continued to cause controversy. The new left, which identified with Third World national liberation movements, began to adopt the Palestinian nationalist cause.

Some parts of this movement articulated an anti-Zionist stand, depicting Zionism as a form of racism and colonialism and the state of Israel as inherently racist on the ground that it was built on the idea of a purely Jewish state (Weinstock, 1979). The disenfranchisement of Palestinians living in the occupied territories and the rise of the Likud right, which led to the 1982 invasion of Lebanon, sharpened the dilemma for the left.

The left's increasing criticism of Israel and the appearance of anti-Zionism led to debates about whether contemporary left-wing anti-Zionism was a new form of anti-Semitism. In Britain, the controversy surrounding Jim Allen's play *Perdition* (Allen, 1987) brought out the significance of this debate. The play's showing at the Royal Court Theatre Upstairs in London was cancelled at the last moment after protests that its central theme, Zionist–Nazi collaboration, was anti-Semitic. In the resulting furore the divisions within the left over Israel came into sharp relief. Lining up with Allen were people such as Noam Chomsky and Maxime Rodinson. Lining up against Allen were people such as the playwright Steven Berkoff (see Allen, 1987).

Reflecting on the Israeli–Palestinian dispute, Barbara Castle remarks:

> Though I was no Zionist, I always had an instinctive alignment with Israel. I was haunted by the horrors of the holocaust and could identify with the Jews' hunger for status and security. At the same time, I had sympathy with the Palestinians who had been turned off their land and out of their homes so that the new state could be formed. It was one of those problems which, like Northern Ireland, seemed almost insoluble (Castle, 1993, p. 242).

In this book I look at how Labour and the other parties under consideration dealt with the dilemmas raised by the postwar developments in this key Middle East conflict, how the policies evolved and what factors structured the policy changes.

The structure of the book

The book is divided into two parts. Part I examines Labour Party policy and Part II considers the British Communist Party and the French left and ends with a general conclusion. In Chapter 2 I look at how Labour's pro-Zionist policy was constructed and the consensus of support for the formation of a Jewish state by the time of the 1945 general election. I then consider the postwar government's subsequent abandonment of its pre-election commitments and the ensuing intra-party conflict. The chapter ends with a look at how the Labour leadership reverted to its pro-Israel stance soon after the new state was created. I consider the way in which internal dynamics, such as factionalism and the dominance of the Labour right, affected the party's attitude towards Palestine and how external pressures, such as the conflict itself and wider foreign policy considerations, influenced government and party policy.

By the time of the Suez War in 1956, Labour was a staunch supporter of the state of Israel. Given Labour's anti-colonialist ideology, Israel's role in the war against Egypt represented a particular challenge. How did the party reconcile its identification with Israel with its part in the anti-war campaign? Chapter 3 looks at the way Labour resolved this challenge to its previous consensus of support for Israel, showing how the consensus was maintained despite the party's impassioned opposition to British and French military intervention in alliance with Israel. I also identify the sources of dissent that emerged as a result of the war and investigate their dynamics as well as the way the leadership dealt with these discrepant voices.

At the time of the 1967 Arab–Israeli War the party's identification with Israel was deeply entrenched. Wilson was notably pro-Israel and the Parliamentary Labour Party (PLP) was similarly inclined. Israel's role in the conflict, especially its decision to continue its military occupation of the West Bank, the Gaza Strip and the Golan Heights, provided a major challenge to this pro-Israel orientation, as did the rise of independent Palestinian nationalism, stimulated by the defeat of the Arab states. These developments forced Labour to confront the opposing claims of the rival nationalisms. Chapter 4 considers the way in which Labour leaders, MPs and factions dealt with the dilemmas raised by the war. Was the party able to stand by its identification with Israel while it was in government? Did the growing divisions within the party over foreign policy affect attitudes towards Israel? Did 1967 stimulate a breakdown in Labour's consensus of support for Israel, and if so, who were the key dissenters? I look also at the leadership's reaction to emergent opposition to Israeli policy.

In the early 1980s Labour's approach to international issues was radicalised. The invasion of Lebanon in 1982 symbolised the rise of the right in Israel, taking place under the government headed by Menachem Begin, who personified Israel's post-1977 shift to the right. The invasion seemed to unleash a torrent of left-wing anti-Zionism in general. Chapter 5 explores how Labour responded to this further challenge to its pro-Israel tradition and the tensions that resulted from the invasion. It investigates how a new consensus emerged around support for Palestinian national rights. It identifies the major sources of the movement for Palestinian national rights within the party and assesses the movement's success in getting Labour to adopt a pro-Palestinian platform. It asks whether sections of the Labour Party, like other strands of the left, became anti-Zionist or even anti-Semitic. Finally, the chapter examines the ways in which the pro-Israel strand of the party tackled this new development and the eventual policy compromise.

Chapter 6 provides an account of the evolution of attitudes within the CPGB. The British party has never been a major political force. After a brief spell of some popular sympathy in the 1930s and 1940s, its history has been characterised by a sharp decline in its membership and electoral base. Consequently it has not constituted a serious rival to the Labour Party, a situation stemming partly from the nature of the political system (Newton, 1969, p. 1). Nevertheless there are good reasons for including the party in this study. First, although the communists' relationship with Labour has been difficult, there have been significant links between the parties, operating principally through the trade unions and the constituency parties. Second, the party's relative distance from the formal political system provides the opportunity to delineate the effects of freedom from the political establishment on policy positions. Third, it is worthwhile including a discussion of the CPGB for intrinsic reasons, namely the historical tie between communism and the Jews.

The communists' position on Zionism, Israel and the Palestinians largely mirrored that of the Soviet Union and fundamental communist principles. However Chapter 6 considers internal dissent over the question of Zionism, Israel and the Palestinians and changes in the party's attitudes. In the case of the Labour Party there was a breakdown in the consensus of support for Zionism and Israel, but the CPGB's position developed in a different direction. It ended up supporting Palestinian national rights, but also adopted a more accommodating approach to Jewish nationalism for the first time. This chapter therefore focuses on the breakdown in the consensus of opposition to Zionism and Israel.

Chapter 7 centres on the French left. The French left differs from the British left because it comprises two major parties, both competing for electoral support. The French Socialist Party, which started off as the Section Français de l'Internationale Ouvrière (SFIO) in 1905, became the Parti Socialiste (PS) in 1969. Like the Labour Party, French socialists have a strong tradition of support for Zionism and Israel. Leon Blum was actively involved in the Zionist effort to establish a Jewish state. In 1956 France allied itself with Israel in the war against Egypt under Guy Mollet's socialist government. In 1967 the SFIO remained one of Israel's strongest supporters. This consensus dramatically broke down in 1982, giving way to a significant pro-Palestinian current. Why did this breakdown occur? How did the French socialists' attitudes compare with Labour's? What kind of external pressures were at work in the French case and absent in the British?

Formed in 1920, the Parti Communiste Français (PCF) enjoyed considerable electoral support until the 1970s and was a serious rival to the Socialist Party. As a member of the international communist movement it maintained an anti-Zionist stand. In 1967 the two parties clashed over their respective responses to Israel's role in the war. Even so, was it the case that the PCF's position never changed? Was the PCF's ideology unaffected by the constraints imposed by its incorporation into the formal political process? Chapter 7 examines the evolution of the French left's approach to Israel. Chapter 8, the conclusion, describes the main themes concerning changes in the left's attitudes and then draws some conclusions about the theoretical question of policy change in political parties.

A note on research method, terminology and sensitivity

The nature of the research topic and the kinds of questions asked should direct the way the researcher conducts her or his research. This study's focus on policy and attitude change over time led me towards qualitative documentary research. Archive documents of the parties under investigation were the only means by which I could ascertain past policy positions and trends in the left's attitude towards Israel. My sources included both published and unpublished documents such as conference reports, biographies, political diaries, party newspapers and journals, parliamentary reports and early day motions (EDMs),[1] interviews and internal policy documents where available or appropriate.[2] The problems associated with archival research are numerous. Unlike other forms of research, such as questionnaire surveys, this type of research depends on finding data rather than generating it (Goldthorpe, 1991, pp. 213–14). This gives rise to a series of difficulties, including document availability, sampling problems when confronted with a profusion of documents and making inferences from factual statements (Platt, 1981a, p. 33). Moreover, once documents have been dug out they can turn out to be 'unyieldingly barren' (Goldsworthy, 1971, pp. 4–5).

During the course of my research I encountered some of these difficulties. Formal government rules such as the thirty-year rule meant that I had no access to cabinet documents on the 1967 hostilities and the subsequent conflicts. Moreover, although the Labour government's Palestine policy in the 1940s has been well researched, some relevant documents have not been released because of their sensitivity. The Labour Party itself operates a fifteen-year rule on its internal documentation, which meant that documents relating to the late 1980s were unavailable. I also came across incomplete archives. Neither Labour Friends of Israel (LFI) nor the Labour Middle East Council (LMEC) appeared to have complete records of their membership over the years, preventing a systematic analysis of trends in participation in these organisations. The British CP's archives contained some interesting internal documents on the 1956 crisis, but very little on the other wars. Rather dubiously, the PCF claimed that it had no internal documents whatsoever on Israel. Dryness was another problem. It was not unusual to trawl through several years' conference reports from the Labour Party, the TUC or Labour Women, only to discover that there was no reference at all to Israel. Alternatively the references were sometimes very dull. For example 'Israel' was listed in the index to one of Tony Benn's diaries, but I was disappointed only to find that Benn had had 'a long talk with Messaoud about Israel' (Benn, 1987, p. 83). Such experiences were not atypical.

These difficulties in turn gave rise to the question of bias and the plausibility of inferences. I tried to resolve these problems by using a plurality of sources in the hope that a consistent picture of party attitudes and policies would emerge. With this in mind I interviewed some people directly involved in the parties' debates over Israel, and although they came from different perspectives, some consistency in their accounts of policy changes did emerge. With respect to the Labour Party in particular, I carried out a quantitative analysis of EDM signatures to show trends in the PLP's attitudes. The use of EDMs is itself problematic, with parliamentary members sometimes signing them in an arbitrary way (Berrington, 1973, pp.

6–11; Norton, 1981, p. 89). Nevertheless groups of MPs have tended to unite around particular issues (Berrington, 1973, pp. 7–9). My own use of them confirmed my perception of opinion changes towards Israel derived from other sources.

A further issue that needs to be addressed here is the use of the categories pro-Israel or pro-Arab in this study. I attribute a 'pro-Zionist/Israel' category to individuals or groups who show a slightly more favourable attitude towards Israel than to the Palestinians, or a definite sympathy in this direction. This orientation may be expressed in assertions about Israel's right to exist, opposition to pro-Palestinian elements in the party and opposition to recognition of the Palestine Liberation Organisation (PLO). A 'pro-Arab/Palestinian' label is attributed to those individuals or groups who show some sympathy for Arab and Palestinian national goals. This may be expressed in criticism of Israel's policies with respect to the Arab countries or the occupied territories, outright anti-Zionism or declarations of support for Palestinian statehood and for the PLO. Such a simple classification obviously obscures subtle differences in positions within both strands. It lumps Michael Foot and David Watkins together as pro-Palestinian but obscures the fact that their views are different in important respects. However it is justified on the ground that it gives a feel for shifts in opinion. Although I have used these categories throughout the study and in different contexts, the categories are useful only as summaries and I have drawn out the more subtle distinctions in the text.

Finally, the sensitivity of the topic being examined should be considered. Research takes place in a political context, either institutional or interpersonal, which can affect the outcome of the work (Bell and Newby, 1977, p. 10). According to Renzetti and Lee (1993, p. 5), a topic is sensitive when it is potentially threatening to the researcher or the researched or both, and when this has problematic consequences in relation to the research. The sensitive nature of the topic in this study certainly had serious repercussions for the outcome of the project. As a researcher who did not belong to any of the constituencies being studied (I am neither Palestinian, Jewish nor a member of any political organisation), I had been unprepared for the consequences of tackling the issue. My motives for engaging in the research were constantly questioned, with some direct implications for access to crucial material. For example Poale Zion refused to allow me access to its internal documents on the ground that the question being addressed in my study was 'too fundamental'. A Palestinian who worked closely with the labour movement in Britain said that he would give me access to campaigning activities amongst the constituency parties if I allowed him to read my work first of all. Finally, a former editor of the *Tribune* newspaper, who had agreed to provide me with material on contacts between the newspaper and Palestinians, became less cooperative after I indicated that my interest in the topic had originally been motivated by an interest in the relationship between anti-Zionism and anti-Semitism. I do not blame these organisations or individuals for their defensive attitudes. Given the way in which people unsympathetic to their goals can exploit their respective positions, they are entirely understandable.

More importantly, however, the sensitivity of the topic was manifest in my often feeling that I was walking on a tightrope in my efforts not to offend either Jews or Palestinians, or sometimes even the left. In relation to the first two groups, the effect of reading an account of the suffering of the Jews under Nazism and then an account of the problems experienced by the Palestinians was very disorientating. I have tried to resolve the dilemmas of dealing with a topic such as this by being as neutral as possible. This has been partly achieved by describing the views of the left instead of entering into the debates that rage over the nature of Zionism, Israel and the Palestinians. However, even description can be infused with values and I do not deny that some of the accounts could seem biased. In conclusion, although I have been systematic and rigorous in my treatment of data, I do not pretend the story told in this book is complete and impartial. This is for two reasons. Firstly, the book is based primarily on 'relics of the past' (Goldthorpe, 1991, p. 213), with all their attendant difficulties. Second, the sensitive nature of the topic has limited the possibility of total impartiality.

Part I
The British Labour Party

2
The Labour Party and the Establishment of the State of Israel

Labour came to power in 1945 committed to anti-colonialism and decolonisation. The rival Arab and Jewish nationalist movements in the period leading up to the formation of Israel, both of which appealed to the party's commitment to national self-determination and anti-colonialism (Howe, 1993, p. 149), were an important test of the party's principles. The 1917 Balfour Declaration had led the Jews to believe that Palestine was to be their national home. They regarded the country as the natural place for a revival of their national identity and freedom from persecution because of its historical and religious significance for the Jews. However, although Zionism grew out of the oppression of the Jewish people, Jewish colonisation of Palestine looked like a continuation of outside domination to the Arabs (Said, 1992, p. 57).

Despite the difficulties posed by the Jewish–Arab conflict, Labour did little soul-searching over the rival nationalist movements in the period running up to the 1945 general election. As Denis Healey recalls, the movement was 'overwhelmingly pro-Zionist' by the end of the Second World War (Healey, 1989, p. 90). Between 1936 and 1945 the party's annual conference had repeatedly backed the creation of a Jewish national home or state. Successive TUC conferences had done similarly, arguing for Jewish refugees to be admitted to Palestine (Alderman, 1983, pp. 124–8). Although the Labour leader, Clement Attlee, was personally anti-Zionist, believing that Jewish nationalism was irrational and romantic, he publicly endorsed Labour's pro-Zionist policy in 1945 (Gorny, 1983, pp. 131, 206–7). Right-wing members of the leadership such as Hugh Dalton and Herbert Morrison

19

were pro-Zionist. Even Bevin backed Zionist goals during the war. The Labour left's identification with internationalism had previously made it sceptical about Zionism. Non-Zionist Jews such as Lucjan Blit, who represented the Bund in London, influenced this faction.[1] The Bund was a Marxist and anti-Zionist party that believed that the Jewish problem could be solved without resorting to a territorial solution (Alderman, 1983, p. 53). Yet Arthur Creech Jones,[2] Aneurin Bevan and Richard Crossman strongly supported Jewish nationalist aims. The radical left also favoured the establishment of a Jewish state. The leader of the Socialist League, Stafford Cripps, welcomed Jewish developments in Palestine as a just response to Germany's persecution of the Jews (Gorny, 1983, pp. 152–3). Fenner Brockway and most of the Independent Labour Party defended Zionist goals (ibid., pp. 185–7). Labour Women also supported the construction of a Jewish national home in Palestine.[3] How was this consensus of support for Zionism constructed?

The construction of a consensus of support for Zionism

To understand how Labour came to adopt this policy in 1945 it is important to consider a whole range of external pressures and internal party pressures and they way they interacted with each other. One of the most significant determinants was the experience of the Second World War and the Nazis' policy of genocide. The wartime atrocities against the Jews gave Zionism a moral legitimacy that transcended party factions. Dalton adopted the nationalist movement as a 'personal cause' after his experience of the war (Pimlott, 1985, pp. 389–90), claiming that the case for a limitation on Jewish immigration into Palestine had collapsed in the face of the 'cold and calculated German Nazi plan to kill all Jews in Europe' and the 'horror of the Hitlerite atrocities' (Dalton, 1957, p. 426). The war also profoundly affected Bevan. When he became the editor of *Tribune* he appointed Jon Kimche and Evelyn Anderson, a former German Social Democrat and refugee, as his assistants (Foot, 1962, p. 302). As a result of the Nazi crimes, the left believed that the Jews' claim to Palestine was morally justified, contending that their right to Palestine lay 'not only from an urge to act as a nation state, but perhaps even more from a primeval desire for a place where they [the Jews] can settle down and feel sure that in a few years they will not be treated as "aliens" and hounded out'.[4] Crossman reasoned that anti-Semitism had prevented the Jews

from committing themselves wholeheartedly either to Jewish nationalism or to assimilation, and that anti-Semitism provided the
historical justification for Zionism. For Crossman, 'history, reaching
its climax in the Nazi persecutions, had made these few survivors
of the Polish, Hungarian and Rumanian Jewish communities into
the members of a Jewish nation' (Crossman, 1946, p. 175). Other
left-wingers, such as Harold Laski, converted to Zionism after the
war. As a Marxist and Jewish, Laski had objected to the idea that
Jews were a separate national group, envisaging a world with 'neither
Jew nor Gentile, bondman nor free' (quoted in Martin, 1953, p. 207).
After the Nazi genocide of the Jews, Laski began to attend Poale
Zion meetings (Kramnick and Sheerman, 1993, p. 462), and in early
1945 he said that he felt like 'a prodigal son returning home'.
Rejecting his earlier view that religion was the opium of the
masses and his belief in Jewish assimilation, he became 'firmly and
utterly convinced of the need for the rebirth of the Jewish nation
in Palestine'.[5]
   The war created a groundswell of sympathy for Zionism throughout the labour movement. Parties in areas with a significant Jewish
community such as Finchley and Friern Barnet, North Hackney,
the City of Leeds Labour Party, Central Leeds CLP and Lewisham
Central Labour Party and Trades Council made a considerable contribution to this.[6] The North Eastern Federation of the Labour Party
at Newcastle Upon Tyne unanimously endorsed the demand that
the Jewish Agency in Palestine be given authority to develop to
the full the capacity of the country to absorb immigrants and called
on the NEC to combat anti-Semitism.[7] The Liverpool Labour Party
and Trades Union Council pledged 'the wholehearted support of
the Labour movement in the fight against anti-Semitism and for
safeguarding the Jewish future in Palestine'.[8]
   The party incorporated Jewish nationalism into its anticolonialist
vision, portraying it as a progressive form of nationalism. An important aspect of Labour's attitude towards colonialism was based
on social engineering or 'modernising imperialism' (Gupta, 1975,
p. 390). Leading party members saw Zionism as a means by which
the Middle East region could be modernised. Dalton, for example,
believed that Jewish immigration into Palestine would facilitate the
economic development of the area, largely through the introduction of advanced irrigation techniques.[9] Labour's Advisory Committee
on Imperial Questions used these ideas in its internal policy documents.[10] Even Bevin said that 'there would be a great welcome for

many more Jewish brains and ability throughout the Arab world. They possess the scientific, cultural and other abilities which the Middle East requires.'[11] This attitude was not confined to the right. The left believed that Jewish immigration would enhance the economic potential of Palestine. They argued that the Middle East was a region of 'vital imperial communications' which had been held back by 'a medieval land system', claiming that there was a need for a 'unified development plan for the Middle East, based on irrigation, land reform and new industries . . . a sort of Tennessee Valley Authority for the whole Middle East. . . . Into such a plan, Jewish colonization in part of Palestine . . . could be fitted without real difficulty.'[12] Left-wingers felt that Jewish colonisation of Palestine would facilitate the development of that country, encourage industrial development and raise the Arabs' standard of living.[13] They maintained that the Jews in Palestine were 'spiritually and physically virile, a progressive, civilised society' whose place in Palestine was of 'paramount importance in relation to the fate of democracy'.[14] Indeed many saw Zionism as a revolutionary movement that would bring Palestine into the modern world. Reflecting on the dilemmas posed by the contending nationalisms, Crossman commented:

> Looking at the position of the Palestinian Arab, I had to admit that no other western colonist had done so little harm. Arab patriotism and Arab self-respect had been deeply affronted . . . by the development of a national home; *but if I believed in social progress, I had to admit that the Jews had set going revolutionary forces in the Middle East* which, in the long run, would benefit the Arabs (Crossman, 1946, p. 176, emphasis added).

The ILP also supported Jewish immigration for this reason. Disaffiliated from Labour in the early 1930s because of its commitment to revolutionary politics, the ILP included ethical socialists such as Brailsford and Brockway, both of whom were principled anti-imperialists (Foote, 1986, pp. 151, 117). However they supported Zionism on socialist grounds, with Brailsford enthusing about the movement's potential for introducing socialism into the region and with Brockway welcoming the Jewish labour movement in Palestine as a 'constructive contribution to socialism' (Gorny, 1983, pp. 154–5).

Developments in Palestine reinforced this position. The Zionist movement was politically heterogeneous, but contained two basic elements: the fundamentalist strand, represented by the revisionists; and the moderate or liberal strand, including people such as Chaim Weizmann and Labour Zionists. Based on the principle of nationalist exclusivity, the Revisionist Party,[15] led by Jabotinsky, adopted a maximalist position towards the Jewish state, opposing any cooperation with the Arabs. In contrast the moderate strand was based on more universalist principles and favoured cooperative policies. These two elements were in conflict in the period running up to Israel's formation; however the moderates dominated both the international Zionist movement and Palestine Jewry. This situation stemmed from the social characteristics of Palestine Jewry. In the pre-state era the majority of the Palestine Jewish community was from Eastern Europe and involved in socialist traditions (Shanin, 1988, pp. 222–9). The Labour Zionist party, Mapai, formed in 1930 and led by David Ben-Gurion, dominated institutions in Palestine such as the quasi-governmental Jewish Agency in the 1940s. Moreover organisations such as the Histadrut (the General Federation of Jewish Workers) were integral to the state-building process (Lucas, 1974, pp. 119–38, 456). This situation produced an alliance between the Palestine Zionist movement and the British labour movement. Ian Mikardo believed that the 'great friendship' between Labour and Israel was based on the fact that

> Israel, the Yishuv, [had been] started by people who had immigrated to Israel mostly from eastern Europe, not entirely but mostly, with socialist ideals. Hence the formation of the Kibbutzim . . . the whole of the leadership of the Yishuv, virtually the whole . . . was of the left – Ben-Gurion, Eshkol, Golda Meir . . . and all the ideologues.[16]

For people such as Bevan and other left-wingers in particular, the idea that Jewish settlement of Palestine was a socialist enterprise was important: 'for these people [Bevan, Foot and others], those Jews in Palestine were socialists . . . socialists were creating Israel. The Labour left could not help but be excited'.[17]

The political alliance between Labour and the Jews also played a part in creating support for Zionist aims. Jews who came to Britain in the late nineteenth century brought with them not only Zionism, but also socialism and trade unionism. These East European immigrants concentrated in urban areas such as London's East End, parts of Manchester and Leeds, forming a significant Jewish working class.

The socialist Zionist organisation, Poale Zion, developed out of this population and affiliated to Labour in 1920, introducing leading Labour politicians such as Ramsay MacDonald to the movement in Palestine (Alderman, 1983, pp. 55–6). In the mid 1930s the Jewish community increasingly turned away from the Liberal Party towards Labour. This shift occurred partly because of the Liberals' decline, but also because of the Jews' economic position. By this time Labour had become the 'normal political home of the mass of poor working class Jews in Great Britain' (ibid., p. 115).

In the run-up to the 1945 general election, political opportunism played a part in Labour's pro-Zionist platform (ibid., pp. 124–5). The party, especially the leadership, saw that it was politically advantageous to adopt a pro-Zionist position. The concentration of Jews in particular parliamentary constituencies opened up the way for a situation of mutual electoral rewards (see Lawson, 1980, p. 14). Labour candidates in areas with a large number of Jewish constituents made explicit appeals to the Jewish vote. In Hackney North, for example, Harry Goodrich informed the Jewish community of Labour's pro-Zionist stand.[18] Two Jewish candidates stood for constituencies with substantial Jewish electorates: Maurice Orbach for East Willesden and David Weitzman for Stoke Newington (Alderman, 1983, pp. 126–7). Orbach made his sympathy for the Zionist cause known at a meeting organised by the Barcai Zionist Society.[19] Both candidates won their seats, although it is not certain that their victory resulted from Jewish votes and the party's pro-Zionist credentials. Candidates who tried to court Jewish voters in Hendon South and Prestwich[20] failed to win their seats (see Alderman, 1983, p. 127). Just before the election the Labour leadership tried to influence Jewish opinion. In May 1945, Dalton declared at the party conference that it was 'morally wrong and politically indefensible to restrict the entry of Jews desiring to go [to Palestine].[21] Whereas in the past Attlee had always objected to Jewish nationalism (Gorny, 1983, p. 137), in the period before the election he emphasised that Labour was the party that would enable the Jews to fulfil their nationalist ambitions (Alderman, 1992).

From the other side, Poale Zion, which had been affiliated to Labour since 1920, acted as a 'powerful pressure group' in the labour movement (Alderman, 1992, p. 315). In the period running up to the election it mobilised electoral support for Labour by stressing the party's Palestine policy.[22] Non-socialist organisations such as the Leeds Zionist Council, the General Election Bureau of the New Zionist

Organisation in Great Britain[23] and the Jewish press[24] also informed Jewish voters of the record of the respective parties on Zionism, suggesting that to vote Labour was to vote for Jewish interests. Labour's pro-Zionist stance was also constructed in the context of heightened inter-party, pre-electoral competition. With respect to Jewish issues, Labour had a distinct advantage over the Conservative Party. No matter how hard Churchill tried to show that the Conservatives had Jewish interests at heart, his efforts fell on deaf ears given the party's track record on Zionism, most notably its 1939 white paper on the restriction of Jewish immigration into Palestine. Moreover, unlike Labour the Conservatives did not have an antifascist current, and even contained anti-Semitic elements. Furthermore the Jewish population's socioeconomic status caused it to be more drawn to Labour than to the Conservatives, a situation that continued until the 1970s and 1980s.

These factors combined to put Arab nationalism at a disadvantage. Unlike Zionism, Arab nationalism had no ideological or political ties with Labour. According to Healey, Labour's overriding pro-Zionism sprang partly from the fact that neither the party nor the trade unions knew much about the Arab countries and that there were no socialist movements in the Middle East to draw attention to the Arab case (Healey, 1989, p. 90). Left-wing movements, either socialist or communist, have traditionally played only a marginal role in Arab nationalism and nationalist movements such as Nasser's have tended to be anti-communist in both theory and practice, implementing severely repressive policies to deal with communist elements (Halliday, 1975, p. 164). In the 1940s pan-Arabists based in Syria made appeals to socialist principles, but their socialism was lukewarm (Ajami, 1992, p. xiii). It was not until the rise of Nasser and Ba'athism in the 1950s and 1960s that Arab nationalism began significantly to draw on socialist ideals and to influence Western liberal or left opinion.

Nor did the Arabs have the moral legitimacy that Zionism enjoyed, resulting from the Arab states' role in the war. As a result of the German occupation of France, Syria and Lebanon came under Vichy control and in 1941 Iraq became pro-Axis (Ovendale, 1992, pp. 15–17). The British wartime government, which included a number of Labour figures such as Attlee, Dalton, Morrison and Bevin, was eager to check pro-German feeling in Arab countries and to this end generated a considerable amount of propaganda.[25] Moreover, during the war thousands of British troops were stationed in the Middle East. At the time, constituents' views on foreign and colonial affairs significantly constrained Labour MPs' positions. People such as Bevan almost certainly took account of popular feeling on this issue. *Tribune*, for instance, made a clear link between the Arab states' behaviour in the war and the refusal to recognise Arab demands. It suggested that the rival claims to Palestine had to be understood in terms of the Arabs' record against Britain and its allies:

> In the present war the Arab leaders, the Mufti, Rashid Ali (both now in Berlin), and their gang have sold themselves for cash to Mussolini, who exterminated thousands of their Libyan co-religionists. They have also sold themselves to Hirohito. . . . Hitler's agents were more difficult to trace, but we know there were many, including some of the most prominent Arabs.[26]

Moreover a fundamental ambivalence in Labour's thought on colonial issues (Howe, 1993, pp. 47–8) shaped the party's understanding of Arab nationalism. Labour's anti-colonialism was 'fragmentary' and 'fragile' (Morgan, 1994, p. 40), and when confronted with the rival nationalist movements this fragility came to the surface. Said has shown that West European colonialism in the Middle East and North Africa produced a belief system that conceptualised Arabs as backward, feudalistic and reactionary, and this lasted well into the post-Second World War period (Said, 1985, pp. 15–19). In particular, colonial history rendered the Palestinian Arabs invisible. Palestine contained a sizeable Arab population with, as a result of living under Ottoman rule and then the British mandate, a significant national consciousness, but Western politicians persistently denied the validity of this consciousness (Said, 1992, pp. 11–19). Despite having achieved paradigmatic status in the study of non-European history, Said has been accused of being theoretically inconsistent (O'Hanlon and Washbrook, 1992, pp. 141, 155–7) and of overstating his case (Ahmed, 1992, pp. 179–91). Although these comments have some purchase, Said's insights are of considerable empirical value and application to the case of the Labour Party, many of whose members held the popular image of Arabs.

For prominent party members, Arab nationalism did not have the same status as Jewish nationalism at a number of levels: economic, political and moral. Labour spokespeople on colonial affairs regarded the Arabs as backward and feudalistic. Arthur Creech Jones was fairly progressive on colonial affairs, having links with organisations such as the Anti-Slavery Society and the Fabian Colonial Bureau (Goldsworthy, 1971, p. 14). However he did not extend his empathy for colonial peoples to the Arabs, portraying the conflict over Palestine as one 'between the new order for which the Jews stand in Palestine and the *crumbling feudal system* for which a few rich Arab landlords stand' (Levenberg, 1945, p. 234). The extra-parliamentary left similarly viewed the Arab–Jewish conflict in terms of the Arabs' cultural, technological and political backwardness, saying that

> the great majority of the Arabs does not really know what Democracy stands for. . . . They were allowed to be led by a few half-educated landowners and greedy politicians who soon enough made their contacts with Fascism. Rashid Ali of Iraq, Haj Amin of Palestine, and Ahmed Maher of Egypt, are not unrepresentative specimens of the Arab ruling classes.[27]

Labour was largely ignorant of the Palestinians' aspirations. Leading party figures took no account of the Palestinians' views on Jewish immigration or their identification with Palestine. Dalton proposed a total transfer of the Palestinians, suggesting that 'the Arabs be encouraged to move out, as the Jews move in', a policy which he thought would make the Palestinians happier (Dalton, 1957, p. 427). This proposal was not merely an expression of Dalton's idiosyncrasy – Labour's annual conference unanimously accepted the policy in 1944.[28] Moreover the Labour left shared these ideas. In *A Palestine Munich?*, Crossman and Foot envisaged the transfer of the Palestinians from certain parts of Palestine. They claimed that this policy would give the Palestinians Transjordan citizenship making them, 'as they demand, citizens of an Arab state' (Crossman and Foot, 1946, p. 3).

So by the time of the 1945 general election Labour was, for a number of reasons, overwhelmingly supportive of the Zionist aim to establish a Jewish state in Palestine. Despite its commitment to anti-colonialism, it had very little sympathy for Arab nationalist aspirations. In July 1945 Labour entered office with an impressive electoral victory, having gained nearly twice as many seats as the Conservatives. The extent of the victory produced a new optimism within the party, raising hopes for radical reforms in both domestic and international policy. With Ernest Bevin as foreign secretary, the party believed that the government would break with past traditions and create a new international order based on stability and peace. Bevin dominated nearly all aspects of the government's foreign policy, including Palestine (Morgan, 1989, pp. 231–6). In the following section, we shall look at what happened when Labour won office.

The government and Palestine[29]

Despite this groundswell of sympathy for Jewish nationalist aims and opposition to Arab nationalism, the new government's policies broke sharply with the party's pre-election commitments. Immediately after taking up his new position as foreign secretary, Bevin told Attlee, 'we've got it wrong. We've got to think again' (Hennessy, 1992, pp. 239–40). As soon as Labour came to power, the leadership decided not to repeal the central clauses of the 1939 white paper, opposition to which was central to Labour's pre-1945 stand (Morgan, 1989, p. 209). In November the government announced the establishment of an Anglo-American Commission of Inquiry to investigate the conditions of Jewish refugees in Europe and the potential for mass Jewish immigration to Palestine. In 1946 the Commission recommended the immediate immigration of 100 000 displaced Jews in Germany, a policy sanctioned by President Truman (Gorny, 1983, pp. 199, 208, 213). Despite the PLP's support for the Commission's proposals, Attlee and Bevin ignored its recommendations.[30] In February 1947 Bevin told the Commons that the government intended to hand the Palestine Mandate back to the United Nations, and the leadership later refused to support the UN's proposal for Palestine's partition.[31] Finally, in contrast to the United States' decision to grant Israel *de facto* recognition upon its formation, the Labour government refused to recognise the new state. Even some of Zionism's most outspoken supporters in the leadership, such as Dalton and Herbert Morrison, sanctioned the anti-Zionist policy (Morgan, 1989, p. 209), and Creech Jones, who felt great sympathy for the aims of moderate Zionism, accepted Bevin's position (Louis, 1984, p. 385). Why did Labour, once in power, deviate so sharply from its pre-election stand?

Opponents of the government's policy have explained the departure from party policy in terms of Bevin's personal antagonism towards Jews. Crossman, Mikardo and Jon Kimche all believed that anti-Semitism played a part (Crossman, 1960, p. 69; Kimche, 1960, pp. 21–2; Mikardo, 1988, p. 4). Other commentators have been more ambivalent. Morgan suggested that Bevin was not anti-Semitic, but was 'without doubt emotionally prejudiced against the Jews' (Morgan, 1989, p. 208), while Louis denied that Bevin was anti-Jewish at all (Louis, 1984, p. 384). Nevertheless the Palestine conflict did bring out Bevin's (in particular) anti-Jewish ideas. In a contradictory way, anti-Semites have traditionally portrayed Jews as both capitalists and communists. They have also suggested that a worldwide Jewish conspiracy exists and have presented Jews as excessively powerful. Bevin drew on these traditional stereotypes. According to Kimche, 'Bevin found often that his bitterest opponents in the union were communists who happened to be Jews or Jews who happened to be communists. Either way, the connection became firmly planted in his mind' (Alderman, 1983, p. 119, note 3).

With regard to a Jewish conspiracy, Bevin claimed that the Jews were involved in a world conspiracy against Britain (Crossman, 1960, p. 69). The foreign secretary explained the outcome of the 1948 Arab–Israeli war in terms of the role of 'international Jewry' (Louis, 1984, p. 43). He made anti-Jewish jokes, attributing the United States' pro-Zionist policy to the 'purest of motives': the fact that the Americans 'did not want too many Jews in New York'.[32] He was also offensive about Jewish members of the party, claiming that the idea of a Jewish state gave him nightmares of 'thousands and thousands of Harold Laskis pursuing him down the road' (Shlaim et al., 1977, p. 61). Even the party's most prominent pro-Zionists held anti-Jewish attitudes. Dalton, for example, was 'a Zionist who could lapse into anti-Semitism' (Morgan, 1992, p. 130), referring to Laski as an 'under-sized Semite' and mocking him for his left-wing 'yideology' (Kramnick and Sheerman, 1993, p. 207). These examples reveal a deeply rooted ambivalence towards Jews even amongst people who were philo-Semitic. Herbert Morrison showed this clearly when he said that 'I have met many Jews in many countries. I know the London Jews very well. But the Palestinian Jews were to me different; so different that a large proportion of them were not obviously Jews at all' (Gorny, 1983, p. 125), implicitly introducing a distinction between acceptable and unacceptable Jews. It is therefore clear that leading Labour people succumbed to popular stereotypes of the Jews, confirming the thesis that anti-Jewish ideas are not restricted to actively racist groups (see Kushner, 1989, pp. 1–13). Such ambivalence has a long history, for example Ben Tillett, a nineteenth-century unionist, qualified his welcome to a group of Jewish immigrants as brothers with the remark 'we wish you had not come to this country' (Husbands, 1983, p. 161).

However it would be a mistake to conclude that these personal convictions dictated the government's policy. While the Palestine conflict exacerbated Bevin's anti-Jewishness, it is unlikely that anti-Semitism determined his position. If this had been the case, one would have expected a consistently anti-Zionist stand. In fact Bevin's attitude towards Zionism was instrumental. He moved from a pro-Zionist position to an anti-Zionist position and back again in a relatively short space of time. Like Attlee, Bevin tended to have personal reservations about Jewish nationalism, believing that the Jews were a religious group and not a nation. However he adopted a utilitarian approach to the question and this explained his support for the movement in the late 1930s and early 1940s. As a member of Churchill's wartime cabinet, for example, Bevin was a 'champion' of the Zionist cause (Gorny, 1983, p. 171).

It was not a sudden change of heart about the merits of Arab nationalism that determined the government's position. In government, Labour's foreign policy was constrained by the need to protect and further British interests abroad. Above all, an instrumental assessment of how these interests could best be served underpinned Labour's postwar refusal to implement its pre-election promises. Once in power, the leadership jettisoned the idea of a socialist foreign policy in favour of realism. From the outset, Bevin made clear that he wished to maintain Britain's international status (Morgan, 1989, p. 240). Moreover the cabinet contained a number of prominent right-wingers who shared this approach. Dalton, for example, was unrelentingly hostile to socialist foreign policy, campaigning against those in the party who did believe in such a notion (Jackson, 1968, pp. 63–4). The international secretary, Denis Healey, also favoured a 'tough, unsentimental' approach and became a 'belligerent supporter of Bevin's stance in foreign affairs' (Morgan, 1992, pp. 316–17) and tried to reconcile government policy with party feeling (Healey, 1989, p. 74). At the time, support for Jewish nationalism was linked with socialist foreign policy.

In the postwar period, Britain continued to have substantial financial and strategic interests across the world, but particularly in the Middle East (Morgan, 1992, p. 154). The foreign secretary thought that Britain's economic well-being depended on maintaining British interests in the region. Bevin's belief in the link between international policy and domestic prosperity was explicit when he said, in relation to Palestine, that Britain must maintain a continuing interest in the [Middle East] area, if only because our economic and financial interests in the Middle East are of vast importance to us and to other countries as well. I would like this faced squarely. *If those interests were lost to us, the effect on the life of this country would be a considerable reduction in the standard of living.* . . . *British interests in the Middle East contributed substantially not only to the prosperity of the people there, but also to the wage packets of the workers in this country.*[33]

The government's approach to the Middle East turned on a policy of non-intervention on the ground that intervention would undermine rather than strengthen British influence in the area. Bevin felt that to alienate the Arabs would jeopardise British interests. His priority was to appeal to the Arab leaders by refusing to use force and to replace the traditionally unequal relationship between Britain and the Arabs with one based on alliances and partnership (Louis, 1984, pp. 16–17).

Moreover the government implemented its policy against the background of the Cold War. Bevin and the rest of the leadership accepted the Cold War consensus, adopting a sharply anti-communist stance. The foreign secretary wanted to curb the Middle East's revolutionary potential and to avoid provoking extreme nationalist sentiment (Weiler, 1988, pp. 8–12). He believed that a Jewish state could be a revolutionary socialist state and that Russia's support for partition was based on the idea that 'by immigration they [the Russians] can pour in sufficient indoctrinated Jews to turn it into a communist state in a very short time. The New York Jews have been doing their work for them' (Louis, 1984, p. 43).

Developments in Palestine also contributed to the government's backtracking. After the war, revisionist Zionists began to challenge labour Zionism's dominance in Palestine, aiming to replace moderate demands with maximalist territorial claims (Shanin, 1988, pp. 226–7). Terrorist groups such as the Stern Gang and Irgun, headed by Menachem Begin, engaged in a series of anti-British attacks, including the bombing of the King David Hotel in July 1946 (Morgan, 1989, p. 211) and, more significantly, the hanging of two British sergeants in 1947. The latter incident caused outrage among the British public and a rise in popular anti-Semitism.[34] British soldiers went on the rampage in Palestine and anti-Semitic riots broke out in London, Liverpool, Manchester and Glasgow (Hennessy, 1992, p. 241). Attlee announced that while he appreciated 'the natural

intensity of the feelings of those who experienced the atrocities of
the Hitler regime . . . this [could] not condone the adoption by Jews
in Palestine of some of the very worst of the methods of their
oppressors in Europe'.[35]

In this context, the government thought it would be politically
popular to adopt an anti-Zionist position. Bevin needed to pacify
people whose relatives were located in the Middle East (especially
Egypt and Palestine) at a time of considerable economic austerity.
Hundreds of thousands of British troops were stationed in the region
in the immediate postwar period at considerable cost to Britain,
leaving the government susceptible to the opposition's jibes. Churchill
constantly exploited this theme (Louis, 1984, p. 11). Moreover the
rise of Jewish terrorism limited people's tolerance of the idea of
British soldiers being based in Palestine (Hennessy, 1992, pp. 241–2).

Nevertheless Labour's Palestine policy came to be known as one
of the government's major failures. Despite the anti-Jewish incidents in the main cities, the popular mood was generally sympathetic
to the idea of a Jewish national homeland. Morgan has suggested
that, in the aftermath of the war, Bevin fundamentally misunder-
stood popular sentiment and failed to understand the political
ramifications of Truman's sensitivity to the Jewish vote (Morgan,
1992, p. 158). Truman put pressure on the British government to
allow Jewish immigration into Palestine almost as soon as Attlee
took office. The United States condemned British policy, exploiting
in particular Bevin's decision to force Jewish refugees arriving in
Palestine to return to refugee camps in Germany (Hennessy, 1992,
p. 241). The Jewish–Arab conflict undermined the government's efforts
to forge a strong relationship with the United States at a time of
mounting tension between the West and the Soviet Union.

How did the government succeed in implementing a policy that
broke with the party's commitments and ideals? To answer this it
is important to look at the internal party dynamics. One factor
was the degree of internal loyalty the leadership was able to command.
In cabinet, Attlee and Bevin 'made an unbreakable combination'
(Louis, 1984, p. 5). Bevin dominated most of the cabinet and particularly the colonial secretary, Creech Jones, leading Zionists to
portray the latter as a sycophant (ibid., p. 453). Only a few cabinet
ministers challenged the policy. Aneurin Bevan argued forcefully
for partition and questioned the view that Britain's interests would
be damaged if the government did not comply with the Arab states'
wishes (Ovendale, 1989, pp. 187–8). He even threatened to resign

over the matter (Dalton, 1962, p. 199). Bevan and John Strachey argued that the Jewish socialist movement would rejuvenate the Middle East, but they and other pro-Zionists such as Emmanuel Shinwell were not sufficiently knowledgeable about foreign policy effectively to oppose the Palestine policy (Morgan, 1989, pp. 214–15, 209).

The leadership also depended on a fairly submissive PLP. Throughout much of the duration of Attlee's governments the parliamentary party was not particularly rebellious, its loyalty springing chiefly from a sense of shared purpose with the leadership. However organisational strategies, including the leadership's decision to divide the PLP into a number of policy-making groups, also played a part. Moreover many of the Labour MPs came from the professional classes, helping to dampen down rebellions (ibid., pp. 59–61). Furthermore, despite the fact that around one third of the PLP objected to aspects of Bevin's foreign policies, these discontented elements did not want to do anything to jeopardise the government's standing in its early years (Schneer, 1988, p. 60).

The government's strength also rested on its relationship with the trade unions, which backed the leadership on most issues in the postwar period (ibid., p. 134). Bevin's ministerial position made him one of the most powerful trade unionists, and as a minister he maintained critical links with the unions (Morgan, 1992, p. 151). The unions controlled the biggest proportion of the total conference vote and a reciprocal relationship existed, where Bevin could count on union support for his foreign policy in return for the representation of union interests in cabinet (Bullock, 1983, pp. 58–9). Despite the TUC's previous pro-Zionism, it supported Bevin's Palestine policy. For example, when the Histadrut asked the TUC General Council to pressurise the government into implementing the Anglo-American Commission's recommendations, the General Council refused and 'strongly urged' acceptance of British policy.[36] At the party conference the leadership consistently defeated the pro-Zionist strand and Bevin succeeded in getting oppositional motions withdrawn, including Poale Zion's[37] – when he advised the conference not to carry any resolution on the matter, the conference complied.[38]

Labour Women also backed the leadership's foreign policy. Mary Sutherland, the chief woman officer, wrote that despite divisions over international affairs 'we can be sure that our Foreign Secretary will continue to work with patience, firmness and frankness, to reach decisions on the issues before the Conference that are in harmony with the Charter of the UNO'.[39] In a later editorial on international affairs, *Labour Woman* commented that if there was no unity among the big powers 'it is fair to claim that the fault does not lie with Ernest Bevin and his colleagues'.[40] This section's reluctance to criticise the leadership reflected its historically weak role. Despite the fact that thousands of women entered the labour movement after women's suffrage in 1918, they remained marginal to policy making. Consequently Labour Women tended to be uncritical of the leadership (Graves, 1994, pp. 1–2, 12).

So, once in office, Labour abandoned its principles in favour of a policy that was broadly in line with the Conservative approach. At the end of the war Zionism was closely associated with the left's international agenda, but Attlee and Bevin rejected it, displaying the tendency for Labour to move to the right once in office. It was not anti-imperialist politics that led the leadership to adopt a pro-Arab stance. Bevin's decision to favour the Arabs over the Jews was rooted in a 'late Forties imperialism,' an approach which aimed to preserve Britain's strategic position and oil interests in the Middle East through a policy of partnership rather than domination (Hennessy, 1992, pp. 239–40). The foreign secretary's primary goal was to maintain British economic and strategic influence in the Middle East (Louis, 1984, pp. 15–17), and the left's hopes for radical changes in foreign policies were dashed. The government managed to implement a basically unpopular policy because of the extent of internal loyalty it could command in the immediate postwar period. Nevertheless the policy did stimulate some dissent. The following section considers the sources of dissent and the leadership's later return to Labour's pro-Zionist tradition.

Intra-party conflict and a return to the old consensus

Despite this support for the government a minority was willing to oppose the government's policy, principally the Labour left and Jewish party members. These groups overlapped because the Jewish members tended predominantly to come from the party's left wing, including people such as Sydney Silverman, Ian Mikardo, Maurice Orbach and Harold Laski. Other Jewish MPs, such as Barnett Janner and Barbara Ayrton-Gould, untiringly criticised government policy both in parliament and in public demonstrations.[41] Crossman and Foot were also vocal critics of the policy in parliament, in public and in the left-wing press. Local parties such as the Glasgow City

Labour Party,[42] the Southport Trades Council and Labour Party,[43] and Hackney North, Manchester Exchange and Leeds Central[44] all condemned the government's policy. At the 1946 annual conference, five critical resolutions called on the government to revert to its pre-election pledges, but were withdrawn at Bevin's request.[45] On the whole, the critics represented the oppositional voice of the left, with Crossman and Foot belonging to the Keep Left group of MPs[46] and Silverman and Laski having a history of rebelliousness (Morgan, 1992, pp. 61–2, 97).

The dissenters condemned the government for refusing to implement the Anglo-American Commission's recommendations. Silverman described the decision as a 'plain, naked war upon the Jewish National Home'.[47] Michael Foot appealed to the government to implement every item of the report in order to avoid a war that would 'leave an indelible and black stain on this country'.[48] They also held the government responsible for the rise of Jewish terrorism. Crossman suggested that the increase in terrorist activities was the direct result of the government's continuation with the policy embodied in the 1939 white paper. He attacked the government for arresting leaders of socialist and trade union organisations and others on the political left in Palestine.[49] In *A Palestine Munich?*,[50] Crossman and Foot systematically rejected the government's justification for the policy. They recalled the party's pledges of support for Zionism, including those made by Labour leaders such as Morrison and Dalton, and condemned the policy as 'appeasement of the Arabs' (Crossman and Foot, 1946, p. 28). They objected to the Palestine policy as one that put expediency before questions of justice and morality. Recognising the impossibility of pleasing both sides, Crossman and Foot commented that 'either course ... involves the risk of bloodshed; either course involves a measure of injustice for one side. The question to be decided is which course involves the lesser injustice, the lesser amount of bloodshed and the lesser risk to world peace' (Crossman and Foot, 1946, p. 4). Crossman's intervention exasperated Bevin, who observed that the former's ideas derived from 'his lack of judgement and his intellectual arrogance' (Louis, 1984, p. 419, note 61).

The 1948 Palestine Bill, introduced to deal with the termination of the British mandate, provoked some parliamentary rebellion. During the bill's second reading, William Warbey moved an amendment for rejection on the ground that it failed to make provision for the 'independence of Jewish and Arab States in Palestine as provided by the United Nations decision'. Silverman seconded the amendment and thirty Labour MPs supported it, including R. Acland, H. L. Austin, J. Baird, A. Bramall, F. F. Cocks, V. J. Collins, L. Comyns, W. G. Cove, R. H. S. Crossman, H. J. Delargy, M. Edelman, W. J. Field, B. Janner, J. Lee, N. H. Lever, B. W. Levy, J. Lewis, J. D. Mack, R. W. G. Mackay, I. Mikardo, E. R. Millington, M. Orbach, J. F. F. Platts-Mills, J. Silverman, S. Silverman, G. Thomas, W. Vernon, W. N. Warbey, L. Wilkes and K. Zilliacus, together with one Communist MP and Denis Pritt, an ILP member (Berrington, 1973, pp. 70–1, Norton, 1975, pp. 44–7). On 2 December 1948 Alice Bacon, Richard Crossman, Harold Davies, Barnett Janner, Ian Mikardo, George Porter and David Weitzman signed an EDM that criticised the government for the 'continued unsatisfactory situation in Palestine' and called for the government to 'support at the United Nations a settlement which would ensure the speedy international recognition of Israel'.[51]

The left's objection to the Palestine policy turned on the view that it represented a continuation of conservative policy and a rejection of socialist principles as the main directive of policy. Keep Left regarded the government's approach to the Middle East as an attempt to create 'an anti-Bolshevik bloc of reactionary Arab states', seeing the Palestine policy in terms of this wider objective (Berrington, 1973, pp. 70–1). The opponents consistently claimed that a conservative and traditionally pro-Arab Foreign Office had dictated the policy in order to preserve British interests, stating that

> It [was] no accident that the Labour Government's outstanding failure . . . occurred in the one field of action where there has been less change of personnel since the Chamberlain era than in any other sphere of the national life. The Middle East has remained untouched by the Labour revolution: the men, the practice and the policy throughout the Middle East . . . continue entirely with the accents of 1939 predominating.[52]

The left believed that the government's Palestine policy was based on 'narrow strategic calculations which would make the Middle East a strategic centre and base'.[53] Criticising the leadership, Laski said that

> neither Arab blackmail nor the strategy on which our policy in the Middle East was based should make these homeless wanderers

the victims of hesitation or timidity in Downing Street. A British statesman who sacrificed the Jews who escaped from the tortures of Hitlerism to the Arab leaders *did not understand the elementary principles of the socialism he professed.*[54]

According to Kimche, the Foreign Office had initiated a 'new look' in terms of its attitude towards the region, involving the establishment of treaties such as the one signed with Iraq in January 1948,[55] aimed at achieving a balance between the removal of British troops and the maintenance of British power. Kimche concluded that a Jewish state had no part in this scheme because the government assumed that Soviet influence would 'seep' into such a state through immigration.[56]

The left's opposition to the Palestine policy stemmed from its broader disillusion with the government's foreign policy. Divisions within Labour during Attlee's government centred principally on foreign affairs. From the beginning, two groups of left-wingers, Keep Left and a small faction of pro-Soviet fellow-travellers, began systematically to condemn Bevin's approach to international issues, disagreeing over ties between Britain and the Soviet Union and specific questions such as that of Indonesia. Keep Left was the most significant group, and Crossman, Foot and Mikardo favoured a neutralist, third-force position whereby Britain would stand between the two major powers (Morgan, 1989, p. 63). Silverman also belonged to the third force movement (Schneer, 1988, pp. 56–7) and advocated a socialist foreign policy (Morgan, 1989, p. 238). This element felt that the leadership had jettisoned its commitment to the principle of socialist foreign policy (Pelling, 1991, p. 99). In a sense the Jewish leadership in Palestine appealed to both of these groups. Its claim to neutrality in the conflict between West and East appealed to Keep Left's neutralism and to the communists, who saw such a stance as potentially pro-communist.

However, during most of the debates over Palestine the dissenters failed to make an impact. This was because the left was relatively weak at the time, having no significant base within the constituency parties or the trade unions (see Coates, 1975). Moreover the Labour left was internally divided and consisted of a number of separate elements, including pacifists, Keep Left and the fellow-travellers (Pelling, 1991, pp. 99–100). The parliamentary left was also numerically small. Keep Left had only 15 members and did not remain cohesive throughout the government. Moreover the leadership formed an organised response to the group, with Hugh Dalton, Morgan Phillips and Denis Healey launching a campaign against the left's idea of a socialist foreign policy. Other party members joined in this campaign, rendering the left incapable of influencing policy (Jackson, 1968, pp. 62–4).

Nevertheless, once Israel was established the gap between the leadership and its opponents narrowed. Attlee and Bevin maintained a publicly hostile attitude towards the Jewish state, criticising the Jewish lobby in the United States and making anti-Israel speeches in the Commons (Pappé, 1990, pp. 565–8). Yet behind the scenes Bevin started to make a series of gestures of friendship. As early as May 1948 the foreign secretary spoke of the need to secure Arab acceptance of the Jewish state and tried to convince Arab governments that the new state was permanent. In October he initiated the opening of a British consulate in the Jewish part of Jerusalem; an action that anticipated recognition (ibid., pp. 562–4). In January 1949 the government responded in a restrained way to the shooting down of five British aircraft over Egypt.[57] At the same time Bevin began to take a more relaxed approach towards Jewish immigration, announcing that Jewish immigrants of military age detained in Cyprus could leave as soon as transport was provided. Bevin's critics took this statement as an indication of a modification of policy towards Israel.[58] At the end of January 1949 Britain gave *de facto* recognition to Israel, and in April 1950 the government conceded *de jure* recognition, although it refrained from acknowledging Israeli sovereignty over the Jewish part of Jerusalem (ibid., p. 574).

The party also began to build bridges with Israel through a spate of networking with Zionist groups in Israel. In December 1949 an official party delegation, including TUC representatives, representatives from the Co-operative movement, Alice Bacon and the party's chair, Sam Watson, visited Israel and met President Chaim Weizmann, Prime Minister, David Ben-Gurion, Foreign Minister Moshe Sharett, Minister of Labour and Social Insurance Golda Myerson and Minister of Finance Eliezer Kaplan, as well as Histadrut representatives and other members of the Mapai Party. In their report, Alice Bacon and Sam Watson recommended full recognition of Israel, assistance with its economic recovery and the establishment of strong relations.[59] Later Herbert Morrison and Morgan Phillips joined the Labour delegation at a reception held by the Israel Histadrut Committee in London, where Morrison said that 'Jewish Palestine was one of the greatest experiments in the modern world'.[60]

What precipitated this policy shift? One factor was a change in the relationship between the leadership and the PLP. As the government's term of office proceeded, the parliamentary party began to challenge the former's dominance. The prospect of a general election made the leadership more vulnerable to internal criticism and the possibility of a divided party. A shift in the party's internal dynamics began, portending a decade of intra-party conflict and dissent, a decline in Labour's popularity and the rise of the Bevanite left (Pelling, 1991, pp. 105–6). The opposition exploited these difficulties and persistently called for the government to recognise the new state of Israel. Churchill argued with Bevin in the Commons over how best to serve British interests, forcefully advocating full recognition of Israel (Pappé, 1990, p. 568). The PLP's growing impatience with the government came to light at the end of January 1949, when at least 50 Labour members abstained from voting on what Attlee saw as a vote of confidence in the government's policy. Although the government won the motion of adjournment, defeating its critics by 283 votes to 193, increasing dissatisfaction within Labour was manifest in the abstentions.[61]

With the new state in existence, recognised by both the United States and the Soviet Union, a new international context existed. Internal opponents of the policy were in a stronger position to voice their dissent and the impact on the leadership was greater. The dissenters enjoyed a new legitimacy as Britain was now clearly out of step with wider international developments, especially with regard to the United States. The critics' claim that the government's policy had created a cleavage between the United States and Britain[62] hit a raw nerve with a leadership that was keen to forge a strong relationship between the two countries. Bevin and Attlee were still bitter about the Anglo-American division over Palestine, which they saw as damaging to the alliance (ibid., p. 565).

However Bevin's policy change stemmed principally from his concern to forge a strong alliance with the United States in the context of the heightening Cold War. After the Korean crisis, the division sharpened between countries falling within the Western alliance and those which were neutral. Israel's support for the UN in Korea was the first sign of its desire to ally itself with the West. The Israeli leadership's earlier displays of neutrality, designed to avoid alienating the Soviet Union and jeopardising Israel's arms supply from the Eastern bloc, began to give way to a shift towards the West. Ben-Gurion and Moshe Sharett both wanted Israel to be included in the Western bloc (ibid., pp. 561–3). The Foreign Office started to see Israel as a country that shared Britain's interests in the Middle East and rejected ideas about Israel moving into the communist camp (ibid., p. 571). The Foreign Office and the US State Department wanted to put the differences between the two countries over Palestine into the past in favour of a coordinated defence strategy. Bevin's aim to secure Anglo-American collaboration to combat the Soviet Union's influence overrode his fears about the Arab–Jewish conflict (Morgan, 1989, pp. 217–18; Pappé, 1990, p. 561).

By the early 1950s, then, Bevin's return to Labour's traditionally pro-Zionist stance was essentially complete. He even told the Israelis that his Palestine policy had been a failure (Pappé, 1990, p. 573). However, practical considerations and not a sudden spurt of pro-Israeli altruism determined the leadership's policy change. As Pappé has observed, 'the dynamism and logic of pragmatic policy . . . ignores past prejudices, psychological barriers, preconceptions or emotions' (ibid., p. 561). Bevin's return to a pro-Zionist stance resulted from his desire to check internal dissent in a climate of mounting unpopularity and, most importantly, to establish a strong Anglo-American alliance in the Cold War period.

Conclusion

A combination of outside and internal party influences therefore lay behind Labour's policy towards Zionism and Israel in the period prior to and after the formation of the Jewish state. External influences included the war, the socialist nature of the Jewish colonies in Palestine, the Arab states' role in the war and the nature of Arab nationalism, as well as domestic political considerations, including the Jewish vote, in a situation of inter-party competition. From the point of view of internal party politics, it was significant that people who worked in the party's decision-making bodies had an attitude towards nationalism that was paternalistic and contained an element of social engineering. This stance influenced how the party chose between the two nationalist movements, given that the one seemed to be based on Western values and the other not.

With the freedom of being in opposition no longer a factor, however, the government, under a mainly right-wing leadership, jettisoned the pre-election commitment to a socialist approach to international affairs. The key external factor now shaping policy was the constraint of having to protect and further British national interests abroad and the Foreign Office's view that a Jewish state could succumb to Soviet influence. The leadership was only able to abandon its position on Palestine and overturn its policy because it was, from the point of view of the party's organisation, now in a stronger position. Having had a massive electoral victory, the leadership could count on the PLP's support; it also had the backing of the trade unions and very little opposition from inside the cabinet. Its main opponent, the Labour left, was relatively weak, having no organisational base in the unions and being outnumbered in the PLP.

A combination of outside and internal pressures also interacted to produce the government's return to the party's pro-Zionist tradition. Once it became clear that Israel wanted to situate itself squarely within the Western domain of influence and had the support of the United States, earlier concerns disappeared and the government was able to reverse its policy without abandoning its basically pragmatic approach to international affairs. This was probably the overriding factor in the government's thinking, but in addition it could not continue to ignore the growing internal disenchantment with its policies, especially among the Labour left, which had begun to gain some ground in the party in the context of the government having lost some of its electoral popularity.

In the next chapter we shall look at Labour's position on Israel's role in the Suez War, the next significant challenge to the party's pro-Israel policy.

3
Labour, Suez and Israel: the End of a 'Special Relationship'?[1]

By 1956 the members of the Labour front bench were the most pro-Israel of politicians (Kyle, 1991, p. 89). Indeed all sections of the labour movement shared this sentiment, which was expressed at successive party conferences,[2] at TUC conferences,[3] in party publications such as *Tribune*[4] and by Labour Women.[5] At the same time the party's anti-colonial outlook had sharpened and anti-colonialism called for a sympathetic attitude towards Nasser's nationalisation of the Suez Canal because it represented an attempt to end colonial domination. Under the leadership of Hugh Gaitskell, Labour engaged in a vigorous campaign against the war and the previously divided party united behind the leader in all-out condemnation of the war. Yet the party's pro-Israel sympathies 'called for a less critical view of Britain's action, if not for outright advocacy, than that which was implied by the Labour Party's all-out opposition to Eden' (Epstein, 1964, pp. 174–6).

Alderman has suggested that Labour's stance ended the 'special relationship' between the party and the Jews (Alderman, 1983, p. 133). To what extent does this claim capture what actually happened? This chapter looks at how Labour reconciled its pro-Israel and anti-government stance. The first section shows that the war did not produce a collapse in pro-Israeli feeling. The second section shows that most of the party, especially the leadership, maintained a negative attitude towards Arab nationalism. The third section considers the reasons for the maintenance of Labour's traditional position on the Israeli–Arab dispute, and the fourth describes the way in which some members of the left started to question Labour's pro-Israel, anti-Arab stance.

Attitudes towards Israel

To some extent the war did produce criticism of Israeli policy. Gaitskell said that if Labour had been in government he would have warned Israel against aggression, and he supported the UN Security Council's resolution against the Israeli attack on Egypt (Epstein, 1964, p. 81). In response to one of Eden's speeches, the Labour leader remarked that the prime minister, instead of acting as a policeman, had gone in to 'help the burglar and shoot the householder' (ibid., p. 192), implying that Israel was the 'burglar', which went down badly within Anglo-Jewry (Alderman, 1983, p. 133). However the conflict did not generate a deep anti-Israel feeling. In fact the party exonerated the Jewish state by distinguishing Israeli actions from British and French ones.[6] Presenting the image of Israel as a small, embattled state surrounded by hostile Arab neighbours, the party depicted the Anglo-French alliance as aggressive and portrayed Israel's part as defensive. Throughout his attack on government policy, Gaitskell contrasted Israeli policy with British policy, saying that 'the devastating mistake that the Government have made in this matter is to mix up the Arab–Israeli conflict with the Suez conflict. . . . I warn them that until and unless they make a sharp distinction between these two problems . . . they will never get themselves right with world opinion.'[7]

Hugh Dalton similarly excused Israel, arguing that its action was a legitimate response to provocation from Egypt and refusing to accept the view that 'Israel [was] a wicked aggressor and Egypt an innocent victim of aggression'. Dalton's support for Israel was so strong that he supported the Conservative government's rejection of a UN Security Council resolution stating that Israel was an aggressor.[8] This exonerative attitude was not confined to the right. Tony Benn believed that the British government's denial of arms to Israel had made the state feel insecure and was responsible for Ben-Gurion's policy.[9] He and five other Labour MPs cabled the Israeli prime minister and asked him to confirm that Israel's action was limited to the 'protection of Israeli frontiers and elimination of Egyptian marauders' and that it had 'no connection with British action'. The message was signed by 'six lifelong friends of Israel' (Adams, 1992, pp. 121–2).

Labour did not view Israel as an equal partner in the tripartite attack on Egypt, believing that Britain and France had exploited the country for their own purposes. In a document circulated at an

NEC meeting it was claimed that while Britain's desire to maintain control over the region and France's aim to deal with Egyptian 'subversion' in Algeria lay behind their actions, the establishment of a unified Syrian–Jordanian–Egyptian Command had provoked Israel into taking defensive action.[10] Nor did the Labour left see Israel as colluding with the West, claiming that the 'imperial powers' had exploited the country's vulnerability: 'They [Britain and France] exploited Israel's difficulties, and the tragic error by which that small nation tried to resolve them, in order to launch a war against Egypt and secure control of the Suez Canal.'[11] The left believed that Britain's Cold War policy made Israel vulnerable because it excluded the country from defence pacts such as the Baghdad Pact, exacerbating the Arab–Israeli conflict (Foot and Jones, 1957, pp. 90–2). The Baghdad Pact was a treaty based on mutual defence and cooperation between Iraq, Pakistan, Turkey, Iran and Britain (Ovendale, 1989, p. 200).

After the war Labour tried to reinforce its pro-Israel credentials, suggesting that Israel should force Egypt to grant it recognition. Gaitskell stated that while Israel should withdraw from the occupied territories, the UN ought to guarantee the passage of Israeli shipping through the Suez Canal and the Gulf of Aqaba and protection from raids from Egypt, concluding that

> While we are completely opposed to the Anglo-French attack on Egypt, we in the Labour Party have always said that Israel could not be expected just to go back to the status quo existing at the end of October. The essential point is that Egypt should recognize publicly that the state of war is now at an end and that she therefore cannot exercise her so-called belligerent rights. The United Nations should insist upon this just as much as on the withdrawal of the Israeli forces.[12]

The Labour leader did not believe that Israel should compromise with the Arab countries, maintaining that if the Arabs had accepted partition in 1947, Israel would have been smaller (Williams, 1983, p. 553). Aneurin Bevan, Labour's foreign affairs spokesperson, objected to US pressure on Israel to withdraw from the Sinai and wanted Israel's position to be used as a bargaining counter to secure Arab recognition of the Jewish state (Foot, 1973, p. 540). After the war, Richard Crossman got in touch with Ben-Gurion with the aim of restoring good relations between Labour and Israel (Howard, 1990, p. 203). The PLP also remained overwhelmingly pro-Israel

Table 3.1 Pro-Israel early-day motions, 1956

Date of first tabling	Number and title	Party support	Main sponsor	Total number of names appended	Number of Labour names appended (and percentage of total names)
11 February 1957	42. Withdrawal of Israeli Forces	Labour Conservative Liberal	Edward Short (Labour)	126	81 (64)

during the crisis. The Labour MP Edward Short sponsored a pro-Israel EDM that attracted 126 signatures, 81 of which were from Labour MPs (table 3.1; see also Appendix 2). There were twice as many labour's supporters of the motion as Conservative supporters, showing that the Conservative government's policy did not stem from pro-Israeli sentiment. Eden accepted the Foreign Office's pro-Arab orientation, believing that Israel should give up some of the territory captured during the 1948 war. Moreover he had previously refrained from criticising Egypt for refusing to allow Israeli shipping through the Suez Canal. Nor did the party have a pro-Jewish reputation at the time, and it even contained people who had sympathised with the British Union of Fascists in the 1930s (Epstein, 1964, pp. 175–7). The Conservatives' unwillingness to sign the motion also reflected the partisan nature of the debates over Suez, drawing attention to the shift away from consensus politics.

For Jewish MPs, the dilemmas of the war were particularly acute (ibid., p. 174). With the Jewish community predominantly behind Israeli policy (Alderman, 1983, p. 131), Jewish MPs came under pressure to oppose Labour's anti-war policy. Barnett Janner, who was president of the Board of Deputies of British Jews (BOD) and the Zionist Federation, came under particular pressure, with the Jewish community challenging his position on the BOD.[13] Even the French General Zionist Party condemned Janner for having voted with Labour against the intervention, stating that the MP's conduct was 'incompatible with the moral obligations of a Zionist', and disqualified him from 'holding any responsible position in the Jewish national movement'.[14] Nevertheless Janner, along with the other sixteen Jewish Labour MPs,[15] voted with Labour in the voting divisions. He only refused to conform to party policy on the vote that took place immediately after the UN's condemnation of Israel and just before the Anglo-French attack because such a vote criticised Israel alone. Justifying his stand, Janner distinguished between the Israeli action and the British action, saying that Labour opposed the latter and not the former (Epstein, 1964, p. 195).[16]

For left-wing Jewish Labour MPs, the difficulty of reconciling their opposition to the war with their pro-Israel sympathies was even more acute because their involvement in anti-colonialist politics put pressure on them to adopt a pro-Nasser position. Ian Mikardo, Maurice Orbach, Sydney Silverman and Barnett Stross all condemned the government's response to Nasser's nationalisation of the Suez Canal.[17] However the stand of these MPs was far from anti-Israel. Like Janner, they distinguished Israel's role from that of Britain and France. Mikardo denied the suggestion that Israel benefited from the Anglo-French intervention, claiming that demilitarisation of the Sinai Peninsula would have been more helpful (Epstein, 1964, p. 195). Moreover he claimed that Israel's objectives were 'limited' and were a legitimate response to Egypt's sponsorship of the fedayeen (saboteurs) and the blockade on Israeli shipping.[18] Most of the Jewish Labour MPs responded to any criticism by saying that they represented their constituents and not the Jewish community, and Mikardo defended his obedience to the party whip in this way (Alderman, 1983, pp. 132, 199, note 27).

There were two exceptions to this pattern. Emanuel Shinwell, who had never forgiven Gaitskell for replacing him as minister of fuel and power in 1947 (Morgan, 1992, p. 222), publicly criticised Labour's policy. Shinwell was not actively involved in Zionist or Jewish organisations, having a background in trade unionism and socialism, and as a socialist he rejected Zionist philosophy. Nevertheless he had a strong emotional commitment to the Jewish state, rooted in his view of it as a refuge for Jews and an experiment in socialism.[19] Although he mainly voted with the party in the divisions, he deliberately abstained from the vote condemning Israeli policy. He publicly accused the government of failing to counter Arab aggression against Israel and suggested that the UN's failure to take speedy action explained Israel's military response. He strongly criticised those who portrayed Israel's action as a violation of international law, including people in his own party (Epstein, 1964, pp. 188–90; Alderman, 1983, pp. 131–2). Harold Lever, who represented the Jewish constituency Manchester Cheetham, also deliberately abstained from the vote that implicitly criticised Israel's action (Alderman, 1983, p. 132). Lever objected to the idea that Israel was the aggressor and supported Britain's alignment with the state and the government's veto of the UN Security Council's condemnation of the Israeli action.

Table 3.2 NEC members, 1956

Pro-Zionist/Israel	Pro-Arab/Palestinian
Alice Bacon	Barbara Castle
Aneurin Bevan	Edith Summerskill
R. H. S. Crossman	
T. E. N. Driberg (vice-chair)	
Hugh Gaitskell	
E. G. Gooch	
A. W. J. Greenwood	
M. Herbison (chair)	
Ian Mikardo	
S. Silverman	
H. Wilson	

Table 3.3 International subcommittee members, 1956

Pro-Zionist/Israel	Pro-Arab/Palestinian
Hugh Gaitskell	Barbara Castle
E. G. Gooch	Edith Summerskill
A. Greenwood	
R. G. Gunter	
M. Herbison	
Sam Watson (chair)	

Although he did not back the British attack on Egypt, he suggested that it showed the government's recognition of Israeli interests (Epstein, 1964, p. 190; see also Alderman, 1983, p. 199, note 26).

The balance in favour of Israel also remained in the party's policy-making sections (Tables 3.2 and 3.3). The NEC and the International subcommittee contained Jewish MPs such as Ian Mikardo and Sydney Silverman and people such as Gaitskell, Anthony Greenwood, Crossman, Bevan and Alice Bacon, all of whom had supported the formation of Israel for historical reasons. Although Barbara Castle sympathised with Nasser, she was not anti-Israel. Edith Summerskill was the only overtly pro-Arab member of the NEC and the International subcommittee and her views brought her into conflict with other NEC members (see Williams, 1983, p. 569).

Nor were there any signs of a grass-roots retreat from Labour's pro-Israel consensus. Speeches at the party's conference stressed the view that Israel wanted peace and that the West should arm the country in order to reduce its sense of insecurity.[20] At the TUC conference, speakers claimed that peace in the Middle East depended

on the Arab states recognising Israel.[21] Labour Women also remained
loyal to Israel. Like the rest of the party, this section exonerated
Israel for its role in the crisis, criticising the government's Middle
East policy on the ground that it threatened the existence of Israel.[22] At its conference in February 1957, Mary Mikardo from Poale
Zion moved a resolution condemning Egypt for its anti-Israel policies and called for a UN guarantee on the safety of Israel's borders
and shipping. The conference carried the resolution and Morgan
Phillips, the general secretary, sanctioned it.[23]

So Labour's anti-war campaign did not undermine the party's basic
pro-Israel orientation. Indeed the party rallied to support the Jewish
state, reconciling its anti-war stance with its support for Israel by
distinguishing sharply between Israeli actions and British and French
actions. This suggests that although the party's policy was badly
received by the Jewish community, the relations between Jews and
Labour were not irreparably damaged, as implied by Alderman's
claim (see Alderman, 1983, p. 133). In the following section I shall
consider the way in which the war affected the party's attitudes
towards Arab nationalism.

Attitudes towards Arab nationalism

Although Labour opposed the war against Egypt, the crisis did not
dramatically change its past hostility towards Arab nationalism. If
anything the hostilities showed just how deeply rooted its anti-
Arab feeling was, paralleling the Conservative attitude. This similarity
between Labour and the Conservatives was most evident at the
start of the crisis, when only Gaitskell's emphasis on Israeli interests
distinguished his position from that of the Conservatives (Kyle, 1991,
pp. 164–5). The Labour leader saw the Egyptian president as a dictator with expansionist aims and he opposed the nationalisation of
the canal, calling for US-backed sanctions against Egypt (Epstein,
1964, p. 66). Dalton went even further, welcoming Israel's defeat
of Egypt and claiming that 'the myth of Egypt as a military power
and a leader of the Arab world is smashed forever. All this is wonderful' (quoted in Pimlott, 1986, p. 687). In a parliamentary debate,
Dalton asked whether ministers had ever thought that Nasser should
have been left to the Israelis, since they 'were doing a very good
job'.[24] Herbert Morrison and other right-wingers such as Reggie Paget,
Frank Tomney and Jack Jones[25] favoured military action against Egypt
(see Williams, 1983, p. 569). Some TUC members also advocated

outright condemnation of the nationalisation of the canal and objected to the idea that force could only be used after referral to the UN. However the mainstream view prevailed in the end,[26] reflecting Gaitskell's influence in the TUC leadership (see Foote, 1985, p. 230). Throughout the crisis the leadership was at pains to show that its position did not imply support for Nasser. Gaitskell was contemptuous of people who sympathised with the Egyptian president, including John Hynd,[27] William Warbey, Tony Benn and Edith Summerskill, challenging what he saw as their automatic defence of any Eastern country and their failure to recognise that Nasser was a dictator. He believed that Summerskill's views stemmed from her being 'a woman whose political views are almost entirely dependent on personal contacts' (see Williams, 1983, pp. 567–9). The Labour leader publicly denied that the party was taking a 'pro-Nasser' line,[28] while Patrick Gordon Walker[29] advised the annual conference not to become 'pro-Nasser' because it was anti-government, distinguishing popular nationalism from the Egyptian leader's nationalism: 'We must come to terms with the genuine nationalism of the Middle East and cut the ground from beneath Nasser's feet by saying openly that we recognise the right of the Arab states to nationalise the oil wells and installations.'[30]

The TUC leadership made a similar distinction. At its conference, the head of the international committee said 'We must not let our legitimate criticism of the Government's handling of this situation be interpreted as praise for Colonel Nasser.... Nasser is a military dictator and this movement has no love . . . for military dictators.'[31] Even Bevan described Nasser as a 'thug' who needed to be 'taught a lesson' (Mikardo, 1988, p. 158). At the 'Law Not War' rally in Trafalgar Square he stressed that although he thought that Eden was wrong, he did not think that Nasser was right (Foot, 1973, p. 526). While opposed to the war, Bevan maintained that even the existence of Western imperialist interests in the canal did not justify Nasser's 'extreme nationalism', contending that 'it is no answer to say that the Suez Canal was an imperialist project from the beginning and that it has been exploited ever since. That does not establish Egypt's right to exploit the Canal in her own interests.'[32] Arab nationalism never had the same emotional appeal as Israeli nationalism for Bevan (Foot, 1973, p. 517). His perception of the Middle East drew heavily on traditional stereotypes of Arabs: 'the collective psychology of the Moslem states is definitely repulsive to me. It is so morbid and wildly irrational that I am conscious of an abiding sense of unease when I am in one of them' (quoted in ibid., p. 547).

Bevan's attitude impressed Gaitskell (Kyle, 1991, p. 190). Prior to Suez, he and the leader had been rivals. Gaitskell saw Bevan as volatile and had once even compared him to Hitler (Morgan, 1992, p. 225). As chancellor, Gaitskell provided the occasion for Bevan's resignation from government over NHS charges. In opposition, the two disagreed over German rearmament and Bevan resigned from the shadow cabinet. However the Suez War united the former opponents and they cooperated over the anti-war campaign. Gaitskell later rewarded Bevan by making him shadow foreign secretary (Pelling, 1991, pp. 107–18).

Bevan's position reflected his ambivalent attitude towards international affairs, putting him at odds with the rest of the left. Mikardo thought that his anti-Nasser statements had 'blunted' his attack on Eden (Mikardo, 1988, p. 157). The press commented on the emerging division between Bevan and the Bevanites.[33] One of *Tribune*'s readers remarked that 'as a disciple of Mr. Bevan, it was most disappointing to see "Our Nye" climbing on to the Eden–Gaitskell bandwagon of hate against Nasser and Egypt' (quoted in Kyle, 1991, p. 190). This development was highly portentous, presaging Bevan's growing alienation from the left wing. His new closeness with the right led to bitter differences with the rest of the Bevanite left, including Crossman, Castle and Foot. This became especially evident during the 1957 annual conference, when Bevan urged Britain to hold on to its nuclear weapons, reversing his previous commitment to unilateralism (see Morgan, 1992, pp. 216–17).

Labour's anti-Arab current was also evident in its treatment of the Palestinian crisis. By 1956 there were about one hundred thousand refugees living in Jordan, Lebanon, Syria and the Gaza Strip. Despite UNRWA's (the UN Relief and Works Agency for Palestine Refugees) efforts to provide the refugees with homes, medical and educational services and the Palestinians' success in finding employment in countries such as Lebanon, many of the refugees lived in very substandard conditions (Rodinson, 1970, p. 52). However the party showed little sympathy for their situation and the leadership marginalised people who drew attention to their position. Before the war, Anthony Greenwood reprimanded Summerskill for suggesting that some of the refugees should return to Israel, claiming that her proposal gave the false impression that Labour held Israel responsible for resettling the refugees.[34] Whenever the issue came up during the war, leading party members portrayed it as a problem that Egypt and the Arab countries should resolve. Dalton argued that the refugees should be resettled in unspecified 'Arab lands' and that Israel had no responsibility for them: 'There is no room for them [the Palestinian refugees] in Israel, that is clear. Their place has been taken by other refugees, by Jewish refugees from Arab lands and we cannot keep turning people round and round.'[35]

Even left-wingers portrayed the Palestinian incursions into Israel as instances of 'mindless terrorism'. As part of a series of visits to the Middle East in the early 1950s, Crossman inspected the refugee camps (Morgan, 1981, p. 195). Before the 1956 hostilities Crossman and Orbach had acted as 'mediators' between Egypt and Israel when the United States and Britain sponsored the peace plan Project Alpha, which involved Israel taking back about seventy-five thousand refugees and compensating the rest in return for a guarantee of Israel's borders and an end to the Arab blockade on Israeli shipping (Shamir, 1989, p. 77; Oren, 1990, p. 358). However the experience did not make Crossman sensitive to the Palestinians' situation. After the war he spoke of the impunity with which the 'Fedayeen gangs' entered Israel and said that he would not blame the Israelis if they tried to 'drive the Egyptians out and clean up the Fedayeen'.[36] Ian Mikardo described the Palestinian fedayeen as 'murder-trained infiltrators',[37] indicating a failure to acknowledge that many of the refugees who crossed Israel's borders were not sponsored by Arab states but trying to return home (see Rodinson, 1970, p. 68).

Labour's anti-war campaign, therefore, did not hinge on pro-Nasser sympathies and the hostilities did not produce a groundswell of support for Arab nationalism, especially on the part of the leadership, but also in the PLP, the NEC and the trade unions. In the next section I shall consider why the crisis did not significantly affect Labour attitudes.

Explaining Labour's policy

One of the reasons why the war did not dramatically affect Labour's outlook was that anti-imperialist politics played no part at all in Gaitskell's campaign against the war. On the contrary, as a member of the revisionist right the Labour leader disapproved of the idea of socialist foreign policy, favouring pragmatism over what he saw as left-wing 'utopianism' (Haseler, 1969, pp. 112–13). Ever since the Korean War, Gaitskell had been strongly pro-American and anti-communist (Morgan, 1992, p. 224). It was the leader's view that Britain's policy undermined the Anglo-American alliance, which principally lay behind his protest against government policy (Foot, 1973, p. 518). Under the Eisenhower government, the United States' desire to improve its position in the region led it to shift from a pro-Israel to a pro-Arab policy (Ovendale, 1992, pp. 157–8). The leadership's respect for the UN also determined its anti-war stance. Gaitskell constantly stressed 'the wrongfulness of acting outside the United Nations and . . . in defiance of the United Nations' (Epstein, 1964, p. 80; see also Morgan, 1992, p. 228), protesting against the government's failure to comply with Britain's pro-UN policy (Epstein, 1964, p. 75). Before the hostilities, Labour claimed that Britain should use the UN Security Council to help it resolve its problems with Egypt, saying that Britain should not contemplate using force without the UN's approval. Gaitskell argued that military intervention disregarded the UN charter. Labour's deputy leader, James Griffiths, centred on this theme in his motion of censure (ibid., p. 80, note 62).

Internal party pressure also persuaded Gaitskell to adopt an anti-war position, with people such as Denis Healey and Douglas Jay on the right and Barbara Castle on the left being particularly influential (Morgan, 1992, p. 228). Healey was more 'pacifist' and 'neutralist' than Gaitskell had anticipated (see Williams, 1983, p. 566), stemming partly from his distaste for the Soviet Union's invasion of Hungary (Reed and Williams, 1971, p. 112). Gaitskell himself admitted that Healey had strongly influenced his decision to oppose government policy (ibid., p. 112). A ginger group called the Suez Emergency Committee, operating from the offices of the Movement for Colonial Freedom (MCF), organised over two hundred and forty protest meetings across the country. Constituency party activists also protested against the intervention (Howe, 1993, pp. 270–2). The Labour left attacked Gaitskell for 'outdoing the Tories' in his response to the nationalisation of the canal and for comparing Nasser to Hitler, suggesting that the leader's proposal that Egyptian funds in Britain be blocked was 'indefensible in law or morality'.[38] Gaitskell's characterisation of Nasser as Hitler also went down badly, with Tony Benn feeling so embarrassed that he 'wanted to shout "Shame"'. As a member of the backbench foreign affairs group, Benn, along with his colleagues, had tried to persuade the leader to take a more oppositional line towards government policy (Adams, 1992, p. 117).

Labour's stance also reflected the shift away from consensus politics, especially over colonial policy. Under the impact of the rise of the Labour left and this faction's pressure on the party to adopt a more confrontational approach to foreign policy, in the mid 1950s the two major parties began to polarise over colonial issues and decolonisation, with Labour adopting a more moralistic opposition to colonialism now that it was in opposition. The previous agreement between the two major parties over the inevitability of decolonisation gave way to Labour strongly opposing the Conservative government's use of force, especially in British Guyana, and the Suez crisis almost led to a 'total break-down in communication' between the two parties (Kavanagh and Morris, 1989, pp. 97–9).

Although the anti-war campaign satisfied a variety of elements in the party, including pacifists, anti-colonialists and UN supporters (Epstein, 1964, pp. 78–9), this unity obscured some fundamental differences between the factions. It was not pro-American feeling that led left-wingers such as Bevan and Crossman to oppose the war. Bevan was deeply suspicious of US motives in the Middle East (Foot, 1973, p. 517). Critical of US and Soviet policy, he wanted the two powers to disengage from the region. In the postwar period Gaitskell went on to support the Eisenhower Doctrine, whereas Bevan opposed it to the same degree as he had objected to the Anglo-French intervention (ibid., pp. 536, 539). Crossman believed that the US policy of appeasement with regard to the Arab states had previously shaped British policy, contending that the consequence of US patronage of the Middle East was 'the job of bribing the Arabs on our side by sacrificing the essential rights of the Jews'.[39]

Labour's reluctance to acknowledge Nasser's nationalist movement also stemmed from the nature of the Egyptian regime. The leadership, in particular, was unwilling to embrace a movement that was not social democratic. Nasser's desire to increase Egypt's independence and modernise the economy by adopting a neutralist position had a progressive element. The Suez campaign turned him into something of a hero within Arab nationalism, scuppering Britain and France's intention to weaken the Egyptian leader (Rodinson, 1970, p. 77). However in terms of internal policies Nasser's promise of progress and democratic control of the economy turned out to be superficial. Through a system of state control over the economy, landowners, officers and bureaucrats continued to have a monopoly over power and the Egyptian people suffered considerably as a result of Egypt's foreign policies (Halliday, 1979, p. 21). Moreover, although Nasser opened up the political system with elections to the legislative assembly and by giving the left greater freedom of expression, the military remained overwhelmingly powerful (Rodinson, 1970, p. 81).

Labour's neglect of the Palestinian refugee question reflected the Palestinians' dependence on Nasser. In the 1950s the Palestinian cause was intimately bound up with Egypt and Palestinian activists were 'drawn into the orbit of Nasserism' (Ajami, 1992, p. xv). Although Nasser's policy towards the refugees was ambivalent and instrumental, Palestinians living in Jordan, Syria and Lebanon saw the Egyptian leader as their natural ally against Israel. While Palestinians in Egypt and the Gaza Strip were more sceptical about the president, Egypt sponsored some (although not all) of the raids into Israel. However there is a sense in which the Suez crisis helped to stimulate Palestinian nationalist consciousness, precipitating the formation of Fatah, which later became the dominant faction of the PLO (Khalidi, 1989, p. 387). This development would later prove critical to Labour's subsequent shift towards a pro-Palestinian stance.

The party's hostility towards Nasserism also reflected its ambivalence towards anti-imperialist movements, particularly on the part of the right wing. Gaitskell, Dalton and Morrison all valued a pragmatic approach to international affairs. The Labour leadership's aims were not dissimilar from those of the Conservative government insofar as they prioritised the protection of British interests. The difference between the two turned on the means by which these interests could best be protected rather than the aims, with Labour believing that force was not the way (see Epstein, 1964, p. 28). Carlton has suggested that this sentiment stirred the leadership's protests over Suez and represented a form of 'inverted jingoism' (Carlton, 1988, p. 107). Gaitskell initially opposed Nasser because he felt that the nationalisation of the canal threatened British interests in the region and he did not believe that these should be sacrificed in favour of anti-imperialist nationalism (see Williams, 1983, p. 558). The Labour leader felt that stability in the Middle East was vital to Britain's oil interests.[40] A number of backbenchers objected to intervention against Egypt because they believed that it would 'inflame the Arab nations against us and have the gravest repercussions in Asia and Africa'.[41] John Strachey,[42] a member of the revisionist right, argued that 'We are supposed . . . to be safeguarding our oil supplies, but where will our oil supplies be if we are at war with every Muslim state between the Persian Gulf and the Atlantic?'[43] Even

Bevan argued that the Suez Canal was critical to Europe's supply of oil, giving Egypt the potential to put 'a stranglehold on the economic life of Europe'.[44]

Nor was it politically advantageous for Labour to identify too closely with Arab nationalism. In an attempt to portray the opposition as unpatriotic, Conservatives derided Labour for being 'Nasser's party' or 'Nasser's little lackey', playing on its reputation for failing to protect national interests (Epstein, 1964, p. 75). By opposing the war and simultaneously objecting to Nasser, Labour could avoid being explicitly jingoistic while continuing to allay public fears by appealing to popular hostility towards Arabs. While the general public was split along party lines over Suez, some leading party members were worried that support for Egypt would alienate working-class voters. Bevan, for example, thought that middle-class ideas overly influenced Labour's approach to foreign affairs (ibid., pp. 147–8). The Arab states' role in the Second World War had created some wariness among the British public. Before the 1956 hostilities, opinion polls suggested that there was widespread opposition to the hostilities. However, once the conflict started the public showed a lot more sympathy for the government and 'rallied to support' Britain's position (Howe, 1993, p. 273).

Labour's continuing sympathy for Israel reflected a number of ideological and non-ideological factors. First, whereas it opposed Nasser for being anti-social democratic, it supported the Jewish state for its commitment to social democratic principles. Defending the Jewish state, Dalton appealed to its democratic nature and said that 'I am not a Jew. But I am a very warm admirer of the achievements of the State of Israel. In this, I am in the mainstream of thought and sympathy of the British Labour Party, which has always been very friendly to the State of Israel.'[45] Greenwood stated that Israel was the only country in the Middle East 'which [thought] and [felt] and [had] the same standards as ourselves'.[46] These ideas were pervasive in the party. The Labour left believed that Israel's socialist experiment would raise the Arabs' standard of living and teach them progressive practices.[47] This sense of common politics led Labour to ignore developments in Israel including the rise of hard-liners such as Ben-Gurion over moderates such as Sharett. As Israel's prime minister between 1953 and 1955, Sharett negotiated with Egyptian officers and his diplomatic approach to the conflict impressed Nasser (Rodinson, 1970, p. 69). Ben-Gurion initiated a campaign against Sharett's moderation, forcing his resignation in 1955 so that he could become leader again. It was Ben-Gurion's tough approach to foreign policy that provided the backdrop to the 1956 conflict (Shanin, 1988).

Whereas Labour had no political links with Arab nationalism, it had strong ones with the Israeli government and Labour Party. Gaitskell's visit to Israel in 1953 had already sharpened his pro-Israeli leanings (Williams, 1979, p. 421). Dalton was also influenced by his links with the Israelis, having met Sharett, a former student of his at the LSE, and other members of the Knesset during one of his visits to Israel. After one visit he claimed that Israel was a country based on the principle of social equality (Pimlott, 1985, p. 615). Bevan was on very close terms with Yigal Allon, the labour minister (Foot, 1973, p. 419; Mikardo, 1988, p. 159). Moreover the Israeli labour movement was well represented at the Socialist International, providing an arena for contact between the two parties.[48] Furthermore there were significant relations between the British trade union movement and the Israeli trade union movement, in the form of reciprocal visits.[49] Finally, there were linkages between Labour Women and the Israeli labour movement through the International Women's School.[50]

These ties enabled the Israeli Labour Party, Mapai, to lobby the British party over Suez. During the crisis Mapai was worried about Labour's policy. Golda Meir recalled that some Israeli socialists felt that Labour had 'swallowed Nasser's line whole'.[51] Israeli politicians tried to rectify this situation, for example Mapai contacted the party about the number of fedayeen attacks against Israel.[52] Moreover talks with the Israeli ambassador in Britain influenced Gaitskell's view that Nasser had expansionist ambitions and that his rise would harm Israel in the long term (see Williams, 1983, pp. 559–60). More locally, Poale Zion put forward Israel's case during debates on the crisis, arguing that the Jewish state put into practice the British labour movement's ideals by trying to build socialism, condemning the Conservative government for refusing to supply Israel with arms and allowing Nasser to prevent Israeli shipping from using the canal.[53] Poale Zion tried to rebuild relations between Labour and the Jewish community, taking part in the creation of Labour Friends of Israel (LFI) in 1957 (Alderman, 1983, pp. 133–4). As a non-affiliated organisation the LFI aimed to lobby opinion on behalf of Israel. It was formed at a public rally at Labour's annual conference and Herbert Morrison was among those who addressed the rally. Anthony Greenwood was its first chair.[54]

Historical considerations also played a part in the maintenance of Labour's pro-Israel sympathies. Leading Labour figures supported Israel because memories of Germany's wartime atrocities were still fresh in their minds. Gaitskell saw the state as the progressive homeland of an oppressed people (Williams, 1979, p. 393) and both he and Bevan were emotionally attached to the country (Foot, 1973, p. 517). Gaitskell's commitment stemmed from his experiences in 1930s Vienna, where he had met Jews brought up in the Central European tradition of Marxism (see Williams, 1979, pp. 53–63), and the collapse of social democracy in Austria had led him to become a strong supporter of anti-fascist causes (Morgan, 1992, p. 222). The 'spirit of the resistance', which was so strong in France (see Louis and Owen, 1989, p. 4), was not lost on this generation of Labour politicians, whose experience of the war had converted them to the Zionist cause. They believed that the survival of the Jewish people depended on Israel's existence and that Egypt threatened this. In fact, recent works on the crisis show that Nasser was not a great threat to Israel at the time and that he wanted to avoid conflict with Israel up to 1955, and for a while opposed Palestinian raids into the country (Khalidi, 1989, p. 390). Nevertheless emotional commitment to the Jewish state remained an important determinant of pro-Israel feeling. Labour continued to regard Israel as a refuge for the Jews from persecution and Shinwell spoke for many when he said that 'When, as a result of Hitler's dastardly acts, millions of people were destroyed in gas chambers, what could one expect? There must be a haven, a refuge for persecuted people, the victims of the pogroms and the rest, and there was the state of Israel.'[55]

There were also compelling political reasons for maintaining a pro-Israel position, rooted in the continuing link between Jews and social democracy. By 1956 there were still significant ties between Labour and the Jews, with the party containing seventeen Jewish Labour MPs. Moreover there was a notable connection between these and the party's left wing. Six of the MPs were among the fifty-seven who joined Bevan in voting against the defence policy in 1952. Ian Mikardo and Sydney Silverman were prominent left-wingers. Mikardo had close ties with the affiliated organisation, Poale Zion, and Silverman had connections with various Zionist organisations (Epstein, 1964, pp. 186–7). In the same way as the Conservatives exploited the party's (largely ungrounded) 'pro-Nasser' stand, they also made much of Labour's apparent 'betrayal' of its friendship with Israel. In one Commons' debate a Conservative MP, Charles Waterhouse, an enthusiastic supporter of force against Egypt, said 'it is a very cruel thing that the Israelis, in this hour of their tribulation, in this hour when every hand is turned against them, should find that many of the voices to which they have been used to listen have been silent' (quoted in ibid., p. 192).

Gaitskell himself represented a constituency (Leeds South) that contained a significant Jewish community. He was married to a Jewish woman and his father-in-law was an active Zionist (ibid., p. 194). Such was the strain between Gaitskell's opposition to the war and his sympathies with Israel that he felt compelled to make clear that he had not given up on Israel. During his anti-government attack Gaitskell telephoned a close Jewish friend in Leeds to reassure her that he was not 'turning against' Israel (Williams, 1983, pp. 243–4). This concern was not groundless. Maurice Orbach's case illustrated the costs of too close an identification with the Arab cause. Unlike the other left-wing Jewish MPs, Orbach clearly sympathised with Nasser, having previously mediated between Egypt and Israel over the Palestinian refugee question (see Shamir, 1989, p. 77). At a public meeting he defended Nasser, eliciting a good deal of anger from the Jewish community.[56] Orbach represented Willesden East, a marginal constituency that contained a significant number of Jews who were in a position to affect election results (Epstein, 1964, p. 185). Local Conservatives exploited the MP's difficulties in the run-up to the 1959 general election and he lost the seat by over two thousand votes (Alderman, 1983, p. 133).[57]

The 1956 war did very little to change Labour's fundamental loyalties in the Israeli–Arab conflict. Ideological and non-ideological factors combined to produce this situation. Committed to social democracy, Labour looked more favourably on Israeli nationalism because Israel was a liberal democracy led by a sister party. In contrast, although Nasserism appealed to progressive values, it was not a social democratic movement and had no political ties with Labour. Moreover, because of the history of Nazism, Israeli nationalism had more of a moral and emotional appeal to the party than Arab nationalism. Even so, instrumental factors also played a part. Despite Labour's commitment to anti-imperialism, it was ambivalent about anti-imperialist movements, sharing with the Conservatives a commitment to the preservation of British interests. Furthermore its pro-Israel stance stemmed also from a rational calculation of the political costs associated with a pro-Arab policy and the benefits arising from a pro-Israel one. However there was some evidence of changing dynamics and I shall consider these in the next section.

Towards dissent

Despite the overwhelming tendency to continue to support Israel and to be sceptical of Arab nationalism, the 1956 conflict did produce a slight shift away from the prevailing Labour views. People such as William Warbey, Edith Summerskill and Tony Benn challenged the leadership's hostility towards Nasser. Benn claimed that 'no country has committed so many crimes against Egypt as this country has' (quoted in Epstein, 1964, p. 28). After a meeting of the executive of Bristol South East CLP in August, he issued the following statement: 'the real issue is very simple. Egypt is a poor country which since 1882 has been fully or partly occupied by British troops. Now free, she is anxious to raise her living standards. Without the Aswan Dam she cannot succeed . . . she deserves the support of the British people' (quoted in Adams, 1992, p. 118). Edith Summerskill knew Nasser personally. After the war, she visited Egypt and found that the Anglo-French attack had caused far more casualties than had been acknowledged (Epstein, 1964, p. 76). Barbara Castle and Fenner Brockway led a march of five hundred people to protest against the government.[58] People linked with the *Tribune* newspaper described the Anglo-French intervention as a 'crime against the world', suggesting that Britain and France had, in defiance of the United Nations, engaged in an 'evil, imperialist struggle against the Arab peoples'.[59]

The rise of the MCF partly accounted for this development. Formed in 1954, it was not linked specifically to one party, however Labour tended to dominate it (Kavanagh and Morris, 1989, p. 99). The organisation aimed to support national liberation movements and decolonisation. It attracted people from the party's left wing, including Michael Foot, Barbara Castle, pacifists such as Frank Allaun, and Tony Benn, who was its treasurer. William Warbey was also closely involved in the organisation, having chaired its London Area Council. There was a particularly strong link between ILP members such as Fenner Brockway and the MCF. The body's links with Labour also operated through affiliated constituency parties and local and national trade unions. It was the MCF that originally planned the anti-war demonstration in Trafalgar Square, allowing Labour to take it over after the latter showed some interest.[60]

Unlike the leadership, these elements did oppose the war on anti-colonialist grounds. Warbey was highly critical of Labour's foreign policy, and although he was not a fellow-traveller he had some sympathy for communist principles. Brockway was a committed anti-colonialist for humanitarian reasons. He believed in the absolute right to national self-determination on moral grounds and wanted Labour to strengthen its anti-colonialist stand and support independence for all the colonies. The Labour left identified with the third-force principle, opposing the Cold War division between the United States and the Soviet Union (see Howe, 1993, pp. 168–9, 171–3, 265). They argued that freeing the Middle East from Cold War ambitions would provide stability in the region and that this depended upon recognition of Arab nationalism.[61] Barbara Castle advocated a new approach to the Middle East, 'based on the political co-operation of all the great powers, including Russia, in an effort to solve the problems of the area'. She claimed that military pacts should be replaced with economic aid through UN agencies and suggested that Nasser's position was a weaker nation's response to 'imperialist policies'.[62] Left-wing opponents of the war were very critical of the United States' decision to withdraw its aid for the Egyptian Aswan Dam project.

Developments in the Middle East also contributed to this shift. In the late 1950s Arab nationalism began to make appeals to socialism and these forms of nationalism went on to dominate in Egypt, Syria, Algeria and Iraq in the early 1960s (see Sharabi, 1966, p. 67). The rise of Nasser was particularly important. Whatever his shortcomings in terms of domestic policy, he was a charismatic leader who won the loyalty of the Arab people and also appealed to Western politicians. Nasser attended the Bandung conference in 1955. The conference's pro-Arab views impressed him and he began to believe that African and Asian states needed to distinguish themselves from the superpowers in order to achieve independence, and he argued that they should act as a third force in international politics. Nasser invented the idea of positive neutrality, which suggested that states such as Egypt could build up their independence if they avoided alignment with the great powers in the Cold War (Dessouki, 1989, pp. 33–6). The Bandung conference as a whole identified with third-force ideas (Howe, 1993, p. 302). Since Labour's anti-colonialists shared these politics they began to sympathise with Nasserism. This faction's concern with anti-colonialist goals allowed it to turn a blind eye to some of the more unsavoury aspects of Egypt's internal regime.

At this stage, sympathy for Nasser did not entail criticism of Israeli policy. People like Warbey and Brockway had been strongly pro-Zionist in the 1940s. Warbey joined Silverman, Mikardo and Maurice Orbach in their condemnation of Bevin's Palestine policy (Howe, 1993, p. 151). Nor was Barbara Castle anti-Israel. She believed that to ignore Arab nationalism and to adopt anti-Nasser policies would exacerbate the Arab–Israeli conflict and threaten Israel's existence.[63]

Only one left-winger, Michael Foot, was openly critical of Israel's policies. He believed that Western Cold War policies such as the Baghdad Pact isolated Israel. However he did not think that this was enough to let Israel completely off the hook (see Foot and Jones, 1957, pp. 90–2), and suggested that although Israel had been subjected to severe provocation, its actions had been 'morally wrong and highly dangerous'.[64] He has claimed that his position stemmed from disillusionment with internal Israeli politics, in particular the marginalisation of moderates such as Sharett in favour of activists such as Ben-Gurion.[65]

These developments later provided the basis of a slight change in Labour's analysis of the Israeli–Arab conflict. Arab socialist groups tried to exploit the anti-imperialist tendency in the party that had come to the fore during the Suez crisis. At the end of 1957 members of an Arab students union approached Tony Benn and proposed the establishment of permanent links with the Labour Party that could be used as the basis of contacts between Labour and Ba'ath Socialists in the Middle East. Although Benn was worried about the Ba'ath Socialists refusal to meet the Israelis, he concluded that such contacts were the only way to progress.[66] John Clarke, the administrative officer of the International Department, welcomed this development.[67] Moreover after the war the NEC asked the International subcommittee to provide a restatement of Labour's Middle East policy. The subsequent document proposed that Labour 'seek out and assist socialist elements among the Arabs'.[68]

A Middle East working party aiming to reconsider Arab nationalism and the Israeli–Arab conflict was set up in 1959. Sympathisers with Israel, including the chair, Ian Mikardo, and Crossman, Philip Noel Baker and Kenneth Younger, were members, so the working party was unlikely radically to change party policy. Nevertheless it gave Arab nationalism serious consideration for the first time.[69] In

August 1959 the secretary of the International Department, David Ennals, went on a fact-finding visit to Israel, Syria, Lebanon and Cyprus. Crucially, he paid an informal visit to the Ba'ath Socialist Party conference in Beirut.[70] One of Ennals' aims was to 'make contact with socialist groups and to see the Palestine refugee problem at first hand'.[71] During his stay he met a number of people involved in the Ba'ath Socialist Party, including Dr Jamal Shaer, a member of its organising committee. In Lebanon he stayed with Nassim Majdalany, a parliamentary representative of the Popular Socialist Party, led by Kamal Jumblat.[72]

This experience was of formative importance in Ennals' approach to the Arab–Israeli conflict. It produced the first indication of a move away from Labour's pro-Israel consensus. In an unpublished report on the Palestinians, Ennals wrote that

> While they [the Palestinian refugees] have eked out their exist-
> ence on the UNRWA rations, maybe supplemented by casual labour,
> they have seen thousands of Jewish immigrants from Europe,
> North Africa and elsewhere pour into Israel. They are aware that
> at the same time as Arabs are refused permission to return, the
> Jewish Agency is negotiating for new immigrants.[73]

However Ennals' views remained those of a minority until well after the 1956 war.

Conclusion

Although the 1956 Arab–Israeli war provided a significant test of Labour's pro-Israel policy, the vast majority of the party remained committed to the Jewish state, refusing to see the Israeli government as blameworthy as the British and French governments for its action against Egypt. Leading the anti-war campaign, Gaitskell went to great lengths to distinguish Labour's opposition to the war from support for Arab nationalism. Labour's exonerative attitude towards Israel stemmed from its strong relationship with the Israeli Labour leadership and lack of equivalent ties with Arab national-ism, together with an awareness of the potentially damaging political effect of adopting an anti-Israel policy given the relationship be-tween Jews and the party. Moreover memories of the Second World War generated an emotional loyalty to the Jewish state, leading party members to rationalise Israeli policy in terms of the country's survival. Nevertheless the war did generate a ripple of dissent from Labour's prevailing hostility towards Arab nationalism and sympathy for Jewish nationalism. Although few members of the Labour left actually challenged Israeli policy, a significant number began to question the leadership's anti-Arab attitudes. The conflict succeeded in putting pressure on the party to take Arab nationalism seriously and set off a series of contacts between members of Labour's internal bodies and Arab nationalist groups. In the next chapter I shall look at how Labour responded to a further challenge to its pro-Israeli tradition.

4

The 1967 War: towards a Breakdown in Labour's Consensus of Support for Israel

At the time of the 1967 Arab–Israeli War Labour had returned to government under the leadership of Harold Wilson, whose background in the party's left predisposed him towards a socialist approach to international affairs (Morgan, 1992, p. 250). Labour entered government committed to continuing the postwar process of decolonisation (Howe, 1993, pp. 306–8) and the new Middle East hostilities again put this commitment to the test, posing a significant dilemma for a party committed to decolonisation and with strong pro-Israel loyalties. The dilemma was especially acute because Israel's definitive victory and subsequent occupation of the West Bank, Gaza and the Golan Heights directly challenged the left's conception of the country as an underdog. These events have been portrayed as a major turning point in Labour's relations with the Jewish community (Alderman, 1983, p. 160). In this chapter, however, I show that the conflict did not produce a dramatic policy shift, and that the vast majority of the party rallied to support Israel.

Solidarity with Israel

Far from condemning Israel's actions in 1967, most of the government stood solidly behind Israel, despite public protestations of neutrality.[2] Wilson himself and leading members of the cabinet, including Herbert Bowden (secretary of state for commonwealth affairs) and Ray Gunter (minister of labour), blamed Egypt for the war and initially wanted Britain to intervene on Israel's behalf. Roy Jenkins (home secretary) also backed the use of force to help the country. John Silkin (chief whip) apparently became a 'fanatical pro-Israeli', despite his anti-Zionist and non-religious Jewish background. It was the view that an Anglo-American intervention would look like an attempt to 're-assert western domination in the Middle East', alienating the Afro-Asian block in the UN, that persuaded the leadership to adopt a more cautious approach (see Wilson, 1971, pp. 395–6; Crossman, 1976, pp. 356–8).

One possible dissenter was the foreign secretary, George Brown, who had a reputation for being pro-Arab. Although he frequently claimed that there was an Arab case as well as an Israeli case,[3] and that Israel should not seek territorial expansion,[4] even he pursued a pro-Israel line behind the scenes by adopting a 'hawkish' attitude towards the blockade, instructing the British delegation at the UN to help the United States to frustrate the Soviet attack on Israel in the General Assembly and trying to persuade King Hussein of Jordan to seek a settlement with Israel.[5] Brown also proposed that political assurances should accompany Israel's withdrawal from the territories.[6] Wilson later recalled that although Brown had never been as pro-Israel as the rest of the leadership, during the war he 'never wavered . . . to make his weight felt against Arab aggression' (Wilson, 1981, p. 332).

This attitude transcended party factions. Crossman, by then the leader of the Commons, also blamed the Egyptian president for the conflict (Crossman, 1976, p. 355). Although he did not favour actively helping Israel, he was clearly torn:

> For once part of me is on the side of military action but another instinct says we shouldn't take part. We should stand aside and let the Americans take the rap, to which my reason replies that if we stand aside the Americans will let the Israelis down, in which case the Israelis will be forced to fight a war on their own and be dubbed an aggressor by the U.N. We would have another Suez on our hands with a Labour Government this time colluding with the aggressor (ibid., p. 356).

Crossman's caution provoked some disquiet in Jewish circles and rumours circulated about his being an appeaser, rumours he quickly dispelled through his contacts with Israeli representatives in Britain (ibid., pp. 358, 365). He later refused to support the UN's demand that Israel withdraw from the territories and was clearly relieved at Israel's victory, saying that it justified having 'left the Israelis alone . . . to let them have their one chance' (ibid., pp. 393, 366).

Most of the PLP shared these views. Of just over three hundred Labour MPs, two hundred were registered and paying members of the LFI.[7] During the war Labour MPs sponsored three pro-Israel EDMs. The most popular motion attracted one hundred and sixty-six signatures, one hundred and five of which were from Labour members (Table 4.1; see also Appendix 3). This motion asserted 'the right of Israel, by her own force of arms, to meet an avowed threat to her existence'.[8] Although there were three Labour-sponsored pro-Arab EDMs, these attracted little support; the most popular had only nineteen Labour names (Table 4.2).

The parliamentary left showed no signs of dissent. For example, Eric Heffer, MP for Liverpool Walton, was one of Israel's most outspoken supporters. Heffer opposed the UN's demand for the state to revoke its law on the status of Jerusalem and defended Israel against reports of its intention to annex the Gaza Strip.[9] Heffer and six other Labour MPs went to Israel after the war to assess the political situation and the refugee problem.[10] He returned fully supportive of the country, writing that 'the Israelis not only want peace with the Arabs, but equally they want justice for the Arabs'. On the refugees, he claimed that he was convinced that 'it has not been the declared policy of the Israeli Government to force the refugees to leave'.[11] Later, Heffer was one of a number of Labour MPs who argued that Israel should not return to its pre-June borders and that the Golan Heights 'should never go back to having gun emplacements shooting at Israel'.[12]

For Jewish Labour MPs, the dilemmas raised by the 1967 conflict were not as acute as those of the 1956 war because the party leadership was not asking them to oppose a war in which Israel was involved. Nevertheless they were under pressure to express outright support for Israel. At the time there were thirty-eight Jewish members of the PLP (see Alderman, 1983, pp. 174–5), some of whom had particularly strong links with Zionist organisations. Barnett Janner, for example, chaired the Anglo-Israel Parliamentary Group, was president of the Zionist Federation of Great Britain, president of the European Council of World Confederation of General Zionists and a member of the World Zionists General Council (Actions Committee).[13] In parliament Janner consistently spoke on behalf of Israel, maintaining that the country wanted peace whereas the Arab states wanted war, supporting Israel's measures in Jerusalem and objecting to the presence of a UN peacekeeping force inside Israel's frontiers.[14] David Weitzman, MP for Stoke Newington and Hackney North,

Table 4.1 Pro-Israel early-day motions, 1967

Date of first tabling	Number and title	Party support	Main sponsor	Total number of names appended	Number of labour names appended (and percentage of total names)
8 June 1967	568. The Middle East	Labour, Conservative and Liberal	David Weitzman (Labour)	166	105 (63)
8 June 1967	570. Defence of peace and Israel	Labour	Arthur Lewis (Labour)	1	1 (100)
27 July 1967	630. Middle East peace	Labour	William Molloy (Labour)	11	11 (100)

Table 4.2 Pro-Arab early-day motions, 1967

Date of first tabling	Number and title	Party support	Main sponsor	Total number of names appended	Number of labour names appended (and percentage of total names)
14 June 1967	573. Plight of Arabs in Sinai Desert	Labour	Jack Ashley (Labour)	19	19 (100)
13 July 1967	606. Ending Israel's occupation of Jerusalem	Labour	Margaret McKay (Labour)	18	18 (100)
No fixed date	78. Her Majesty's Governments' policy towards Arab/Israel dispute	Labour	Margaret McKay (Labour)	1	1 (100)

made similar claims.[15] Other Jewish MPs, such as Ian Mikardo, Leo Abse and John Mendelson, actively campaigned in favour of Israel by organising 'solidarity with Israel' meetings.[16]

The internal decision-making bodies also remained largely pro-Israel. The NEC and the Overseas Department contained many more pro-Israel members than pro-Arab ones (Tables 4.3 and 4.4). There were few indications of a shift in these sections' attitudes. Internal documents that did suggest that Israel should give up the territories and cooperate with the Arabs[17] did not find their way into official policy. In the postwar period the NEC adopted UN Security Council Resolution 242[18] as central to its policy, but added a clause that stressed Israel's 'absolute right to exist'. The Jewish press welcomed the NEC's position as confirmation of Labour's continuing support for Israel.[19]

More surprisingly, given the growing divide between the leadership and the grass roots over foreign policy, the constituency parties also supported Israel. Five CLP resolutions submitted to the NEC backed the government's position.[20] Although there was a groundswell of grass-roots opposition to the government's other foreign policies, such as Vietnam, Rhodesia and South Africa, there was none on the Middle East generally or the Israeli–Arab conflict specifically.[21] This situation continued until well after the war. While Labour activists were generally hostile to the government's foreign policy in the late 1960s, they did not attack Wilson's attitude towards the Middle East[22] and the annual conference unanimously accepted the leadership's policy.[23] Moreover Labour members of the GLC showed solidarity with Israel, supporting a policy of sending people to Israel to give advice on the rebuilding of East Jerusalem and backing Soviet Jewry's right to emigrate (Alderman, 1989, p. 116).

Throughout the conflict the TUC remained pro-Israel too. The union leaderships strongly supported Israel's aims, calling for the Arab countries to recognise Israel and for direct negotiations between the two sides.[24] Labour Women also continued in the party tradition. At the first of its postwar conferences it expressed its 'full solidarity with the people of Israel who are defending their existence and their liberty against aggression'. Although Doris Young from the National Labour Women's Advisory Committee raised the matter of the Palestinian refugees, she supported the resolution and the conference carried it.[25] Later she and another member of the committee attended an International Council of Social Democratic Women seminar in Israel. After meeting representatives from the

Table 4.3   NEC members, 1967

Pro-Zionist/Israel	Pro-Arab/Palestinian
A. Bacon	F. Allaun
E. M. Braddock	T. Benn
J. Callaghan	B. Castle
T. Driberg	
A. Greenwood	
J. Lee (chair)	
J. Lestor	
I. Mikardo	
H. Wilson	

Table 4.4   Overseas Department members, 1967

Pro-Zionist/Israel	Pro-Arab/Palestinian
J. Callaghan	B. Castle
T. Driberg	
A. Greenwood	
M. Herbison	
J. Lee	
G. Morgan	
H. Wilson	

Histadrut, the Israeli Labour Party and the Israeli women's movement, these women reported sympathetically on Israel's situation in the Middle East, calling for the establishment of the 'closest possible links' between the British and Israeli labour movements to help counter the threat to Israel.[26]

Despite Labour's commitment to anti-imperialist politics, it showed little sympathy for Arab nationalism. In the late 1960s important sections of the labour movement still operated within the tradition of thought that characterised Arabs as backward and feudalistic and denied the existence of a Palestinian identity. Wilson believed that responsibility for the war lay squarely with 'Arab aggression' and Nasser's 'great fanfare of aggressive speeches' (Wilson, 1971, pp. 395–6). The trade union leadership also spoke of 'Arab backwardness' and 'fascism'. At the TUC conference Frank Cousins, the TGWU leader, referred to the Arab states' 'feudalism'. In the debate on the Middle East, Fred Hayday, chair of the International Committee, said that 'the Arab countries' war aims [were] clear, simple and specific – that is, to drive the Israelis out of Israel and to extinguish them as a people'. Another trade unionist spoke of the Arab states'

'Fascist' and 'Nazi' ideas,[27] and these themes were common in sections of the labour movement.[28]

The 1967 conflict also drew attention to the Palestinian question. The PLO was formed in 1964 with the aim of uniting expatriate Palestinians. It had a government in exile in Gaza and an army consisting of refugees, and Nasser was one of its main sponsors (Ovendale, 1984, pp. 170–1). Having abandoned pan-Arabism in the aftermath of the war in the belief that the Arab states were powerless in the face of Israel, Palestinian nationalism focused on the figure of Yasser Arafat and called for independent national rights for the Palestinians (Ajami, 1983, p. 123). However key members of the government paid very little attention to the refugee question. Although in a speech at the UN, Brown called for a solution to the refugee crisis, he did not identify Israel as responsible.[29] In their postwar reflections on the conflict, neither Wilson nor Crossman mentioned the Palestinians (Wilson, 1971; Crossman, 1976). Many party members continued to argue that the Arab states should take responsibility for resettling the refugees.[30] Moreover, although Labour's rank and file took up other aspects of Third World politics, such as the anti-Vietnam War campaign and anti-apartheid, it did not adopt the Palestinian cause. The party as a whole showed little sympathy for this movement, condemning the rise of Palestinian terrorism and the activities of the Popular Front for the Liberation of Palestine (PFLP) at the 1970 annual conference.[31]

There is little evidence, then, that the war significantly altered Labour's traditional sympathies. Indeed the conflict led most of the party, from the leadership to the constituency parties, to rally behind the Jewish state and condemn the Arab countries for aggression. Why, given Labour's anti-colonialist outlook, did it take this stand?

Explaining Labour's policy

Once again, one has to consider a whole range of external and intra-party factors. The fact that Israel had a decisive victory and went on to maintain military control over the territories and to annex East Jerusalem was of little consequence to party policy. One of the reasons why Labour continued to support Israel during the hostilities was essentially ideological, that is, based on a sense of shared political purpose with the Jewish state. Heffer, for example, defended Israel's continued occupation of the territories on the ground that Israel was 'the only genuine democratic and socialist oriented state in the Middle East'.[32] The MP Raymond Fletcher said 'I support the socialist dockers of Haifa, the socialist builders of Beersheba, the socialist farmers on the shores of Galilee, the socialist mayor of Nazareth, who has given his Arab people better houses and better conditions than they would get in Jordan.'[33]

Labour's political identification with the Israeli Labour Party led to considerable networking, enabling Labour to hear the Israeli case. Wilson, for example, was on very close terms with Golda Meir (see Alderman, 1983, p. 160), Abba Eban and Yigal Allon, describing Allon as his 'closest friend among the Israelis' (Wilson, 1981, p. 380). During the war Wilson entertained the Israeli prime minister, Levi Eshkol, at Chequers and Downing Street (Eban, 1972, p. 192). Crossman was close to Labour politicians in Israel and people in Britain who had links with Israel, such as Marcus Sieff and the Israeli ambassador, Aharon Remez. Sieff was vice president of the Joint Palestine Appeal and Crossman kept in touch with both people throughout the conflict (see Crossman, 1976, pp. 364–5). George Brown publicly announced that his concern for Israel's safety arose out of his being married to a Jewish woman (Litvinoff, 1969, p. 3). Furthermore a number of cabinet ministers, including Crossman, Greenwood, Bowden, Edward Short, Tony Benn, Patrick Gordon Walker, Arthur Bottomley, George Thompson (minister of state for foreign affairs) and Jennie Lee, were members of the LFI.[34]

Similar links existed between the TUC and the Israeli labour movement. Throughout the 1960s the TUC leadership and representatives of powerful unions such as the TGWU exchanged visits with the Histadrut executive. From the early 1960s the TUC provided the Histadrut with financial assistance for its Afro-Asian Institute in Tel Aviv, which awarded scholarships to students from countries such as Nigeria, Southern Rhodesia, Ghana, Grenada, Uganda and Zambia for training in trade unionism.[35] Left-wing Israeli critics of Israel's role in Africa and Asia have suggested that the institute was a primary means by which Israel could try to 'build economic and political ties with non-Arab Afro-Asian states and to strengthen pro-Israeli influence there' (Hanegbi *et al.*, 1971, pp. 12–13). Given the unions' block vote at the annual conference, these links had significant policy consequences. Other sections of the Israeli labour movement had links with the British movement. For example Pioneer Women of Great Britain was a UK affiliate of Mapai. Mary Mikardo was a member of this organisation, which sent representatives to the Labour Women's conference.[36]

Labour's solidarity with Israel was also due to a continuing emotional commitment, leading it to exonerate the country for policies that it would normally have criticised. For instance the occupation of the West Bank and Gaza involved the disenfranchisement of the Palestinian population in these areas, contravening the state's liberal democratic principles. However Labour chose to gloss over this development. For people who had been around during the Second World War the sight of Arab armies converging on Israel's borders struck a deep emotional chord and memories of the war continued to be salient. Referring to public sympathy for Israel, Wilson said that it was 'understandable after two thousand years of history and the sufferings of the Jewish people, including the massacres of the last war' (Wilson, 1971, p. 403). Defending Israel's postwar policies, Crossman claimed that the country had 'raised the status of the Jew and banished his sense of insecurity which provided for centuries the basis of antisemitism'.[37]

These ideological and historical factors gave Israel an advantage over the Arab nationalist leadership. Arab nationalism was not based on social democratic principles. In the period after the Second World War, Nasserism was the dominant anti-imperialist movement in the Arab world, opposing Western control over the Egyptian economy and apparently empowering the masses through state control of the economy. However its socialist rhetoric betrayed the fact that Nasser did not allow mass political organisation (Halliday, 1979, pp. 21–4). Furthermore, at the time there were no Arab members of the Socialist International with whom the party could identify. Although the Palestinians had begun to organise themselves, their cause was still subordinated to pan-Arabism, being physically dependent on the Arab states' sponsorship. The PLO's lack of independence meant that the Palestinians had yet to touch Western opinion. Just before the war, people living in Western Europe were almost completely unaware of the Palestinian refugee crisis, despite the fact that there were already over a million refugees (Ovendale, 1984, pp. 172–5).

However external political considerations also played an important part in shaping the government's policy. In office, Labour was constrained by the need to protect British interests. Despite the left's expectations, Wilson's approach to international affairs departed little from the Conservative tradition (Wrigley, 1993, pp. 123–5). The anti-colonialist left's hopes for the government had been premature, evidenced especially by Wilson's attitude towards Rhodesia and Vietnam (Howe, 1993, p. 308). The government's commitment to Atlanticism was also an important factor in its support for Israel. Wilson enthusiastically supported a strong alliance with the United States in opposition to the Soviet Union, and his tacit support for US involvement in Vietnam was the most controversial expression of this tendency (Pelling, 1991, p. 148). Wilson's belief that Britain should form a special relationship with the United States shaped his general attitude towards foreign affairs (Foot, 1968, pp. 207–13); indeed all the key players at the time – Wilson, Brown and Healey – accepted the need for Britain to ally itself with the United States in opposition to the Soviet Union. Brown, for example, subordinated his pro-Arab inclination to his fear of the Soviet Union. Being a pragmatist, Healey, the defence secretary, prioritised the alliance with the United States and was keen to maintain a British presence in areas such as South-East Asia and the Persian Gulf, and even supported the supply of arms to South Africa (Morgan, 1992, pp. 317–20).

Under Wilson, between 1964 and 1970 the Labour government preserved aspects of the postwar consensus in its foreign policy, including the nuclear deterrent and pro-Americanism, despite Wilson's short-lived spell of unilateralism. At the end of his second term, Wilson even approved the updating of the Polaris system (Kavanagh and Morris, 1989, pp. 102–3). This continuity between Labour and the Conservative tradition expressed itself in the government's attitude towards the Middle East. There was considerable agreement between Labour and the Conservatives over the 1967 war. The leader of the opposition, Edward Heath, welcomed Wilson's approach (Wilson, 1981, pp. 336–44), and in none of the four Commons debates was there a division or a motion of censure,[38] contrasting sharply with the Suez crisis.

The West's identification with Israel and the Soviet Union's support for the Arabs was most pronounced in 1967 (Halliday, 1975, pp. 161–2). Israel's alliance with the United States had been sharpened in the years preceding the 1967 war, and the United States provided Israel with ideological, economic and military support (Chomsky, 1986, pp. 1–27). In the previous wars the United States had been more ambivalent, supporting the formation of the state in 1948, but opposing its role in the 1956 war in the belief that Israel was not in sufficient danger to warrant US support. However in 1967 it saw Israel as an ally in its attempt to counter revolutionary movements (Halliday, 1975, pp. 161–2). Leading Israeli

Labour politicians such as Shimon Peres made it clear to key party members that Israel's ambition was to integrate itself into the industrially advanced West (see Benn, 1987, p. 489). Israel's pro-Western orientation made it an obvious ally for a Labour government that wanted to strengthen its relationship with the United States.

Domestic political considerations were also important. In 1967 Labour lost control of the GLC and a number of inner London districts that the party had controlled from the 1930s (Pelling, 1991, p. 140). The Conservatives took the lead in the opinion polls, largely because of the government's unpopular economic policies. Wilson and the chancellor, James Callaghan, presided over a government whose determination to prevent devaluation led to a series of badly received economic measures, including a wages and price freeze (ibid., pp. 140–1). During the war, public opinion was predominantly pro-Israel (Ovendale, 1984, pp. 174–5). Two Gallup polls showed that one fifth of the British public wanted Britain actively to help Israel, in contrast with the 1 per cent who wanted Britain to fight on the Arabs' side.[39] A poll conducted by the Opinion Research Centre for *The Sunday Times* showed that whereas 56 per cent of those polled supported Israel, only 2 per cent supported the Arab states.[40] Popular support for Israel was also expressed in the high level of participation in 'solidarity with Israel' rallies, with around ten thousand people attending a pro-Israel demonstration on 5 June.[41] Wilson and people such as Crossman were acutely aware of the weight of public opinion in favour of Israel (see Wilson, 1971, p. 403; Crossman, 1976, p. 370), and this was likely to have played a part in their thinking.

In this context, too, the leadership took notice of Jewish opinion. Jewish members of the party were quick to condemn any public signs of a moderate approach to the Arabs, with Poale Zion warning of the alienation of Jewish opinion.[42] The Jewish community and a number of Jewish Labour MPs characterised the government's ostensible non-alignment as a betrayal of the party's pro-Israel tradition, portraying the policy as one of non-intervention in favour of the Arabs. The Jewish press maintained that 'the Foreign Office, from Bevin to Brown, has based its policy on its so-called Arab friends'.[43] The Labour MP Emmanuel Shinwell forcefully attacked the leadership for failing to take positive action in favour of Israel.[44] Paul Rose, David Weitzman, Sydney Silverman and Barnett Janner all reacted sharply to Brown's pro-Arab tone at the UN, as they saw it.[45] Poale Zion's general secretary, Sidney Goldberg, told the party that the organisation was dismayed at Brown's UN speech, saying that 'appeasement' would be counterproductive for Britain's relations with Israel and the Arab states.[46] The organisation sent a delegation to the prime minister to complain about the UN speech and to seek confirmation of Labour's commitment to Israel. Concerned about these developments, Wilson instructed Gerald Kaufman, then the parliamentary press liaison officer, to clarify the government's position: that it did not advocate an Israeli withdrawal in the absence of a guarantee of its recognition.[47]

The PLP chose to support Israel for much the same reasons as the government, namely a strong ideological and emotional attachment to the country. However its failure to challenge the leadership's position reflected its conservative and pro-leadership tendency in the 1960s. The parliamentary left had begun to grow, partly as a result of new recruits after the 1964 and 1966 elections (Berrington, 1982, p. 81), and partly as a result of the establishment of the Tribune Group in 1966 (see Seyd, 1987, p. 77). However it was not a strong oppositional force at this stage, lacking a well-defined programme and constrained by its ties with Wilson (ibid., p. 16). During the first years of the Wilson government, much of the left supported the new leader and the PLP was very loyal to him (see Foot, 1968, pp. 301–9). A similar situation existed in the NEC. Its left-wing members included people such as Mikardo, Greenwood and Jennie Lee, all of whom belonged to the generation who had welcomed the establishment of a Jewish state in the 1940s for humanitarian reasons.

However the grass-roots' sympathy for Israel was paradoxical because the United States' support for Israel was related to its desire to gain political, economic and military control over other parts of the Third World (Deutscher, 1967, p. 31). Given the activists' hostility towards US foreign policy and Wilson's pro-American orientation, one might have expected a different outcome. The fact that there was not testifies to the idiosyncratic nature of Israel's appeal and the continuing Jewish presence in left-wing politics at the time, with prominent Jewish members of the left, such as Ian Mikardo and Frank Allaun, reinforcing the idea of a link between Jews and socialist politics.

Claims that the 1967 war ended Labour's traditional sympathy for Israel (see Alderman, 1983, p. 160) therefore fail to capture the extent of pro-Israeli feeling within the party during the war. A number of factors, including international allies and national opinion, determined Wilson's foreign policy generally (Wrigley, 1993, p. 125), and these, together with a strong ideological and emotional commitment to the state, played a part in Labour's views. Yet despite the weight of opinion in favour of Israel, there were signs that the pro-Israel consensus was starting to break down.

Dissent from the pro-Israel consensus

Only a small minority dissented from the party's conventional position. However, whereas in 1956 only a few individuals challenged the pro-Israel consensus, in 1967 the dissenters were more organised, more vocal and more systematic. The war marked the start of a trend that intensified throughout the 1970s and reached a peak in the 1980s. Labour had always contained a pro-Arab minority, following in Bevin's tradition. George Brown, for example, had pro-Arab sympathies, although he forsook these for what he perceived as higher objectives during the war. Douglas Jay, president of the Board of Trade and one of the party's revisionists, also sympathised with the Arabs.[48] In the PLP, Christopher Mayhew was the most notable advocate of the Arab cause – Crossman described him as a 'fanatical pro-Arab' (Crossman, 1976, p. 370). Others included Margaret McKay, Andrew Faulds and David Watkins.[49]

Whereas cabinet ministers were constrained by their offices and had to moderate their positions, backbenchers were freer to voice their opinions. In the period immediately after the war some backbenchers attacked Israel for occupying the captured territories and annexing East Jerusalem. Margaret McKay sponsored an EDM that called for an end to the Israeli occupation of Jerusalem. The motion also urged the country to implement the UN General Assembly resolution that declared the annexation of East Jerusalem invalid, and to observe the UN charter, which stated that war should not lead to territorial expansion.[50] The EDM attracted eighteen Labour signatures, including those of Mayhew, Watkins and Faulds and Will Griffiths from the left (see Appendix 4). In a Commons debate on the Middle East, Mayhew accused Israel of the 'arbitrary annexation' of Jerusalem.[51] They also challenged the party's view of Arabs, objecting to the idea that Arab aggression had caused the war. In Mayhew's opinion,

We should stop labelling the Arabs the aggressors. . . . It is not true that either the Arabs or the Jews are the aggressors in this

quarrel. It depends where in time one takes one's stand. If one
takes one's stand on 5th June, the Israelis were the aggressors;
but if one takes one's stand a fortnight earlier, at Aqaba, then
the Egyptians were the aggressors.[52]

In a private meeting of the Labour foreign affairs group, Mayhew
denied that Nasser was a racist, saying that when the Egyptian president spoke of the liberation of Palestine he did not mean the
annihilation of Jews.[53] He also appeared on a *Panorama* programme,
expressing sympathy for Nasser (Crossman, 1976, p. 364). Moreover the right-wing pro-Arabists drew attention to the Palestinian
refugee crisis, comparing the Palestinians' situation with Jewish
historical experience. Mayhew maintained that while the establishment of Israel had seemed to the Jews 'a miraculous homecoming
after two thousand years of dispersion', for the Palestinians it had
meant 'dispersion from the land of their fathers and their holy
places, eviction from land which they . . . had occupied for longer
than the Jews'.[54]

Some of these MPs took part in the formation of the Council for
the Advancement of Arab–British Understanding (CAABU). CAABU
was formed in 1967, apparently in response to the revelation that
98 per cent of the British public had no knowledge of the Arab
world.[55] It aimed to strengthen economic, political and cultural links
with Arab countries. Although CAABU was not exclusively a Labour
organisation, it lobbied on behalf of the Arab cause within the party.
In 1967 it held a meeting at the party conference, with Bob Edwards
MP presiding and Mayhew speaking.[56] Mayhew also played a central part in the formation of the Labour Middle East Council (LMEC)
in 1969 and Faulds and Watkins later became deeply involved with
the Council. LMEC's goal was to persuade the Labour Party to take
up the Arab cause. It published pamphlets and organised meetings
at the annual conference in order to put forward the Arab case.
LMEC sought the same affiliated status as Poale Zion, although without
success, with the NEC consistently rejecting the organisation's requests for affiliation.[57]

The 1967 conflict also precipitated a left-wing move away from
the party's traditional stance. Barbara Castle (minister of transport)
opposed the leadership's original decision to rally around Israel with
the United States. Castle viewed Wilson's plan to 'stand by the US'
and 'enforce the right of innocent passage through the Gulf' as 'no
better than 1956' (Castle, 1984, p. 258). In the PLP, the left-wingers

Will Griffiths and Stanley Orme, MPs for Manchester Exchange and Salford West respectively, adopted a pro-Arab stance. Crossman contemptuously described them as 'left-wing Nasserites just back from Egypt' (Crossman, 1976, p. 361). In the Commons, Griffiths forcefully argued for a re-evaluation of Arab nationalism, contending that it represented an understandable response to Western interference in the Middle East, especially after the Suez War.[58] Griffiths was one of three Labour MPs who moved a critical amendment to the pro-Israel EDM of 8 June, calling for the right of Egypt, Jordan and Syria to 'live without breach of their territorial integrity' in accordance with the UN Charter.[59]

Outside parliament, the *Tribune* left began to question the party's conventional approach to the conflict. Previously one of Israel's most enthusiastic supporters, it now condemned the country's decision to annex East Jerusalem and remain in the territories captured during the war on the ground that these acts breached international law.[60] The shift in this strand's position was sharply illustrated in *Tribune*'s contention that 'sentimental Israelis are wont to excuse this [annexation] on the grounds that Jerusalem means so much to the Jews. It means a lot to the Moslems too, but no one is being sentimental about them.'[61] The *Tribune* left now explicitly challenged the customary conception of the Arabs as feudalistic, backward and reactionary, arguing that Nasser's Egypt represented a source of 'stability and moderation' in the region and denouncing 'hysterical comparisons with Hitlerism'.[62] It also took up the Palestinian cause and claimed that peace between Israel and the Arab states depended upon Israel accepting its obligations to 'the hundreds of thousands of Arab refugees who lost their homes when Israel was created'. *Tribune* carried a cartoon by Abu that depicted Moshe Dayan sending Palestinian refugees back to where they *'didn't'* come from'.[63] Furthermore a leading member of the group, Michael Foot, was one of LMEC's sponsors.

Although the party's right- and left-wing dissenters were united in their challenge to the pro-Israel tradition, their reasons for doing so were not the same. The right's dissent was not motivated by a socialist-inspired, anti-imperialist ideology. Rather their support for the Arabs lay more in a desire to protect British interests in the Middle East than in idealistic concern for Arab nationalist aspirations. Although CAABU wished to be independent of party politics, conservatives and business sponsorships originally dominated the organisation.[64] Following in Bevin's footsteps (see Haseler, 1969, pp.

112–37), the Labour right was highly pragmatic and objected to the notion that socialist foreign policy was unrealistic.

Brown subordinated his pro-Arabism to the demands of office, but he did sympathise with Arab aims. Reflecting on his position, he claimed that it had arisen from his 'oddly inherited Irish background, which made [him] an anti-imperialist and gave [him] sympathy for people who were trying to throw off the yoke of imperialism' (Brown, 1971, p. 227). This interpretation was rather romantic, contradicting the foreign secretary's reputation as strongly pro-American and hostile to the Soviet Union. Moreover Brown's links with the Middle East had developed from commercial contacts (ibid., pp. 227–8). During the 1950s Brown had got to know a number of Arab leaders, including a member of the Lebanese parliament, Emile Bustani, who had wanted to put the Arab case to Western politicians. Through Bustani, Brown had made contact with King Hussein of Jordan and, most importantly, President Nasser, whom he admired greatly (ibid., pp. 229–31).

Turning to the other dissenters, Douglas Jay was once associated with *Socialist Commentary*, a journal that advocated the maintenance of British influence in the colonies and promoted a paternalistic type of imperialism (Foote, 1986, pp. 203–4). Mayhew had been Bevin's parliamentary undersecretary during the 1945–51 Labour governments and had backed the government's Palestine policy in the 1940s. Some suggested that McKay's support for the Arabs derived from her dedication to the monarchies in Jordan and Saudi Arabia.[65] McKay eventually retired to Abu Dhabi in the United Arab Emirates.[66]

The left-wing dissenters' views sprang from a different set of factors. This faction's previous sympathy for Israel had arisen from its identification with moderate members of Mapai, such as Sharett.[67] However developments within Israeli politics had undermined this identification. Although the Israeli Labour Alignment, formerly Mapai, was still in power, it had moved rightwards in terms of external affairs and the Palestinians. The Israeli government's postwar policies reflected the subordination of the moderate strand of Zionism, represented by Sharett, to the activist strand of Zionism, represented by people such as Ben-Gurion and Golda Meir. The entry of former military people into politics was partly responsible for this development (Shanin, 1988, p. 244). People known as hard-liners on external policy, such as Moshe Dayan and Shimon Peres, entered politics from the military under Ben-Gurion's patronage (Peri, 1983, pp. 71–3; Medding, 1972, pp. 252–3). Peres was deputy minister of defence between 1959 and 1965, while Dayan was minister of agriculture from 1959 to 1966 and minister of defence from June 1967 (Ovendale, 1992, pp. 156, 180–1). The Labour left in Britain did not identify with the new, activist type of Israeli politician, seeing Dayan's rise in politics as an obstacle to peaceful settlement in the Middle East.[68]

Moreover, by the time of the war this element had become more sensitive to anti-colonial politics. The United States' involvement in Vietnam generated a wave of protests. The 1967 Arab–Israeli hostilities took place in the midst of these developments, and left-wing activists began to make connections between Israel's role in the Middle East and the United States' involvement in Vietnam, and to see Israel as a major inhibitor of Arab nationalism.[69] Griffiths argued that 'it [was] the conviction of Arab nationalists everywhere that Israel was created as an instrument of imperialism and not a refuge for persecuted Jews', and that the current crisis was a direct result of the West's use of Israel to defend its interests in 1956.[70] Left-wing dissenters from Labour's pro-Israel tradition tended to be involved in the anti-colonialist and anti-racist movements. For example Castle was a long-time member of the anti-colonialist left and between 1960 and 1964 she was president of the Anti-Apartheid Movement (see Howe, 1993, p. 250); David Ennals chaired the Anti-Apartheid Movement between 1960 and 1964.[71] As a backbencher, Ennals was one of the few MPs to oppose the government's position on Vietnam (Foot, 1968, pp. 319–20). *Tribune* was a forum for protesting against US involvement in Vietnam, and it was no accident that the paper chose to serialise the reflections of the radical American journalist I. F. Stone on the Israeli–Arab war.[72] Stone was a sharp critic of US foreign policy.

The rise of Nasser as a figurehead in the fight against Western neo-colonialism appealed to these new sentiments. Despite Arab nationalists' ambivalent relationship with socialism, they began to exploit socialist language (see Ajami, 1983, p. 42). Arab, especially Palestinian, politics started to converge with other major issues and people such as Frantz Fanon, Mao and Guevara entered the Arab 'political idiom' (Said, 1992, p. xi). Arab nationalists' appeal to socialist principles led the Labour left to ignore the unsavoury aspects of movements such as Nasserism and Ba'athism, including the repression of communist elements. Some of those who sympathised with the Arabs were aware of these movements' shortcomings but were willing to tolerate them. For example Ennals believed that Labour should form good relations with Ba'athist socialists despite the fact that they were not democratic socialists.[73] These developments provided fertile ground for the creation of contacts between Arab groups and the party, serving to counter the ties between Jewish groups and Labour. Links between Labour and the PLO were also established. *Tribune* had made contact with Palestinian refugees and the PLO before the 1967 war,[74] and the PLO's decision to forge a separate identity in the postwar period further generated support for Palestinian nationalism in this faction.[75]

However the introduction of pro-Arab views into the party provoked a furore. In a Commons debate Janner attacked McKay, suggesting that she read 'the scurrilous, venomous-Hitlerian' literature of the Arabs.[76] Pro-Israel activists such as Paul Rose, Edward Rowlands and David Weitzman moved critical amendments to the pro-Arab EDMs. Mayhew's appearance on *Panorama* provoked an angry response, with a number of Labour MPs writing to the chief whip to complain that the MP's presence on the programme had given the impression that his views represented those of the Labour Party.[77] Thirty-five Labour backbenchers signed the letter, including Ted Rowlands, Edwin Brooks, John Dunwoody, Myer Galpern, Arnold Shaw, Daniel Jones, Lena Jeger, Raymond Fletcher and Paul Rose.[78] The political costs of appearing to sympathise too closely with the Arabs were most clear in the case of McKay. McKay entered into a debate with her constituency party over her pro-Arab activities and the NEC authorised a reselection meeting to solve the difficulties. However she withdrew from the contest before the meeting was held (Butler and Pinto-Duschinsky, 1971, pp. 295–6).

On the party's left, a rift developed between previously close colleagues. Ian Mikardo was deeply distressed by *Tribune*'s line on the conflict. In his article 'Who let Nasser off the leash?',[79] he deviated from the newspaper's editorial position. Mikardo resigned from *Tribune* shortly after this episode and it is possible that the newspaper's movement towards a more critical position on Israel contributed to his resignation. *Tribune*'s position on the war also led to a debate with the Israeli party, Mapam, which was to the left of Mapai, over the paper's refusal to accept that Nasser was intent on territorial expansion.[80] Moreover Abu's cartoon led to accusations of anti-Semitism, but Michael Foot and others on the newspaper's board denied these accusations and defended the decision to publish the cartoon.[81]

Did these developments result in Labour anti-Semitism? In the first place, very few Labour members adopted an anti-Zionist stance, defined in terms of opposition to the existence of a Jewish state. Even the strongest pro-Arabists in the party, Mayhew and McKay, defended Israel's right to exist,[82] although, in a private meeting of the party's foreign affairs group Mayhew advocated the reconstruction of Israel as a 'non-Zionist, multi-racialist state'.[83] At this stage too, the Labour left explicitly did not adopt an anti-Zionist standpoint and consistently defended Israel's right to exist. For example *Tribune*'s pointed critique of Israeli policies also stated that 'the Arabs have got to accept the existence of Israel. They must recognise as every sane person does, that Israel ... has the "right to live"'.[84] In 1967 this faction was wholly free from anti-Jewish stereotypes.

However some individual members of the pro-Arab strand did use anti-Jewish ideas. Although anti-Zionism and anti-Semitism are analytically distinct, they can overlap in practice. The theme of Jewish 'dual loyalty' and a conspiracy theory of Zionism have been central to traditional anti-Semitism and there is clear evidence of these themes appearing in the views of prominent pro-Arab members of the party. Mayhew, for example, consistently exaggerated Zionist power, holding that the 'Zionist lobby' was responsible for Labour's policy (Mayhew, 1975, p. 27). Mayhew later defected to the Liberal Party. In the early 1970s Young Liberals such as Peter Hain, now a Labour MP, were at the forefront of the anti-apartheid and anti-Zionist campaign inside the Liberal Party, leading to Lord Beloff's resignation (Alderman, 1989, pp. 117–18). Andrew Faulds and David Watkins also used anti-Jewish themes. For example in a Commons debate on the Middle East Faulds made a very explicit appeal to the idea of Jewish dual loyalty when he said that

> It is time some of our colleagues on both sides of the House forgot their dual loyalty and another Parliament. They are representatives here and not in the Knesset ... it is undeniable that many MPs have what I can only term a dual loyalty, which is to another nation and another nation's interests (quoted in Alderman, 1983, p. 150).

Wilson later removed Faulds from the front bench for 'uncomradely behaviour' in 'impugning the patriotism' of Jewish MPs (Ziegler, 1993, p. 389). In his pamphlet *Labour and Palestine* (1975), Watkins argues that Zionism is a nationalistic philosophy that opposes the

basic principles of democratic socialism. In his account of the relationship between Zionism and the labour movement, he draws heavily
on a conspiracy theory of Zionism, maintaining that 'the infiltration of the Labour Party has always been the policy of British agencies
of the world-wide Zionist movement'; he says that this infiltration
began in 1906 and that it was 'under Zionist influence [that] Labour
adopted double standards towards the Middle East in the year of
the Balfour Declaration'. Explaining the pro-Zionist tradition of the
party, Watkins argues that 'during the 1930s and '40s, the Zionists
consolidated their grip on the Labour Party and came completely
to control its policy towards the Middle East' (Watkins, 1975, pp.
3–14). This crude conspiracy theory of Zionism runs through Watkins's
pamphlet, completely ignoring the fact that Labour frequently
exploited Zionism for its own purposes and abandoned it when it
wanted to, as in the postwar government.

Despite these signs of dissent, criticism of Israel and sympathy
for the Arabs remained marginal in the Labour Party. At the 1970
conference, in its statement on the Middle East the NEC condemned
the activities of the Popular Front of the Liberation of Palestine. It
claimed that UN Resolution 242 provided the best basis for peace
in the region but added a series of clauses that prioritised Israel's
right to exist as a sovereign state. David Ennals asked the conference not to support the statement on the ground that the NEC
had added the party's 'own gloss' to the UN resolution. Ennals'
request was overwhelmingly defeated.[85] The conference also refused
to observe a minute's silence in memory of President Nasser, who
had died that year.[86] In the period after the war the NEC consistently rejected the LMEC's requests to affiliate.

Conclusion

Labour mainly responded to the 1967 Arab–Israeli War by maintaining its pro-Israeli stance. Indeed the hostilities succeeded in uniting
the leadership, most of the PLP, the NEC, the trade unions and the
constituency parties behind the Jewish state, cutting across party
factions. This virtual consensus existed because the Israeli Labour
Alignment shared significant ideological and political links with
Labour, and the Israeli right wing had yet to dent the left's hege-
mony. It also existed because the Palestinian nationalist movement
had only just emerged as an independent force and had not managed to influence international opinion. Partly because of this, it

was more politically advantageous for Labour to adopt a pro-Israeli than a pro-Arab position. The weight of sympathy for Israel in the party made it impossible for the small minority of dissenters from the pro-Israel consensus to affect any policy change. All the more so since those who challenged the leadership's stance were either mavericks such as Christopher Mayhew or elements from the Labour left, which was relatively powerless at this stage. Nevertheless the 1967 conflict represented a turning point insofar as the seeds for change were sown and a further crisis in the Middle East, in which Israeli policies appeared to depart even more from socialist principles, would almost certainly generate a greater level of dissent. In the following chapter I shall look at Labour's reaction to the Israeli invasion of Lebanon in 1982.

5
Israel in Lebanon: a New Labour Consensus?

In the late 1970s and early 1980s Israel made a series of incursions into Lebanon. The 1982 invasion was the most controversial, unleashing an unprecedented level of international condemnation. Although the attempted assassination of Shlomo Argov, the Israeli ambassador to London, was the pretext for the strike, Israel's real aims were to undermine the PLO's military and political base in the country, to forge links with its Lebanese allies and to improve its border security (Lesch and Tessler, 1989, p. 63). The government believed that a heavy military blow to the PLO would render it incapable of carrying out terrorist activities and erode its support among moderate Palestinians (ibid., pp. 36–7). In September the Lebanese Christian militia massacred Palestinians in the Sabra and Chatila refugee camps in Beirut. The massacre took place within the sight of the Israeli army (ibid., p. 63), creating the view that Israel's decision to send the militia into the camps rendered it responsible for the subsequent events.

The invasion and the massacre dramatically undermined Israel's international standing and drew attention to a new form of left-wing anti-Zionism, found mainly within new and far left groups and the women's movement (see Chapter 1). How did the social democratic left react? In this chapter I look at the way in which the British Labour Party responded to Israel's policy towards Lebanon. The first section illustrates the shift in the party's attitudes and the second considers the reasons for this shift. The third section explores the emergence of anti-Zionism and the fourth investigates the intra-party conflict resulting from the policy change and the leadership's subsequent efforts to moderate the party's position as part of the 1987 policy review process.

The collapse of the pro-Israel consensus

The 1982 war in Lebanon precipitated a wave of Labour grass-roots condemnation of Israeli policy and revealed how far the party's activists had moved in the direction of the Palestinian national cause. Local parties in London and Scotland spearheaded the campaign against Israel and in favour of the Palestinians. In London, Hackney North and Stoke Newington, Brent South, Paddington and St Pancras North actively championed the Palestinian cause.[1] Later on the Chipping Barnet CLP endorsed a pro-PLO motion (Alderman, 1989, p. 136). In Scotland, Aberdeen South, Dundee East, Dundee West and West Renfrewshire were the main pro-Palestinian CLPs. The Dundee CLP was especially active. It forged links with Palestinian activists studying at Dundee University such as Yousef Allen, who later became the British representative of the Palestinian Trade Union Federation.[2] It also organised meetings that were open to the general public and addressed by PLO representatives.[3]

Although particular CLPs in London and Scotland dominated the pro-Palestinian campaign, a more general shift was taking place. At the annual party conference, held immediately after the Sabra and Chatila massacres, forty-six emergency resolutions were passed condemning Israel.[4] Grass roots' sympathy for the Palestinians escalated during the 1980s and reached a peak in the late 1980s. By this time nearly all the constituency parties in the Greater London region and the south were consistently turning down the LFI's offers of speakers for their meetings.[5] Conference decisions reflected the trend. At the 1988 conference the pro-Palestinian motions won the two-thirds majority needed to become policy (Table 5.1).

A similar development took place in some Labour councils. Both the GLC and Brent began actively to promote Palestinian national rights. In the May 1982 borough elections the Jewish Labour candidate for Cricklewood (Brent), Alf Filer, declared that Israel should become a secular state (Alderman, 1989, p. 126). In the 1980s the GLC embarked on a number of measures to promote the Palestinian cause. County Hall became the base for the Labour Committee on Palestine (LCP). In 1984 the Council launched an anti-racist year and the Ethnic Minorities Unit (EMU) provided funding to the Palestine Solidarity Campaign (PSC) for a conference on racism against Arabs (ibid., pp. 130–4).[6] Dundee District Council played an important part in campaigning for the Palestinian nationalist cause. The council was twinned with the West Bank town of Nablus and

Table 5.1 Pro-Palestinian resolutions, Labour Party annual conference

Year	Votes for	Votes against
1982	3 538 000*	3 263 000
	3 318 000**	3 308 000
1988	4 163 000	1 943 000
1989	4 645 000	1 394 000

* Composite motion.
** Emergency resolution.

the PLO flag flew over the Dundee City chambers. After the invasion of Lebanon, the council unanimously adopted a resolution condemning Israel for its actions in Lebanon and its occupation of the West Bank and Gaza. The resolution also spoke of the 'genocide' of the Palestinian people.[7]

The trade unions also began to challenge the pro-Israel consensus after the invasions. At the TUC conference in 1982 the General Council and Tom Jackson (chair of the International Committee) opposed a pro-Palestinian motion on the ground that condemnation of Israel would hinder the prospects of peace. However the conference overwhelmingly backed an FBU-sponsored resolution condemning the 'death and destruction' caused by Israel's invasion and saying that only recognition of the national rights of the Palestinian people would provide security for all the states in the Middle East, including Israel.[8] The TGWU also put its weight behind the Palestinians. In response to the war, in 1982 it asked the TUC to organise an air and sea boycott of Israel until the country's troops left Lebanon.[9]

During the 1980s a number of unions sent delegations to the occupied territories as a result of Trade Union Friends of Palestine (TUFP) coordination. These included the FBU, the GMB, the MSF, the NGA, NUPE, SOGAT 82, the TGWU and UCATT, as well as non-affiliated unions such as the AUT, NALGO and the NUT. At the same time branch-level unions increasingly participated in TUFP activities.[10] NALGO, NUPE, the NUCPS, the ACCT, COHSE, the GMB, the FBU, the NUM and SOGAT affiliated to the TUFP. Although the TGWU was not affiliated, it had good relations with the organisation and both sent and received delegations to and from the West Bank.[11] The support of unions such as the NUM, the TGWU and NUPE was vital since these unions controlled a large proportion of the conference vote (see Koelble, 1987, pp. 260–1). As the 1980s proceeded the unions continued in this trend. SOGAT 82 played a particularly active part in the late 1980s, sponsoring resolutions at the party conferences in 1988 and 1989 that, in the context of the intifada, attracted overwhelming support.[12]

The new generation of Labour women also challenged the party's pro-Israel tradition. Clare Short played a high-profile role in the campaign for recognition of Palestinian national rights and became an active member of the Labour Middle East Council (LMEC). Harriet Harman, Maria Fyfe, Kate Hoey and Marjorie Mowlam also sympathised with Palestinian nationalism and joined LMEC. Dawn Primarolo, Alice Mahon and Anne Clwyd did not join LMEC but sympathised with its aims.[13] The agendas for the National Conference of Labour Women (NCLW) in 1984 and 1986 indicate a shift in favour of Palestinian national rights and a more critical attitude towards Israel.[14] These developments represented a significant policy change. In the early 1980s the NEC for the first time adopted a resolution that called for the establishment of a Palestinian state, with the PLO involved in any negotiations. Benn described the decision as a 'major development in Labour policy' (Benn, 1992, p. 240).

Israel's involvement in Lebanon sparked an unprecedented critical reaction within the PLP. An analysis of EDMs put down on the Palestinian–Israeli conflict in 1948, 1956, 1967 and 1982 indicates a sharp decline in pro-Israel feeling in 1982 and a corresponding increase in support for Palestinian nationalism. However sympathy for the Palestinians did not reach the level of pro-Israel feeling in the preceding years (Figure 5.1; see also Appendix 5). There were no Labour-sponsored pro-Israel EDMs between April and June 1982, but there were three Labour-sponsored pro-Palestinian ones (Table 5.2). Pro-Israel activists did not sponsor any motions, confining themselves to moving critical amendments to EDMs that criticised Israel.

The party leadership played a part in this shift. In June 1982 Michael Foot sponsored an EDM that condemned Israel's invasion of Lebanon, endorsed the UN Security Council's call for an immediate ceasefire and demanded the withdrawal of all Israeli forces from Lebanon, although it should be noted that the motion also included a condemnation of the attempted assassination of the Israeli ambassador to Britain, Shlomo Argov.[15] Foot's stand was consistent with his earlier departure from the party tradition. However even prominent right-wing members of the leadership began to criticise Israeli policy and support Palestinian national aims. In June Denis Healey, then the shadow foreign secretary, warned Israel

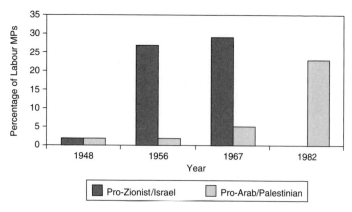

Figure 5.1   Top Scoring Early Day Motions

that humiliation of the Arabs in Lebanon would have repercussions throughout the Arab world and play into the hands of 'Arab fundamentalism'.[16] Elsewhere Healey sympathised with the idea of Palestinian statehood.[17]

In the 1980s, then, most of the party's sections began to challenge Labour's traditional loyalty to Israel and to advocate a policy in favour of Palestinian national rights. In the following section I shall consider the reasons for this development.

Explaining Labour's policy

A good deal of Labour's early sympathy for Israel depended on the identification of Zionism with socialism and progress, and the idea that Israel was the only progressive and democratic regime in the Middle East. From the state's inception the Israeli Labour Party was politically dominant, thus reinforcing these conceptions. Israel's shift to the right challenged these views. In 1977 the right-wing Likud Party won power. Made up of a number of independent factions – including Herut, headed by Menachem Begin (Lesch and Tessler, 1989, pp. 143–4) – Likud was ideologically committed to a 'Greater Israel' and embarked on a series of uncompromising policies towards the Palestinians and the Arab countries, including intensive settlement of the occupied territories and annexation of the Golan Heights.

These political changes caused a number of Labour people to consider that Israel's policies now betrayed the country's original

Table 5.2 Early-day motions, 1982

Date of first tabling	Number and title	Party support	Main sponsor	Total number of names appended	Number of labour names appended (and percentage of total names)
29 March 1982	372. Israeli action against Palestinians	Labour, Conservative and SDP	David Watkins (Labour)	30	18 (60)
22 April 1982	422. Israeli attacks on Lebanon	Conservative and Labour	Tony Marlow (Conservative)	44	22 (50)
26 April 1982	426. Congratulations to the Institute of Contemporary Art*	Labour and Conservative	David Watkins (Labour)	13	8 (62)
9 June 1982	510. Israeli invasions of Lebanon	Conservative and Labour	Dennis Walters (Conservative)	60	25 (42)
9 June 1982	512. The conflict in the Lebanon	Liberal and Labour	David Alton (Liberal)	14	6 (43)
10 June 1982	519. The Middle East	Labour	Michael Foot (Labour)	64	62 (97)

*The ICA had shown films promoting the Palestinian nationalist cause values. On the left, Eric Heffer's support for Israel had been based on the idea that Israel was a progressive and democratic state, but its involvement in Lebanon forced him to question his convictions. At the LFI's annual dinner in November 1981 he responded to Shimon Peres's criticism of the European conception of Palestinian self-determination by dropping his prepared speech in favour of a proposal for Palestinian national self-determination and negotiations with the PLO.[18] Eric Heffer and Tony Benn resigned from the LFI in 1982 in protest against Israel's position on the question of Palestinian statehood and its involvement in Lebanon.

Prominent right-wingers responded similarly. Although Healey had never been as emotionally committed to Israel as Heffer (his pragmatism had led him to support Bevin in the 1940s), in the 1980s he argued that Begin's and Sharon's policies were a threat to peace in the region and to Israel's continued existence.[19] Gerald Kaufman, in his personal account of Israeli politics in the 1980s, argues that the country was in political and moral decline (Kaufman, 1986). Leo Abse, MP for Pontypool, summed up the general feeling when he said that Begin's policies represented a 'vulgar nationalism quite contrary to the founding principles of the Israeli state'.[20]

The developments in Israel dovetailed with political changes in the Jewish communities outside Israel. In a number of Western countries Jews began to drop socialism in favour of conservative politics, largely as a consequence of changes in their socioeconomic status, but also because of their disillusionment with left-wing anti-Zionism (Rubinstein, 1982, p. 118). Commenting on US Jewish attitudes, Healey claimed that Jewish intellectuals had evolved from anti-communist Marxists to 'hard-line Zionists of the radical right' and that this had detrimentally affected US policy towards the Middle East (Healey, 1989, pp. 200–1). The Jewish community in Britain, as a result of increasing prosperity and disproportionate membership of the upper and middle classes, started to adopt conservative politics and the Jewish electorate moved to the right (see Alderman, 1983, pp. 135–8, 154–60). Although Jewish Labour MPs continued to outnumber their Conservative counterparts, the gap between the two narrowed (ibid., pp. 174–5). Jews started to perceive the Conservative Party as the best representative of their social and economic position, eroding the 'traditional affinity' between Labour and the Jews (see Rubinstein, 1982, p. 156).

As Israeli and Jewish politics moved to the right, Palestinian politics became more accommodating. From the early 1980s the PLO be-

gan to move from a maximalist position that called for Israel's
destruction to acceptance of its existence, and also began to accept
a two-state solution to the conflict. In 1986 it offered to acknowledge UN Resolution 242 in return for Israeli recognition of Palestinian
national rights (Lesch and Tessler, 1989, p. 282). The organisation's
shift towards a more moderate policy legitimised the Palestinian
aims. At the same time PLO representatives in Western countries
helped it to win international recognition. In Britain, Palestinian
activists carried out solidarity work aimed at influencing party policies,
working with party activists and members of the PLP.[21] PLO representatives in London, such as Said Hammani and Nabil Ramlawi,
forged links with MPs such as Ernie Ross in order to influence
opinion.[22] London representatives of the PLO were also in touch
with Labour front-benchers, notably Gerald Kaufman. In 1988
Kaufman shared a platform with Edward Said and Faisal Lweida, a
London-based PLO representative, at a meeting organised by LMEC.[23]
   Other developments affected the party's perceptions of Israel. During
the 1980s organisations such as UNESCO, the Socialist International
and the EEC began to take up the Palestinian nationalist cause (Said,
1992, p. xx) In June 1980 the EEC stated that the Palestinian people
had a right to self-determination and that the PLO should be involved
in all peace negotiations. More generally, by 1989 ninety-six states
had given Palestinian representatives diplomatic recognition
(Ovendale, 1992, pp. 202, 294). As early as the 1970s the Socialist
International had started to establish links between European socialists
and Arab socialist groups, causing some debate in Labour's internal
policy-making bodies.[24] Nevertheless these developments clearly
affected Labour policy. Healey, for example, referred to them in his
justification for supporting Palestinian self-determination.[25]
   In the latter part of the 1980s the intifada attracted widespread
sympathy for the Palestinians. Starting in December 1987, the intifada
involved a series of riots and protests that began spontaneously
but were subsequently directed by local committees. The uprising
was a grass-roots movement, spearheaded by young people living
in the occupied territories rather than political leaders or academics.
It galvanised Israeli Arabs into asserting their Palestinian identity
and it represented the Palestinians' attempt to act independently
of the Arab countries (Lesch and Tessler, 1989, pp. 272-3). The
intifada had major implications for international politics. It affected
the policies of the PLO as well as other important actors in the
Middle East conflict, including the United States (Hunter, 1991, p. 4),

and it provided a significant backdrop to Labour's overwhelming support for Palestinian nationalism at the 1988 and 1989 annual conferences.

Nevertheless these developments would have been less effective without the rise of the Labour left, which made the party particularly receptive to the Palestinian cause. In the 1970s and 1980s the party began to attract people from middle-class professions, including teachers, lecturers and social workers, displacing traditional working-class activists. Ethnic minorities and women's groups also began to enter the party, introducing distinctive 'voices of protest' (Morgan, 1992, p. 8). The new activists tended to be young and influenced by movements such as the Anti-Apartheid Movement, CND and the women's movement (Seyd, 1987, pp. 40–50). The left began to organise itself into groups such as the Campaign for Labour Party Democracy (CLPD) and the Labour Co-ordinating Committee (LCC). The former was established in 1974 and fought mainly for constitutional changes, whereas the latter was formed in 1978 and focused mainly on political ideas and policies (ibid., pp. 83–94). Labour councils, especially in London, became the site of considerable left-wing activism. In London the GLC was the most notable case. After the May 1981 elections to the council, the new Labour majority introduced a more radical outlook (Alderman, 1989, p. 127). Under the leadership of Ken Livingstone[26] the GLC introduced a new left agenda, incorporating a multiplicity of causes such as feminist and anti-racist politics. This development influenced other London councils, for example Brent borough council, and Labour councils in Scotland also became more radical in the 1980s (Wainwright, 1987, pp. 94–105).

Although the unions were not politically unified, having both a right and a left wing (see Dunleavy, 1993, p. 139), they too moved to the left in the 1980s. The unions' dissatisfaction with the party leadership and the new left activists' strategy to mobilise union support for their aims accounted for this shift (Koelble, 1987, pp. 255–8). The formation of Trade Union Friends of Palestine (TUFP) was part of this process. Established in 1980, its sponsors included Bill Speirs (assistant secretary of the STUC), Ernie Ross (Labour MP for Dundee West), Brian Price (president of the AEUW and TASS), Jim McCafferty (member of the Scottish executive of the NUM), William McKelvey (MP for Kilmarnock), George Galloway (vice chair of the Labour Party in Scotland) and Councillors Colin Rennie and Tom McDonald from Dundee District Council.[27] The TUFP aimed explicitly to mobilise support for the Palestinians within the trade union movement. Prior to the recent introduction of one member one vote (OMOV), Labour's industrial wing had a disproportionate influence at the annual party conference because of the block vote (Koelble, 1987, p. 255). The party's structure in the 1980s meant that these campaigners had no chance of affecting a policy change without the support of the trade unions. The TUFP's tactics were partly responsible for the high levels of conference support for pro-Palestinian resolutions in the 1980s.

Labour Women's support for the Palestinians also resulted from these internal changes. In the 1970s and 1980s a new generation of women who had been involved in the feminist movement entered the party (Seyd, 1987, p. 49). These feminists radicalised the women's organisations, politicising institutions such as the NCLW (Lovenduski and Randall, 1993, p. 142). The women's movement outside the party had already taken up the Palestinian cause under the impact of Third World feminism, developments in the UN and trends within socialism, such as those towards anti-racism and anti-imperialism (see Pope, 1986, pp. 13–25). The new generation of women brought these ideas into the party.

Similar developments occurred in Labour's internal organisations. External advisers began to play a part in formulating policy. Left-wingers such as Fred Halliday and Christopher Hitchens joined Labour's Middle East Sub-Committee (MESC) – Halliday was a regular contributor to *New Left Review* and Hitchens was a radical journalist and author. Although Halliday was not prominent in the campaign for Palestinian national rights, he had some sympathy for the cause. From 1967 the NLR pursued a consistently pro-Palestinian line. Halliday himself contributed to a volume entitled *Israel and the Palestinians*, where he argued that the Arab states could force the United States to pressurise Israel into conceding Palestinian statehood (Halliday, 1975, pp. 169–70). Hitchens' pro-Palestinian views were expressed in a book he authored jointly with Edward Said, *Blaming the Victims* (Said and Hitchens, 1988). Although the MESC had previously been extremely divided over Palestinian nationalism, it played a part in getting the party to call for PLO participation in peace negotiations in the early 1980s.[28]

The PLP's position also stemmed from a shift to the left. Since the 1964 elections the number on the parliamentary left had grown progressively. Incoming MPs were disproportionately left wing and the constituency parties were tending to select more left-leaning candidates (Berrington, 1982, pp. 69–94). These developments contributed to Michael Foot's election as leader in 1980 (Seyd, 1987, p. 128). In 1982, twenty-three Labour MPs formed the left-wing Campaign Group (ibid., p. 165). As the 1980s progressed the PLP's left-ward trend intensified as a result of the entry into parliament of the 'new urban left'. This new element introduced a soft left agenda that included a sensitivity to issues such as gender and minority rights (Dunleavy, 1993, pp. 140–1), predisposing them to Palestinian nationalism. Members of LFI parliamentary group noted that new MPs were reluctant to join the organisation.[29]

A striking number of left-wingers were actively involved in the campaign for recognition of Palestinian national rights. Although David Watkins and Andrew Faulds were not left wing, a number of the other pro-Palestinian activists were (see Appendix 6). Martin Flannery, Joan Maynard, William McKelvey, Robert McTaggart, Robert Parry, Reg Race, Allan Roberts and Ernie Ross were all members of the Campaign Group. Albert Booth, Dale Campbell-Savours, Stanley Newens and Martin O'Neill were members of the Tribune Group. Many TUFP sponsors were from the Labour left, such as Dennis Canavan, who was a member of the Campaign Group (Seyd, 1987, p. 222, note 18), and George Galloway, who was involved in the formation of the Labour Co-ordinating Committee (LCC) in Scotland (Heffernan and Marqusee, 1992, p. 172). Moreover the pro-Israel–pro-Palestinian division mapped on to the right–left divide in the unions. While a good number of unions had begun to take on the Palestinian cause, the right-wing EETPU remained pro-Israel. At the 1983 conference the EETPU moved a resolution that gave priority to recognition of Israel's borders. The motion was defeated.[30]

Generational changes also played a vital part in the party's adoption of the Palestinian cause. Whereas the sight of Jewish refugees had touched Labour's older generation and created a groundswell of sympathy for Zionist aims, the Palestinian refugee crisis was more salient for the 1980s generation, hence the Palestinian cause attracted a greater proportion of the younger-generation Labour MPs than the Israeli cause. An analysis of activists[31] in the PLP for the respective causes shows that 9 per cent of pro-Israel activists were born in or after 1935 compared with 32 per cent of pro-Palestinian activists. After taking into account other sources of data that give a broader picture, around 6 per cent of the Labour MPs who sympathised with Israel were born in or after 1935 compared with around 29 per cent of the Labour MPs who identified with the Palestinian cause. Furthermore, 32 per cent of the pro-Israel Labour MPs entered parliament after 1970 compared with around 62 per cent of pro-Palestinian MPs.

The left's rise led the party to adopt a broad approach to foreign policy that was particularly amenable to Palestinian demands. Labour contained a strong undercurrent of anti-American feeling, being particularly critical of US involvement in the Third World. At the same time the party adopted anti-racist politics, protesting against South African apartheid, and it took up the campaign for nuclear disarmament. These developments coincided with Israel's increasing identification with US foreign policy. The United States provided Israel with a significant amount of financial and political support and the Likud government helped the United States to implement its foreign policy agenda in the Third World. It sold arms to countries such as Nicaragua and Guatemala and it also had links with South Africa (see Said, 1988, pp. 24, 33). Furthermore Israel had begun to develop a nuclear capacity. The Vanunu affair in 1986 drew attention to this development and sparked off a series of protests. In an interview in *The Sunday Times* Mordechai Vanunu claimed that Israel had developed and stockpiled nuclear weapons. Mossad subsequently captured Vanunu in Rome and he was imprisoned for treason (Ovendale, 1992, pp. 303–4). According to Healey, the fact that the US authorities knew about Israel's nuclear weapons programme provides further evidence of the United States' commitment to Israel (Healey, 1989, p. 315).

The significant localisation of pro-Palestinian and anti-Israel activism in London and Scotland deserves special consideration. The case of London is particularly interesting because the pro-Palestinian movement occurred in traditionally Jewish areas such as Brent. However, demographic trends had resulted in black and Asian communities being established in boroughs such as this and relations between these minorities and the Jewish community were tense, with some Asians and Afro-Caribbeans adopting anti-Zionist politics (Alderman, 1989, pp. 118–25). This coincided with Labour's efforts to appeal to black and Asian voters (Peele, 1990, p. 81). During the 1982 local elections in particular, Labour candidates, amongst others, made a concerted effort to attract the votes of these minorities (Charlot, 1985, pp. 139–54). Consequently the new, anti-racist left's links with black and Asian communities replaced the traditional alliance between Labour and the Jews.

These factors did not account for the high degree of pro-Palestinian activism in the Scottish labour movement. Rather the Scottish left's support for the Palestinians reflected their tradition of radicalism and independence: the Scottish Labour Party and the Scottish TUC (STUC) had never felt compelled to stand by the national party's policy positions (Wainwright, 1987, pp. 144–9). Hence the Scottish labour movement's independent spirit enabled it to identify with movements for self-determination such as the Palestinian one. Also important was its identification with other left-wing causes, such as the anti-apartheid campaign. Although not on the far left, the Dundee Labour Party had long been committed to the Anti-Apartheid Movement and various anti-imperialist movements.[32] Political activists such as Abe Sirton, who had spent his life campaigning on behalf of oppressed groups, played a part in getting the Scottish Party to take up the Palestinian cause by helping to establish the Scottish Friends of Palestine (SFP).[33]

Like other left-wing movements, then, in the 1980s the Labour Party broke away from its pro-Israel tradition and moved towards support for Palestinian national rights. External factors, including developments in Israel, the British Jews' shift to the right and the rise of the PLO and the intifada, all contributed to this shift. However the rise of the Labour left was the most important factor. In the following section I shall discuss the question of anti-Zionism in the party and whether the party succumbed to anti-Jewish themes.

Anti-Zionism

It would be misleading to suggest that the Labour Party has never contained anti-Zionist elements. The traditional pro-Arabists, Mayhew and Watkins, were anti-Zionist (see Chapter 4). However their views were very marginal before the 1980s, when new elements began to elaborate anti-Zionist themes. For example at the 1982 annual conference Ted Knight, a Workers' Revolutionary Party (WRP) plant, moved an emergency motion that called for the replacement of Israel with a democratic secular state of Palestine.[34] In his supporting speech, Knight compared Zionism to Nazism, claiming that it was the 'Zionists who . . . feed antisemitism by working hand-in-glove with the Nazi Falangists in Lebanon'.[35] At the party conference in 1986 Jeremy Corbyn chaired a meeting of the Labour Campaign for Palestine (LCP). One of the speakers at the meeting was Tony Greenstein, who[36] espoused an especially extreme form of anti-Zionism, claiming that Zionism justified the National Front's views

period/of young people revolt?
era

and even questioning the extent of the Nazi genocide of the Jews (see Billig, 1984b, p. 31). Ken Livingstone allegedly referred to Israel as a country based on 'racism and the murder of Arabs' (Alderman, 1989, p. 133), and at a rally held in Trafalgar Square in August 1982 he compared the Israeli cabinet to the Galtieri regime in Argentina.[37]

The far left Labour press also provided a platform for anti-Zionist views. In June 1982 the *Labour Herald* carried a cartoon that showed Begin, dressed in a Gestapo uniform, standing over the bodies of Palestinians. The cartoon was entitled 'The Final Solution'. The newspaper also described Israel as a 'state entirely built on the blood of Europe's Jews, whom the Zionists deserted in their hour of greatest need' (Alderman, 1989, pp. 132–3). The ILP newspaper, the *Labour Leader*, used similar images. In September 1982 it published a photograph of Jews in a Nazi concentration camp next to a picture of Begin, who was described as the 'former leader of a terrorist gang'.[38] By the mid 1980s far left ideas had evidently affected Labour Women. NCLW resolutions began to use characteristic anti-Zionist themes. In 1984 the Bootle Women's Section tabled a resolution that stated that the Palestinian–Israeli conflict was the result of the 'intervention of imperialism'.[39] Two years later Leicester South Women's Section called on the NEC to demand Israel's withdrawal from the occupied territories and stated that it was 'opposed to the Zionist state as racist, exclusivist and a direct agency of imperialism'.[40] International developments underpinned this trend, including a 1976 UN Security Council resolution that condemned Zionism as a form of racism, the shift to the right in Israel and the rise of Palestinian nationalism.

However Trotskyist entryism was also responsible for introducing anti-Zionism into the party. Trotskyism has a strong anti-Zionist tradition and contemporary groups continued in this tradition, but also added a new theme, replacing the idea that Zionism splits the working class with the view that Zionism is a form of racism or even fascism (see Billig, 1984b, pp. 28–34). In the 1970s various far left groups entered the party. The Militant Group, which was strong in Merseyside and to a lesser extent London, was the most significant of these (Lovenduski and Randall, 1993, p. 138) and its membership tripled between 1976 and 1982 (Crick, 1986, p. 315). Other Trotskyist groups included the Socialist Organiser Alliance (SOA) and the Chartist Group, which seceded from the SOA in 1980 and published *London Labour Briefing*. The Chartist Group was active primarily in the GLC and Labour borough councils in London (Seyd, 1987, p. 52). Ted Knight, the controversial leader of Lambeth council, was a member of the WRP (Lansley *et al.*, 1989, p. 6). Knight had links with people such as Ken Livingstone and Jeremy Corbyn, all of whom were involved with the *Labour Herald*, which was published by Gerry Healy's WRP (Crick, 1986, p. 257). The *London Labour Briefing* was also anti-Zionist. A committee of WRP members ran this newspaper and Livingstone, representing the Labour Party, was a committee member.

Did this wave of anti-Zionism incorporate anti-Semitic themes? Billig argues that anti-Zionism is anti-Jewish when it singles out Jewish nationalism for special criticism. Hence it is not anti-Jewish to oppose Jewish nationalism on the ground that nationalism generally contradicts socialist principles (Billig, 1984a, pp. 8–9). The question of whether opposition to Israel is anti-Jewish can only be settled at the empirical level. At this level, it cannot be denied that some party members' anti-Zionism had an obsessive quality and included typical anti-Jewish themes. The *Labour Leader*, for example, conceptualised Jews as a race, claiming that Israel had given 'exclusive civil and political power to the race which had habitually been denied such power'.[41] The portrayal of Begin as a bloodsucker and the claim that Israel was based on the 'blood of Jews' resonated with the anti-Semitic theory of 'blood libel'.

Some members of the far left and pro-Palestinian strand also gave voice to a conspiracy theory of Zionism. Knight spoke of 'Zionist forces' and claimed that 'Zionist organizations, particularly in this country and throughout the world, have attempted to silence the critics of what has gone on in the Lebanon'.[42] Some members of LMEC referred to the 'conspiracy of silence' over Labour's policy on Israel.[43] The conspiracy theory of Zionism exaggerates the power of Zionist organisations in the same way as anti-Semites have traditionally exaggerated Jewish power. More sensitive members of the campaign for recognition of Palestinian national rights noticed the tendency towards conspiracy theory. For example, after attending a Poale Zion fringe meeting on 'Racism, Antisemitism and the Socialist Agenda', Clare Short said that supporters of the Palestinian cause were in danger of 'slipping into the language of conspiracy'.[44]

Nevertheless it would be wrong to conclude, as Alderman does, that the anti-Zionist element of the party had taken control of the NEC by the early 1980s (Alderman, 1989, p. 125). Although in 1982 the NEC endorsed the principle of Palestinian self-determination and statehood, it was not anti-Zionist. Indeed the NEC explicitly opposed hard-line opposition to Zionism or Israel. Speaking as its representative at the 1982 annual conference, Healey opposed two resolutions on the ground that they failed to include clauses that conceded Israel's right to exist.[45] Moreover it is important to distinguish between the views of the far and the soft left. Whereas the former saw class conflict as fundamental, the latter was interested in divisions other than class ones (see Seyd, 1987, pp. 168–9). Consequently the far left refused to recognise Israel and proposed the establishment of a democratic, secular state, whereas the soft left tended only to criticise Israeli policy, which is not necessarily anti-Zionist. Michael Foot, for example, did not question Israel's right to exist. Nor did he depict Israel as a racist or fascist state. The same was true of the younger generation of soft left activists. Clare Short, for example, advocated a two-state solution to the conflict and explicitly opposed Trotskyist demands.[46] Even Palestinian activists believed that the far left's call to abolish Israel was impractical and damaged their cause.[47] So although the anti-Zionist elements did seek to influence policy, their views were in the minority. In the following section I shall consider the intra-party conflict that followed Labour's move away from a pro-Israeli perspective and its implications for policy.

Conflict and retreat

However widespread the shift towards recognition of Palestinian national rights, it produced a serious rift within Labour's ranks. Jewish members of the party played an active part in seeking to stem the tide of the new current, including prominent backbenchers such as Ian Mikardo. Although Mikardo accepted the principle of Palestinian self-determination,[48] he strongly opposed the move in the party towards recognition of the PLO. In the past[49] he had objected to internal party criticism of Israel and the Socialist International's decision to establish links between European socialists and Arab socialist groups.[50] Following a fact-finding trip to Lebanon after the 1982 invasion, the MP told a meeting of LFI's parliamentary branch that there had been a 'gross exaggeration' of the number of casualties and people made homeless and that the Lebanese people were grateful to Israel for freeing them from PLO control.[51] At the party conference he opposed the pro-Palestinian resolutions on the ground that they sought the 'extinction' of Israel.[52]

In response to the cluster of pro-Palestinian resolutions submitted
to the conference in 1982, Greville Janner, MP for Leicester West
and president of the BOD, complained that he and the Jewish
community could not understand how a democratic body such as
Labour could have relations with the PLO. He added that Jewish
delegates at the conference would do their best to overturn the
resolution.[53] Kaufman's contacts with the PLO alienated certain
sections of the Jewish community and press; and some Jews felt
that his links with the PLO invalidated his claim to be a Zionist.[54]

In their efforts to counter the pro-Palestinian movement, Jewish
Labour organisations began to operate in areas that were at the
forefront of the campaigns. In particular, Poale Zion and LFI organised in the Scottish labour movement. In the summer of 1982
the LFI arranged a demonstration against a Scottish TUC meeting
in Perth. A leader of the Dundee Jewish community, Albert Jacobs,
supported LFI's director, Valerie Cocks.[55] In June 1982 Poale Zion
formed a Scottish branch and the MP for East Kilbride, Maurice
Miller, became its chair.[56]

Some Jewish Labour members and groups tried to influence political opinion by appealing to the Jewish vote. In the Brent borough
elections in May 1982, John Lebor advised electors not to vote for
Labour on the ground that around one fifth of all Labour candidates in the borough supported the PLO. The local Rabbi, Dr Harry
Rabinowicz, warned congregants not to vote for Alf Filer, the Jewish
Labour candidate for Cricklewood, because Filer favoured the
establishment of a secular state of Israel. During the May 1982 elections Labour lost two Cricklewood seats and its share of the poll
decreased quite considerably compared with 1978. Some attributed
Labour's poor results to the rows between the Brent Labour Party
and the Jewish community (Alderman, 1989, p. 126). The BOD also
tried to influence the Jewish electorate. In the 1983 election Dr
Jack Gewirtz, its director of defence, expressed concern about 'activities within the Labour Party of groups and individuals which
work closely with the PLO'. The BOD identified the Labour candidate for Westminster North, Arthur Latham, as a PLO supporter.[57]
The organisation also made direct appeals to the party leadership.
For example just before the annual conference in 1988 a BOD delegation, headed by its president, Dr Lionel Kopelowitz, met Neil
Kinnock to express concern about the anti-Israel motions that had
been tabled.[58]

The Labour councils' shift towards the Palestinian movement revealed sharp differences in opinion between the old Labour left and the new Labour left (see Alderman, 1983, p. 114). John Lebor, a former leader of Brent council and a member of LFI's national executive, claimed that 'militant leftists' were responsible for this development (Alderman, 1989, pp. 125-6). The protest focused on Ken Livingstone. Some Labour members of the GLC objected to Livingstone's outspoken criticisms of Israel, and especially his claim that Jews on the extreme right had taken over the BOD. The GLC chair, Illtyd Harrington, suggested that Livingstone's remarks had made the GLC seem anti-Semitic and damaged relations with the entire Jewish community. Gladys Dimson, former chair of the GLC's Housing Committee, threatened to resign unless Livingstone apologised for the remark about the BOD. The Labour Group subsequently voted for Livingstone to withdraw his claim (ibid., p. 134). The policy changes also split Labour Women. The party's older generation of women and the incoming generation disagreed over a range of issues (Seyd, 1987, p. 49; see also Wainwright, 1987, pp. 165-71). This split played itself out on the question of Israel. Prominent women in Labour's older generation, such as Gwyneth Dunwoody and Jo Richardson, remained strong supporters of Israel and active members of LFI. In the 1980s Dunwoody and Richardson continued to champion Israel and to resist the impetus towards the Palestinian cause, especially recognition of the PLO. This conflict also took place in Labour councils. For example in April 1983 women members of Poale Zion were prevented from attending an International Women's Day seminar at County Hall. In June 1984 four Labour members of the GLC council, including Gladys Dimson, voted with the opposition in protest against the GLC's Women's Committee's alleged anti-Zionist comments (Alderman, 1989, p. 135).

The debates drew attention to the potential costs to Labour of too strongly identifying with the Palestinian cause. The party's officials and leadership tried to diffuse the tension. In response to the NEC's endorsement of a policy document drafted by MESC, Joan Lestor, chair of the international committee, suggested that the reference to the PLO be omitted.[59] At the 1983 conference the NEC decided to withdraw resolutions on the Palestinian–Israeli conflict for the sake of unity and its statement on the Middle East did not include a reference to the conflict.[60] The new leader, Neil Kinnock, adopted a more conciliatory approach towards Jewish opinion and tried to rebuild bridges with Jewish Labour groups in Britain and Israel. Kinnock always attended the LFI reception held at the party's annual conference. He expressed particular sympathy for Israel and was close to Shimon Peres and other leading Israeli politicians.[61] In June 1987 Kinnock told the *Jewish Chronicle* that Labour was 'a strong supporter of Israel' and that he had campaigned strongly for changes in Soviet policy on the question of Jewish emigration.[62] Labour's attempts at reconciliation with the Jewish community had direct implications for candidates' policies in the 1987 general election in Jewish areas. The candidate for Hendon South, Louise Christian told the *Jewish Chronicle* that she 'fully supported Israel's right to exist as a separate state'. She also said that although the PLO should be included in peace talks, she opposed the view that Zionism was a form of racism, clearly seeking to distance herself from the anti-Zionist left. Poale Zion backed her. In Finchley John Davies, leader of the Labour group on Barnet Council, campaigned primarily on issues irrelevant to Jewish voters. However his agent, Mick O'Connor, said that the party was going to draw attention to Thatcher's refusal to pursue Nazi war criminals.[63] Thatcher had long been personally committed to Israel, being one of the first members of the Conservative Friends of Israel (Rubinstein, 1982, p. 95). However she was vulnerable to Labour's exploitation of her government's record as its Middle East policy had tended to be pro-Arab (ibid., pp. 154–5).

Even Ken Livingstone, the candidate for Brent East, began to moderate his views. Livingstone replaced the Jewish Labour MP Reg Freeson, who had been particularly upset by the developments in London (see Alderman, 1989, pp. 126–7). In an interview with the *Jewish Chronicle*, Livingstone said that if anyone thought he was anti-Semitic they should not vote for him, but 'it would be difficult for anyone to explain how [he could] support every single minority except the Jewish minority'. He added that he had always defended the rights of Jews to live in Israel. He dismissed the charge that he had described the BOD as fascist and added that he did not think Zionism was a form of racism,[64] signalling a definite shift in his position. Livingstone's new moderation on this issue reflected his increasing alienation from far left groups (see Seyd, 1987, p. 168).

In the late 1980s the tide began to turn on the question of Labour's policy towards Israel and the Palestinians. The leadership sought to replace the earlier radicalism with a more moderate position. The NEC opposed the resolutions at the 1988 and 1989 conferences,[65] despite the fact that they included references to Israel's right to exist. Whereas in 1982 the NEC's policy statement had included an explicit reference to Palestinian statehood, its policy statement in 1988 referred to the Palestinians' right to self-determination and a 'homeland'. The pro-Palestinian activists were not happy with this shift.[66] Kaufman's and Tony Clarke's policy review on 'Britain and the World', included a diluted form of previous policy commitments to the Palestinian cause. The statement recognised that the Palestinians had been prevented from having their own chosen form of government, called for the government of Israel to enter into dialogue with the PLO and supported a UN-sponsored International Conference to negotiate a settlement of the Palestinian–Israeli conflict.[67] At a meeting in May 1989 the NEC discussed the review document. During the discussion on the Middle East, Tony Benn proposed a motion in favour of acceptance of a Palestinian state. He was defeated by eighteen votes to five. Ken Livingstone proposed that Palestinian refugees be allowed to return to Israel. This motion was defeated by twenty votes to three (Benn, 1992, p. 565). These votes showed very clearly the change that had taken place since the early 1980s.

The battle over the party's policy towards Israel and the Palestinians was part of a wider battle. The Labour right launched a counter-attack on the left and the left started to fragment and divide (see Seyd, 1987, pp. 159–71). As the 1980s proceeded the left's dominance declined. With the election of the new leadership in 1983 the balance of power between the factions shifted. The Kinnock–Hattersley partnership tried to restore a more centralised style of leadership, characteristic of the Wilson era (Dunleavy, 1993, pp. 139–42). Although Kinnock was from the party's left, under his leadership the left divided over a series of issues, in particular the miners' strike (Seyd, 1987, pp. 166–7). After Labour's electoral defeat in 1987 the leadership's desire to reconstitute the party intensified. The 1987 policy review process aimed to transform the party by dropping apparently unpopular policies (Peele, 1990, pp. 79–80). By the late 1980s the left's retreat was evident in Labour's decision to drop its commitment to unilateralism and withdrawal from the EC (Morgan, 1992, p. 339).

Nevertheless a new (if imperfect) Labour consensus emerged, based on a compromise between the two sides. The policy included three main principles: recognition of Israel, support for a UN-sponsored peace conference and support for Palestinian self-determination. With respect to the first principle, the pro-Palestinian activists conceded the leadership's demand for a policy that included explicit recognition of Israel's right to exist within secure borders.[68] The activists' concession reflected developments in the PLO. Under Yasser Arafat's leadership the PLO had moved towards coexistence with Israel in addition to Palestinian statehood (Said, 1992, p. xiii, see also Lesch and Tessler, 1989, p. 282). The two sides also agreed on the idea of a UN peace conference. At the party conference in 1990 Kaufman said that there had to be an international conference that would provide 'justice and self-determination' for the Palestinian people.[69] Later the NEC overwhelmingly backed this policy. Ernie Ross's support for the NEC's decision indicated agreement between the activists and the leadership.[70] The two sides also agreed on the principle of Palestinian self-determination. Although the leadership's statements tended to use the ambiguous concept of 'homeland' rather than statehood, irritating some of the pro-Palestinian campaigners,[71] Kaufman claimed that a peace conference should aim to achieve self-determination for the Palestinians.[72] Moreover LMEC members felt that the party could not go back on its commitment to this principle. In any case, Labour's sanctioning of this policy was not politically risky. By this stage there was a significant current of support for Palestinian self-determination, both internationally and nationally. An implicit consensus also emerged on recognition of the PLO as the legitimate representative of the Palestinian people. Although the leadership did not include this principle in official policy statements, it gave the principle its unofficial support. Kinnock stated that a future Labour government would be willing to meet the PLO if such a meeting would assist the peace process.[73] Moreover Kaufman told a meeting of Poale Zion and LMEC that the PLO should be included in any peace talks. He suggested that the Palestinians should be able to choose their representatives in the same way as the Jews had been able to choose theirs during the British mandate.[74]

Conclusion

In the early 1980s Labour moved decisively towards recognition of Palestinian national rights. Previously, dissent from the pro-Israel consensus had been confined to a small number of pro-Arab MPs, some elements in the Labour left and the constituency parties. However the breakdown in support for Israel in the 1980s embraced all sections of the party, including the PLP. The rise of the right in Israel, the movement of British Jews towards conservatism and the increased activism of the Palestinian nationalist movement in Western politics all contributed to this shift. However the key dynamic was the rise of the Labour left. Although identification with Palestinian nationalism cut across party factions, the Palestinian cause became closely associated with a new kind of left activist. The party's policy in favour of Palestinian statehood in the early 1980s was part of a wider process that led to the adoption of unilateralism and a policy of withdrawal from the EC.

This trend towards greater sympathy for Palestinian nationalism did not go uncontested. The minority who continued to be ideologically committed to Zionism and Israel campaigned against the pro-Palestinian element. Alderman's description of the 1980s as a decade marked by a 'descent into war' between the Labour Party and the Jews (Alderman, 1989, p. 111) somewhat exaggerates the state of affairs, but the Israeli–Palestinian conflict did reveal intra-party divisions. The debates drew attention to the potential costs of the party identifying with the Palestinian cause, in terms of both intra-party division and electorally. The election of a new leadership in 1983, intent on weakening the left as part of a drive to make Labour more electable, had repercussions for policy on the Palestinian–Israeli conflict. In the late 1980s a new division emerged when the leadership marginalised some of the pro-Palestinian demands in its attempt to rebuild the party. This gave way to a new consensus, based on recognition of Israel's right to exist and the Palestinians' right to self-determination.

Although intra-party developments were behind this shift towards a more moderate stance, external factors made it easier for pro-Palestinian activists to accept it. In the first place, the PLO itself had dropped its wholesale opposition to Israel, advocating a two-state solution to the conflict. Second, Israel's shift to the right, which had so alienated traditional Labour supporters of the Jewish state, had sparked off a counter-reaction and given rise to progressive forces such as the Peace Now movement. Its effect had not been to unite Israelis but to polarise them, creating a sharp division between right and left, with the former rallying behind Begin and the latter strongly opposing the Israeli government's policy (Lesch and Tessler, 1989, pp. 39–40). These developments provided the momentum for the Israeli Labour Party's move towards negotiation with the Palestinians, propelling leaders such as Shimon Peres to adopt a more accommodating attitude and ending with the current peace negotiations. The British Labour Party could now safely support a two-state option without alienating the Jewish community.

To what extent did the evolution in Labour's thinking take place in other left-wing groups? Did the processes behind its policy changes operate within the communist left and other social democratic parties? Part II of this book addresses these questions. It looks first at the way the British Communist Party responded to Israel during the postwar period and then at the French left's attitudes.

Part II

The CPGB, the French Left and Conclusion

6
The British Communist Party and Israel: From the Establishment of the Jewish State to the Invasion of Lebanon

As a member of the international communist movement, the British Communist Party (CPGB) had a strong internationalist current, holding that international socialism prevailed over national culture and that the cause of the international working class took priority over nationalism (Hobsbawm, 1977a, pp. 5–6). Supporting only those nationalist movements considered capable of overthrowing capitalism and imperialism, the CPGB had a long tradition of hostility for Zionism and support for Arab nationalism. With respect to the conflicting nationalist claims to Palestine, the party opposed the Jews' claims on the grounds that Zionism divided the working class and only paid lip service to socialism. Moreover it believed that the Zionist movement depended upon an alliance with imperialism, whereas Arab nationalism represented a 'struggle for national independence against imperialism' (see Rennap, 1943, pp. 73–87).

As the Cold War intensified, the CPGB's support for anti-imperialist national liberation movements sharpened. Perceiving Western imperialism as the major threat to progress, the party supported national liberation movements irrespective of their relationship to communism or socialism so long as they were anti-imperialist (Howe, 1993, pp. 288–93). To what extent did communist principles determine the party's policy position during the various Israeli–Arab conflicts? Was the party's attitude unchanging and monolithic or was there dissent? How did the communists' stand compare with that of Labour? In this chapter I shall consider these issues. The first section describes the way in which the CPGB interpreted the Israeli–Arab conflict from the postwar period to the 1980s. The second section explains its various policy positions and the third compares the evolution of its approach to Israel with that of Labour.

Changing attitudes towards Israel

Given the CPGB's traditional hostility towards Zionism, one might have expected it to oppose Jewish migration to Palestine and the establishment of a Jewish state. However during the 1940s the CPGB abandoned its principles and adopted a number of pro-Zionist policies, including the formation of a National Jewish Committee (NJC) in 1943 and supporting Jewish migration to and land purchases in Palestine (Kushner, 1990, pp. 67–70). Phil Piratin, MP for Mile End, and Jack Gaster, the communist representative for Mile End on the LCC (Alderman, 1992, p. 317), in a statement to the Anglo-American Committee of Inquiry said that although Jewish development in Palestine had contributed to a large mass of landless Arabs, the existing Jewish community had earned the right to 'develop their new home as free and equal citizens of Palestine'.[1] In 1948 the CPGB wholeheartedly supported the establishment of Israel, seeing the state's foundation as 'a big step toward fulfilment of self-determination of the peoples of Palestine' and 'a great sign of the times'.[2] The party's past support for Arab nationalism gave way to a hostile characterisation of the nationalist movement as reactionary and feudalistic, the CPGB suggesting that there should be an 'ultimatum to the Arab feudal lords, who are truly puppets of Anglo-American oil – an ultimatum to lay down their arms'.[3]

This position brought the communists into conflict with the Labour government. The CPGB condemned Bevin's Palestine policy, accusing him of having committed a 'shameful betrayal' of the Jews and claiming that 'Bevinism leads to anti-Semitism and all that follows' (Kushner, 1990, pp. 70–1). In parliament William Gallacher (MP for West Fife) and Piratin sponsored an EDM that stated that the government was responsible for the Arab states' invasion of Palestine, urging recognition of Israel and recommending the immediate withdrawal of military aid to the Arabs. The fellow-travellers Denis Pritt and John Platts-Mills added their signatures.[4] The party declared that the war in Palestine was 'British sponsored' and the direct consequence of 'imperialist policy': 'This reactionary war conducted by the chieftains of the Arab League under British control is entirely against the interests of the Arab masses, who in all the countries of the Middle East are striving for freedom from imperialist domination.'[5] The communists portrayed the Jews' protest against British policy as anti-imperialist, declaring that 'the days of imperialism are numbered'.[6]

However the party's ideological opposition to Zionism and support for Arab nationalism quickly re-emerged. Its initial support for Israel gave way to a strong anti-Zionist stand during the Slansky trials in Czechoslovakia and the 'Doctors' Plot' in the Soviet Union,[7] with the party asserting that the Slansky trials 'revealed the now familiar pattern of American espionage and sabotage against the People's Democracies. . . . The fact that eleven of the fourteen conspirators were of bourgeois Jewish origin . . . proved beyond doubt the complicity of the Zionist organization and Israeli government in the plot.'[8] Now that the CPGB saw Israel as an imperialist state. Harry Pollitt, the party's secretary, said that the Zionist movement had always been a 'tool of British imperialism' and that it was 'increasingly shifting its allegiance to the stronger American imperialism'. He claimed that Israel had become a 'pawn of the USA' and that Zionism was 'a ready-made tool and weapon for the American-backed spies, traitors and wreckers' (Pelling, 1975, pp. 167–8).

The party adopted a pro-Arab position in the 1956 hostilities, seeing Nasser's nationalisation of the Suez Canal as 'Egyptian defiance of western imperialism',[9] and viewing the Anglo-French attack as a manifestation of the West's intention to undermine national liberation movements in the Middle East and North Africa. The communists claimed that the British government's

> only friends are rabid French imperialists, who, having got themselves embroiled in large-scale warfare in Algeria, would like their British allies and rivals embroiled up to the neck in Egypt. . . . Their only semblance of a policy consists in the assumption that if Britain and France can overthrow Nasser, the Arab world will quieten down.[10]

Citing Lenin's theory of imperialism, the party argued that the Anglo-French invasion happened because 'while there is capitalism in the world, the forces of reaction, representing the interests of capitalist monopolies, will persist in military gambles and aggression'.[11]

The CPGB accused Israel of allying with Western imperialism, suggesting that Israel's role in the war served 'the interests of the foreign colonialists' and was motivated by a desire for 'territorial expansion'. It claimed that the Ben-Gurion government had 'entered

into a dangerous plot, together with the British and French imperialists, against neighbouring peoples defending their national
independence and sovereignty'.[12] Bert Ramelson, head of the NJC,
said that Israel's part in the conflict reflected the country's 'imperialist alliances'.[13] The conflict revived the party's views on the nature
of Zionism and anti-Semitism. It claimed that anti-Semitism was
the 'weapon of reactionary ruling classes' and 'split the working
class', and reiterated the view that Zionism could not combat anti-
Semitism since it was based on the premise that anti-Semitism was
'ineradicable'. However the 1956 crisis produced an unprecedented
groundswell of internal dissent over the party's position on Israel.
Chimen Abramsky and Hyman Levy began to challenge communist policy and the view that the Soviet Union was a haven for the
Jews. In September 1956 the International Department and the NJC
held an emergency meeting on the question of Soviet anti-Semitism,
revealing a split between some Jewish members and the leadership.
Members of the NJC stated that the *Daily Worker* had suppressed
debate on anti-Semitism in the Soviet Union and had given the
impression that the party condoned socialist anti-Semitism. The majority of the NJC refused to accept Palme Dutt's defence of the Soviet
Union (Kushner, 1990, pp. 71–2). Levy and Abramsky in particular
challenged the party's line on Zionism and Israel. In their short
book *Jews and the National Question* they called for a re-evaluation
of communism's attitude towards Jewish nationalism and the party's policy towards Zionism and the Arab–Israeli conflict (Levy, 1958,
pp. 12–7).

The breakdown in the anti-Zionist consensus reflected the wider
developments that resulted from Khrushchev's revelations about
Stalinist repression. Those who disagreed with the party's attitude
towards Zionism were also involved in the movement for greater
internal democracy. Abramsky argued that the party should learn
from the Khrushchev revelations and that it should re-examine the
principle of democratic centralism. He objected to the way in which
ordinary party members played no part in the formulation of party
policy and the tendency for 'blind loyalty to Moscow'.[14] His and
Levy's eventual departure from the party was part of a much wider
exodus that included people such as Edward Thompson and John
Saville: between 1956 and 1959 about ten thousand members left
(Callaghan, 1990a, pp. 186–7). Thompson and Saville took part in
the establishment of *The Reasoner*, which also found the Soviet Union's
attitudes towards Jewish nationalism disturbing (Saville, 1976, p. 6).

The affair split the Jewish communists. Chimen Abramsky later told Zaidman that members of his former branch regarded him as an 'untouchable' (Kushner, 1990, p. 72). Later Jack Woddis, an active member of the MCF, also broke with the party's line on Jewish nationalism, claiming that the Soviet Union was hostile to Jewish cultural expression.[15] Ramelson, Zaidman and Solly Kaye chose to remain in the party and conform to its anti-Zionist position. Reflecting on the affair, Solly Kaye has said that although he could now see that what Levy said was well founded, at the time he had been impressed by Dutt's expertise on international affairs.[16]

The leadership responded by trying to repress the dissent. Palme Dutt disowned Levy's book on the ground that it contradicted basic Marxist tenets, saying that Jewish nationalist aspirations could only be realised by 'methods of colonial conquest or imperialism' and that it provided 'fodder for anti-Semitism'.[17] Bert Ramelson, head of the NJC, objected to Levy's call for a re-evaluation of the party's stand on Zionism and described the book as a 'thinly disguised defence of Zionism', attacking Levy for praising the Israeli party Mapam (to the left of Mapai) on the ground that the party shared responsibility for the Israeli government's 'deeds'.[18] Idris Cox recommended a review of the NJC's activities.[19] Palme Dutt imposed handpicked members on the committee on the ground that there was an 'urgent need for a strong and effective Jewish committee', and insisted that the committee should put forward the communist perspective on the Jewish question as 'part of the general fight against imperialism'.[20] The new NJC complied with this imperative. In a subsequent policy statement it said that Zionism falsely claimed that Jewish workers had something in common with 'Jewish supporters of imperialism'; that Zionism was a reactionary doctrine and had rightly been condemned as such by the international socialist movement as early as the First World War. The committee further maintained that Zionism was integrally linked with imperialism and that 'No-one is Socialist – certainly not Marxist – who divides workers of a given country, city or locality, from each other and finds greater unity between capitalists and workers of one religion or race than among workers of the same class who may have different religions.'[21] With respect to anti-Semitism in the Soviet Union, the committee contended that 'bourgeois Jews' who 'could not believe that there [was] a difference between hostility to Zionism and hostility to Jews' had made the accusations.[22]

The CPGB's anti-Israel and pro-Arab position was maintained

throughout the 1967 hostilities. Supporting the Arab countries, John Gollan, the general secretary, stated that the struggle against imperialism demanded support for the Arab liberation movement.[23] The party claimed that the 'imperialist powers' had 'stirred up conflict between Jews and Arabs to safeguard their own economic and strategic interests in the Middle East'.[24] It said that the West's principal aim was to overthrow the Syrian and Egyptian governments and to bring these countries back into the 'imperialist orbit' in order to secure oil supplies and remove Soviet influence from the region (Ramelson, 1967, p. 24).

As for Israel, the communists said that its role in the war was the result of 'imperialist alliances', with the political committee stating that 'Israel can never enjoy security and peace as long as it acts as an ally of imperialism, denies the rights of Arabs and ranges itself on the side of the forces opposing the Arab liberation movement.'[25]

The 1967 hostilities produced another spate of anti-Zionism. Ramelson's pamphlet on the Middle East crisis contended that Zionism was a 'false' and 'reactionary' doctrine whose sole aim was to 'weaken the class sense of Jews by preaching a non-existent "common national interest"' (Ramelson, 1967, pp. 7–10). His exposition of the party's position included a conspiracy theory of Zionism. He claimed that Israel's military, financial and strategic force rested on 'Zionist inspired financial, economic and "pressure group" support from the widespread Jewish communities, conditioned by years of Zionist propaganda to believe that they owe allegiance to the Zionist state of Israel' (ibid., pp. 36–7) and that 'It is . . . no accident that the "new found" friends of the Jews and Israel during 1956 and 1967 are often the same ones who supported Munich and the rise of Hitler and Mosley, and for exactly the same reasons – considerations of imperialist advantage' (ibid., p. 41).

The party's policy generated further dissent, with some members challenging the idea that Israel was the aggressor and suggesting that the Arab states had deliberately whipped up the Palestinian refugee crisis. They also queried the CPGB's support for Egypt in the light of Nasser's anti-communist policies. Other party members began to question the leadership's defence of the Soviet bloc against accusations of anti-Semitism. Referring to the Polish Communist Party's repression of Jewish cultural activities, the dissenters accused the British party's leadership of refusing to take seriously the possibility of anti-Semitism in Eastern Europe. In particular they attacked Bert Ramelson and Maurice Lichtig for failing to provide information on Poland's anti-Zionist propaganda.[26] The leadership again tried to repress disquiet over its Arab–Israeli position. Idris Cox and the International Department decided to reestablish the Middle East subcommittee and to merge it with the NJC.[27] Cox was responsible for the choice of potential members of the new subcommittee and decided that Maurice Lichtig should be chair.[28] This decision was significant because Lichtig was highly committed to the traditional communist view of Zionism and the idea that the Soviet Union had solved 'the Jewish problem'.[29]

So, for most of the postwar period the CPGB maintained a pro-Arab, anti-Israel stance. However Israel's involvement in Lebanon in the 1980s drew attention to some significant changes in the party's outlook. By this time the party had split between the traditionalists and the reformist new times faction. The traditionalists clustered principally around the *Morning Star* and the revisionists or the new times faction around *Marxism Today*. The key difference between the two factions rested on their analysis of the role of class in contemporary society. The former strand believed that communism's appeal to the working class should remain a priority, and although it recognised the importance of non-class identities, it maintained that it was wrong to understand them separately from class (Pitcairn, 1985, pp. 102–20). The new times strand included people such as Martin Jacques and Beatrix Campbell and believed that there was a deep-seated weakness in the labour movement, arising primarily out of the decline of the working class. This faction challenged what they saw as an indiscriminate tendency to apply class analysis to new social divisions (see Callaghan, 1988).

With respect to the Palestinian cause in the 1980s, the CPGB as a whole was committed to Palestinian nationalist aspirations, claiming that Britain should 'recognise the Palestinian people's right to establish their own national state and the PLO as the sole voice of the Palestinians'.[30] After the invasion Gerry Pocock, head of the international department, said that the party favoured 'full recognition of the PLO and the right of the Palestinian people to establish their own state in the occupied territories'.[31] An article in *Marxism Today* suggested that the decline of the communist Rakah party in Israel stemmed from its unwillingness to acknowledge the 'unity of the Palestinian people'.[32] The CPGB supported Labour's shift towards recognition of Palestinian national rights and called on the labour movement to follow the pro-PLO resolutions at the annual conference and the TUC conference.[33]

However this consensus over Palestinian national rights did not extend to views on Israel, with the traditionalists maintaining the party's previous anti-Zionist approach and the reformers rejecting it. Pocock argued that the Israeli attack was part of a long-term plan to destroy the Palestinian people and extend Israel's territory. He believed that the UN should impose sanctions against Israel in order to enforce a withdrawal.[34] Just before the invasion the *Morning Star* condemned Lord Carrington, the foreign secretary, for refusing to meet PLO representatives and claimed that Britain was providing Israel with 'tacit support' for its expansionist policies.[35] Moreover it drew parallels between the invasion and the Nazi holocaust, saying that Israel had used 'Blitzkrieg tactics' 'modelled on the military theories of Nazi strategists'.[36] The party's traditional strand portrayed Menachem Begin and Ariel Sharon as 'Nazi monsters', stating that General Sharon seems to have regarded this operation as some sort of Israeli version of a "Final Solution" but against the Palestinians'.[37]

Some of the traditionalists' coverage of Israel was anti-Semitic, drawing on anti-Jewish themes couched in biblical references. In response to the massacre, for example, the *Morning Star* declared that 'the mark of Cain is clearly on Sharon's forehead' and

> 'thy brother's blood cries out from the ground' needs to be inscribed in letters of blood over the courtroom in Jerusalem. . . . For these lines from the biblical story of Cain and Abel have been in the minds and mouths of millions the world over as ever more horrific details emerged of the monsters who masterminded it.[38]

In a pamphlet on Israel and the Palestinians, the party published a cartoon that depicted Begin salivating over skulls, with his mouth open and revealing the teeth of a vampire.[39]

In a sharp break from party orthodoxy, the reformists adopted a more moderate attitude towards Israel and Jewish nationalism, rejecting traditional communist rhetoric and confining its criticism to specific Israeli policies such as the military occupation of the West Bank and Gaza on the ground that it breached human rights and to the rise of the Israeli far right, most notably, the Kach Party.[40] Whereas in the past the CPGB had believed that there was no progressive left wing in Israel, the reformists sympathised with the Israeli *New Outlook*, edited by Simcha Flapan, which urged the return of Zionism to its socialist roots,[41] and they supported members of the Israeli peace movement such as Uri Avineri.[42] In the late 1980s this, by now dominant, faction's new approach was sealed when it explicitly condemned left-wing anti-Zionists such as Lenni Brenner for being apologists for 'Marx's anti-Semitism' and rejected communism's 'simple binary theory' – which posited that Jews were good but Zionists were bad – as 'sloganism which equates Zionism with imperialism or Israel as a tool of the US'. It further objected to a fixation on Zionist collusion with the Nazis and asked the left to take on board 'the experience of the Jew who has ingested the knowledge of the holocaust and now finds it uncomfortable to feel at home anywhere'.[43] What accounted for the CPGB's various positions?

Explaining the evolution of the CPGB's attitudes

The CPGB's early attitude towards Israel and the Israeli–Arab conflict stemmed principally from its historical subordination to the Communist Party of the Soviet Union (CPSU). Although the British party was one of the smallest in Western Europe, it belonged to the Communist International from 1920 until the International's end in 1943. While it was not formally a member of the Cominform, established in 1947, it tended to adopt the Cominform line. The formation of the Cominform meant that the British party came under greater pressure from Moscow to conform. In relation to colonial and imperial affairs, it accepted the view of the Russian leader, Andrei Zhdanov, that the world was split into an 'imperialist and anti-democratic camp' and an 'anti-imperialist and democratic camp', the first seeking to establish US imperialism across the world and the second dedicated to undermining imperialism and installing democracy (Pelling, 1975, p. 141). The intensification of the Cold War led the international communist movement increasingly to pressurise the party into rejecting any possibility of a third way between the Soviet Union and the United States (Howe, 1993, p. 160).

It was primarily the CPGB's relations with the Soviet party that caused it to make various pro-Zionist gestures in the 1940s. As part of its attempt to mobilise Jewish support after Germany's invasion of Russia, the CPSU set up the Jewish Anti-Fascist Committee (JAFC) and declared that the Jews had a 'right to political independence in Palestine' (Wistrich, 1979b, pp. 277–8). Moreover Soviet officials made contact with Zionists and supported the Haganah's illegal efforts to bring Jewish survivors to Palestine (Brod, 1979, pp. 53–5). As part of the Soviet Union's efforts to obtain Jewish support for its fight against Germany, the Soviet leadership sent the actor Shloime Mikhoels and the poet Itzik Feffer to Britain to publicise the Soviet Union's pro-Jewish activities. The CPSU directed Jewish communists in Britain to mention specific issues in their electoral campaigns, such as Mikhoel's Moscow Yiddish State Theatre, the activities of the JAFC and Birobidzhan (an autonomous Jewish region established in 1934). Piratin and other candidates dutifully complied with the directive (Srebrnik, 1986, pp. 285, 295–300). The British party's recognition of Israel directly mirrored the Soviet position. Stalin's immediate postwar policy was pro-Israel, as symbolised by Golda Meir's visit to Moscow's Grand Synagogue soon after Israel's establishment. At that time the Soviet Union had no allies in the Middle East and the Zionist movement in Palestine was anti-British. The Soviet Union supported Israel because it wanted to weaken the Western alliance by exploiting the disagreement between Attlee and Truman over Jewish immigration and to obstruct Western control over oil resources (Wistrich, 1979b, pp. 278–9, 281).

The British party's position in 1956 also arose out of its identification with the Soviet Union, which had intensified in the early 1950s. During the Suez crisis Nikita Khrushchev, the Soviet leader between 1953 and 1964, denounced Britain, France and Israel for their war against Egypt, saying that the Soviet Union would help Egypt militarily if the three countries did not withdraw their forces (Campbell, 1989, pp. 246–7). In an effort to improve the Soviet Union's position in the Middle East, Khrushchev adopted a pro-Arab stance, seeing the non-aligned states of the Third World as potential allies and portraying Arab nationalists such as Nasser as progressive, as well as providing Egypt with military aid (Wistrich, 1979b, pp. 285–6). As the Soviet Union's relations with Egypt improved, its relations with Israel deteriorated. The Soviet Union's identification with Third World neutralism and Egypt occurred when border clashes between Israel and Egypt had exacerbated relations between the two Middle Eastern countries. The Soviet premier, Bulganin, declared that Israel's role in the war would alienate it and even threaten its existence (Brod, 1979, pp. 64–6). Under Khrushchev the Soviet Union continued to repress Jewish nationalist expression and its media consistently linked Zionism and Judaism with reaction (Wistrich, 1979b, p. 286).

The CPGB's position in 1967 again reflected that of the Soviet Union. The Soviet Union was neutral about the war at first (Golan, 1991, p. 67), but soon adopted an anti-Israel stance and broke off diplomatic relations with Israel. Other East European countries quickly followed suit (Laqueur, 1969, p. 59). The Soviet Union protested against Israel's aggression and called on it to give up the occupied territories. The Soviet leader, Brezhnev, said that 'the Israeli aggressors [were] behaving like the worst of bandits. In their atrocities against the Arab population . . . they want to copy the crimes of the Hitler invaders' (Wistrich, 1979b, pp. 287, 302, note 39). This position stemmed from the Soviet Union's continuing pro-Arab strategy, aimed at strengthening its position in the Middle East by establishing a military presence there (Golan, 1991, p. 58). In this context the Soviet Union presented itself as the Arabs' natural ally by identifying with Third World liberation movements. The Soviet leadership described Nasser as a 'Hero of the Soviet Union', portraying the Egyptian leader's actions as preparing the way for socialism (Wistrich, 1979, p. 286).

The CPGB's anti-Zionist campaign in 1967 directly mirrored developments in the Soviet Union. The new rivalry between the Soviet Union and the United States over the Middle East expressed itself in the former country in an extreme anti-Zionist campaign (Wistrich, 1979, pp. 137–52). The postwar Soviet press constructed a conspiracy theory of Zionism, claiming that Zionism was a 'ramified system of agencies and political practice of the Jewish big bourgeoisie closely linked to the monopoly groups in the United States'.[44] In the late 1960s the Polish Communist Party embarked on a campaign against Zionism, accusing Zionists of being lackeys of imperialism and warmongers, and of wanting to isolate Poland from the Soviet Union; a campaign launched in response to economic problems and internal unrest, despite the fact that Polish opinion was sympathetic to Israel.[45]

The British CPGB, like the CPSU, opposed Israel because it was a Western ally. Almost from its inception Israel had adopted a pro-Western orientation, identifying with the West over the Korean conflict and seeking to join the Western alliance in the early stages of the Cold War (Pappé, 1990, pp. 561, 578). In the 1950s the Israeli government became increasingly anti-communist. After the Slansky trials, Ben-Gurion began actively to oppose the Israeli Communist Party. The Histadrut banned communists from its trade unions, the government stopped the distribution of the communist daily newspaper and Ben-Gurion wanted to expel communists from the Knesset.[46] Later Israel moved increasingly towards a pro-US stance as it depended upon alliances with powerful countries such as the United States to fulfil its military, economic and political needs.

This coincided with the United States' need to find suitable allies to protect its interests in the Middle East. Israel's original pro-Europe orientation gave way to a pro-US alignment and hostility towards the Soviet Union, condemning the latter for supporting the Arabs (Shanin, 1988, p. 248). In contrast Nasser began increasingly to stress socialist values (Ayubi, 1994, p. 168), and in international affairs Egypt increasingly identified with the Soviet Union (Laqueur, 1969, pp. 67–8).

The CPGB's loyalty to the Soviet Union at the height of the Cold War meant that it had very little internal democracy. After 1947 the CPGB initiated procedural changes that undermined its earlier openness. In 1945 the executive committee had been chosen by open ballot, but by 1952 the Political Committee was drawing up a list from which an open ballot was then conducted. In the same year the leadership decided that the rank and file could only discuss party policy and could not actively take part in its formulation (Pelling, 1975, p. 160). The Khrushchev revelations did not unduly upset the leadership, with Palme Dutt describing them merely as 'spots on the sun' (Callaghan, 1990a, pp. 186–7). The lack of internal democracy and loyalty to the CPSU accounted for the way in which the party dealt with members who deviated from the anti-Zionist line. The leadership's attack on Levy was part of its wider campaign against party intellectuals and marked the start of the party's attempts to establish a division between intellectuals and industrial workers (Saville, 1976, pp. 16, 20–2). Although under Gollan between 1956 and 1975 the CPGB was supposed to have become more democratic, its subordination to the Soviet Union remained entrenched (Miliband, 1976, p. 136).

The party's relationship with the CPSU also partly influenced its reaction to Israel's invasion of Lebanon in the early 1980s. Although the traditionalists were not uncritical of the Soviet Union, having objected to its intervention in Czechoslovakia and Afghanistan (Pitcairn, 1985, p. 110), they continued broadly to follow Moscow policy. From the mid 1970s the Soviet Union consistently supported Palestinian nationalism, recognising the PLO as the sole representative of the Palestinians and supporting the establishment of a Palestinian mini-state (Wistrich, 1979b, p. 299). The invasion of Lebanon occurred when the Soviet Union's relations with the United States had deteriorated further, partly as a result of the Soviet Union's invasion of Afghanistan and partly the election of Reagan as president. Moscow provided the PLO with arms supplies, paralleling its previous policies towards Egypt. The Soviet Union's support for the PLO arose from its desire to undermine US influence in pro-US Arab countries (Golan, 1991, pp. 126– 32). The CPGB's traditionalists held the United States responsible for the events in Lebanon through the use of its veto in the UN and its economic and military aid to Israel.[47]

However the British party's policies did not always flow from Soviet policy. When its relationship with the CPSU loosened, national factors played a part. Between 1943 and 1947, for example, there was a relatively high degree of intra-party democracy and the party tried to integrate more directly into the British democratic system (Pelling, 1975, p. 129). This situation played out in the party's attitude towards the Palestine conflict. While pro-Zionist policies mirrored Soviet initiatives, they also stemmed from internal factors. For instance the party had significant political ties with the Jews, especially in London's East End, to the extent that Poale Zion had been worried about Jewish support for communism. At the end of the war the Zionist movement had only managed to attract about 7 per cent of Britain's Jewish population (Alderman, 1992, p. 315). Jews accounted for 10 per cent of the CPGB's national membership (ibid., p. 317) and for an even greater proportion of membership of London branches, making up at least half of the Stepney party's membership in 1945 (Kushner, 1990, p. 66). Many of the party's Jewish members were actively involved in organisations such as the Bundist Workers' Circle Friendly Society (WCFS) and local trade unions (ibid., pp. 66–7). The NJC contained a number of Jewish communists, such as Chimen Abramsky, Hyman Levy, Mick Mindel, Alec Waterman, Lazar Zaidman and Issie Panner (ibid., pp. 67–70).

The identification between Jews and the CPGB depended partly on the level of pro-Soviet feeling within the Jewish community. Those of East European origin were committed to socialism, having been impressed by the Soviet Union's post-revolutionary attempts to deal with the Jewish question, including the establishment of Birobidzhan, a Jewish national region, and the Soviet Union's role in the war (Srebrnik, 1986, pp. 285–8, 298; Kushner, 1990, p. 70). It also sprang from the party's history of actively seeking to combat anti-Semitism and fascist groups such as the British Union of Fascists (BUF), activities that contrasted favourably with the Board of Deputies of British Jews' (BOD) non-confrontational approach (Alderman, 1992, p. 316). The Jewish left has traditionally been hostile towards the BOD's passivity (Kushner, 1990, p. 68). Solly

Kaye, for example, joined the party because of the communists' participation in anti-fascist campaigns.[48] The communists believed that the Nazis' anti-Jewish activities justified limited immigration into Palestine.[49]

This link provided the basis for the party's attempts to exploit the Jewish vote during the 1945 general election campaign. Wanting to pre-empt the Zionist movement's influence in the Jewish community (Kushner, 1990, p. 69), communist candidates such as Phil Piratin and William Rust, the candidate for South Hackney, tried to attract Jewish voters by moderating the party's assimilationist principles. Piratin stood as a 'communist and a Jew' and both candidates called for anti-Semitism to be outlawed and for measures to satisfy Jewish cultural needs (ibid., p. 70). Communist candidates did not do well in the general election and won just two parliamentary seats: William Gallacher was re-elected for West Fife and Phil Piratin took the Mile End seat from the Labour incumbent (Pelling, 1975, pp. 131–2). Nevertheless their limited success was largely due to Jewish electoral support, with about half of Piratin's vote probably coming from Jews (Alderman, 1992, p. 31).

In the 1980s, when the party's reformists began to dominate, the CPGB's more moderate attitude towards Zionism and Israel reflected its distancing from the Soviet Union. From the late 1970s the British party came under the influence of Eurocommunism, a term that refers principally to the French, Italian and Spanish parties' attempts to create a more distinctive national identity by distancing themselves from the Soviet Union and emphasising integration into their own democratic systems. Eurocommunist strategies reflected the national parties' efforts to enhance their domestic image and increase their electoral strength after years of being marginalised because of their identification with Moscow (Webb, 1979, pp. 3–6).

The British reformists' attitude sprang from their move away from Soviet politics. Although they were not strongly anti-communist (Miliband, 1985, pp. 24–5), they refused blindly to follow the Soviet Union's line. This meant that they refrained from judging nation-alist movements only in terms of their contribution to Soviet interests and started to support them for intrinsic reasons. The new times manifesto called for a greater sensitivity to ethnic and national identities for their own sake. Their sympathy for both Palestinian and Jewish nationalism came from a new emphasis on national identities: 'The character of the working class is changing . . . other sources of collective identity among women, black people, and other

social groups will be central to progressive politics. Progressive politics has to realign itself to changes in its potential constituencies of support.'[50]
The revisionists' position stemmed from an attempt to create a new alliance with Labour. In their efforts to rejuvenate socialist politics the new times people began to forge links with Labour's soft left, in particular with members of the Labour Co-ordinating Committee (LCC) (Heffernan and Marqusee, 1992, pp. 63–4). This Labour faction, like the revisionists, began to stress the importance of identities such as gender and ethnicity as well as class. Although in the 1980s hard left Labour activists such as Ted Knight tried to persuade Labour to adopt an anti-Zionist agenda, they failed when the Kinnock leadership embarked on a programme to make the party more electable. After the divisions of the early 1980s, Labour eventually adopted the soft left's support for a two-state solution to the Palestinian–Israeli conflict as policy. The CPGB's move towards a more moderate attitude towards Jewish nationalism represented an attempt to appeal once more to left-wing Jews. In the late 1980s Jewish groups such as the Jewish Socialists' Group (JSG) continued to draw on the Jewish communist tradition, being attracted to Bundist ideology and celebrating the Bund's 90th anniversary in 1989 (see Kushner, 1990, p. 72, for details of this group).

So although communist principles played a significant part in shaping the CPGB's policy on Israel, by the late 1980s other factors, including intra-party changes and political expediency, directed the party away from orthodox communist policy. In the following section I shall consider the way in which the CPGB's attitude towards Israel and the Arab–Israeli conflict compared with that of Labour.

Conclusion: comparing the CPGB and Labour

There were significant differences between the Communist Party's and Labour's approach to Israel in the postwar period. Immediately after the war the Labour leadership jettisoned the party's electoral commitment to the establishment of a Jewish state in favour of an anti-Zionist policy. In contrast the CPGB abandoned its traditional hostility towards Zionism and support for Arab nationalism in favour of a pro-Zionist policy, supporting the creation of Israel and opposing the government's approach to Palestine. During the Suez War, although both parties campaigned against the tripartite attack on Egypt they differed considerably in their attitudes towards Israel and Nasser. Labour explicitly tried to separate its anti-war stance from an anti-Israel one and made clear that its opposition to the war did not entail support for Nasser's nationalist aims. The CPGB, on the other hand, strongly identified with Arab nationalism and reverted to its previous anti-Zionist ideology, condemning Israel for being an imperialist state.

The CPGB and Labour diverged even more sharply over the 1967 Arab–Israeli War. The majority of the Labour Party, including the leadership, the PLP and most of the extra-parliamentary party, rallied behind Israel, claiming that Arab aggression had caused the war. The CPGB adopted a completely different policy, showing solidarity with the Arab states and arguing that Israeli aggression had caused the war. It accused the Labour government of colluding with the United States and Israel in the war against the Arab countries, saying that Wilson and President Johnson supported Israeli aggression. Ramelson wrote that both leaders had threatened Egypt with force, had failed to act to help stop the aggression and had prevented a ceasefire decision at the UN (Ramelson, 1967, pp. 19–25). Moreover the 1967 conflict led the CPGB to reassert its anti-Zionist views, whereas anti-Zionism barely existed in the Labour Party at this time, being confined to a tiny minority of people, including Christopher Mayhew.

The two parties also differed in the direction in which their respective dissenters from their traditional attitudes towards Israel tried to push them. In 1956 Labour's dissenters, including people such as Michael Foot and David Ennals, began to move towards a more sympathetic approach to Arab nationalist claims. The CPGB's dissenters, including people such as Levy and Abramsky, went the other way, urging the leadership to refrain from unquestioningly adopting a pro-Arab stance and to re-evaluate its attitude towards Jewish nationalism. In 1967 Labour's dissenters comprised a small group of right-wingers, most notably Christopher Mayhew, and some left-wingers such as Michael Foot, who began to criticise Israel's postwar policy and tried to persuade the party to recognise Arab grievances. The former saw the conflict as a chance to air previously held views in the tradition of Bevin, whereas left-wing critics began to support the Arabs as a result of their involvement in anti-colonialist politics. The CPGB's dissenters again challenged the idea that the Arabs were victims of Israeli aggression and accused the leadership of pandering to anti-Semitism in its anti-Zionism.

What lay behind these differences? In the first place the CPGB had never constituted a serious rival to Labour, partly because of the nature of the political system (Newton, 1969, p. 1). At its high point in the 1945 elections it only won two parliamentary seats. Thereafter the party suffered a drop in its membership (Morgan, 1989, p. 295), and both local and national decline. During the 1950 election the CPGB fielded 100 candidates, but only three managed to keep their deposits (Pelling, 1975, p. 163). Piratin and Gallacher both lost their parliamentary seats in 1950, with Piratin attracting the lowest number of votes in his constituency. Moreover communist representation on the LCC collapsed (Alderman, 1992, p. 318). By the 1980s the party had irretrievably lost its industrial base, rendering it unable to influence the trade union movement, and was completely unable to attract the younger generation into its ranks (Callaghan, 1990b, p. 74).

Furthermore the relationship between Jews and communism broke down in the aftermath of the 1956 events. Although by 1957 every communist candidate elected to Stepney Borough Council was Jewish, this situation was confined to Stepney (Alderman, 1992, p. 318). Although Jewish support for communism still existed in 1967, with Jews making up around 10 per cent of the party's membership, the new crisis further undermined the link between Jews and communism (Litvinoff, 1969, p. 158). While the CPGB recognised the political advantages of adopting a pro-Zionist platform in the immediate postwar period, it did not appeal to Jewish opinion again until the late 1980s. In contrast the relationship between Labour and the Jews, despite a couple of hiccups, remained significant until the 1970s. Unlike the CPGB, Labour's integration into formal politics and its continuing links with Jews meant that it continued to appeal to Jewish opinion in the postwar period. In 1956 Gaitskell was worried that Labour's anti-war stance would jeopardise the party's ties with the Jews and he tried to reassure Jewish opinion about Labour's continuing identification with Israel. In a period of some unpopularity, members of the Wilson government were aware of the weight of popular and Jewish sympathy behind Israel during the 1967 hostilities and realised that sympathy for Israel would do its image no harm.

The parties' different approach to the Israeli–Arab conflict also reflected the rivalry between them in the postwar period. Relations between the CPGB and Labour deteriorated after the war as a result of the Cold War, the communist leadership's pro-Stalinism and the Labour leadership's anti-communism (Howe, 1993, p. 263). The postwar Labour government was strongly anti-communist, believing that communist infiltration into the unions would damage government policy (Pelling, 1991, p. 101). With the start of the Cold War and communist opposition to the Marshall Plan,[51] the government began to clamp down on communists, with Attlee refusing to allow communist civil servants to handle sensitive documents. Attlee, Morrison, Dalton, Shinwell and Morgan Phillips saw people such as Platts-Mills and Konni Zilliacus as subversive elements (Schneer, 1988, pp. 110–12) and initiated a policy to purge the party of such 'fellow-travellers', expelling Platts-Mills and his colleagues for their pro-Soviet sympathies (Howe, 1993, pp. 160–1, note 55).

The rivalry between Labour and the CPGB in the 1940s expressed itself in the parties' respective attitudes towards the Palestine conflict. Believing that the Middle East was critical to Britain's economic and strategic needs, the Labour government began to regard communism as a threat to its interests in this region and the Soviet Union's support for the Jewish state reinforced Bevin's fears (Callaghan, 1993, p. 128). Thinking that Israel could 'turn red' as a result of an influx of Jews from Eastern Europe (Pappé, 1990, p. 563), Bevin became obsessed with preventing the Soviet Union from gaining strength in the Middle East (Morgan, 1989, p. 218). In contrast, having decided to join the anti-imperialist side, the CPGB thought that a pro-Soviet Jewish state would undermine Britain's imperialist interests in the region. Many of Israel's founders were Russian Jews who sympathised with the Soviet Union. The Yishuv contained people such as Moshe Sneh, who had led the Haganah between 1940 and 1946 and believed that the Yishuv should support the Soviet struggle against British imperialism. Left-wing Zionists in the Palmach, the Haganah's elite force, and Mapam shared this view (Wistrich, 1979b, p. 283). Moreover the CPGB believed that in Palestine, as well as India, the eradication of colonialism would end local conflicts (Howe, 1993, pp. 157–8).

Gaitskell was as opposed to communist links with Labour as his predecessors had been, denouncing communist activism in the constituency parties (Haseler, 1969, p. 38). He belonged to the revisionist right, a faction that was notoriously suspicious of Soviet foreign policy (Haseler, 1969, p. 120). Labour's opposition to the war arose from a number of factors, but anti-imperialist politics did not play a part in the leadership's stance. Gaitskell took an anti-war line because he feared that Britain's action would jeopardise the Anglo-

American alliance. His faith in the UN's authority also led him to oppose the war on the ground that it breached international law because the UN had not sanctioned the tripartite attack on Egypt. The motivation behind Gaitskell's opposition to the war contrasted sharply with that of the communists. By now, having made the defeat of imperialism its overriding priority, the CPGB supported anti-imperialist nationalist movements irrespective of their character, arguing that even bourgeois nationalist movements were progressive (Howe, 1993, p. 290), an outlook that informed the communists' attitude towards Nasser. The party had little in common with the Labour leadership, saying that 'The battle for a socialist foreign policy has not yet been won in the Labour Party and the trade unions: and that showed itself in ... November 1956, in spite of the wonderful and heartening protests against the attack on Egypt.'[52]

In 1967 the two parties' different allegiances in the Cold War and the rivalry between them were mirrored in their positions on the war. Wilson's pro-Israel orientation sprang from his commitment to the Atlantic alliance. The CPGB's pro-Arab position stemmed from its pro-Soviet orientation. In the 1960s the communists' commitment to anti-imperialist nationalist movements had intensified (Howe, 1993, pp. 290–3), justifying their support for non-communist movements such as that of Nasser on the grounds that imperialism had prevented the growth of a working class in colonial regions by preventing industrial development (Ramelson, 1967, p. 17). The communists' opposition to Labour's attitude towards the hostilities was part of its wider disillusionment with Wilson's foreign policies, especially the Labour leader's refusal explicitly to condemn the United States' involvement in Vietnam and his failure to prevent Southern Rhodesia's unilateral declaration of independence from Britain. The CPGB supported a Labour back-bench rebellion over this issue.[53]

However there were some similarities between the CPGB and Labour, especially between the communists and the Labour left. Both parties adopted a pro-Zionist platform in the 1945 general election campaign. The CPGB's attempts to forge links with Labour and integrate into the political system made it subject to some of the same constraints as Labour, including an appreciation of popular and Jewish opinion. Aware of the political advantages of adopting a pro-Zionist stance, both parties did so for electoral gain. Once Labour won power, the CPGB allied with the Labour left in protesting against Bevin's Palestine policy, a unity that stemmed from a shared disappointment with the government's approach to foreign policy. Both the Labour left and the CPGB believed that the government had jeopardised its commitment to a socialist foreign policy. The communists' protests against Bevin's Palestine policy were part of a campaign against other aspects of the government's policies abroad, including, most notably, the government's response to the insurgency in Malaya (see Howe, 1993, pp. 159–60).

There were also some similarities between the two parties in 1956. The CPGB joined the anti-war demonstration in Trafalgar Square, along with the Labour Party, the TUC and other Labour organisations such as Labour Women from Scotland.[54] It particularly sympathised with the Labour left, portraying this faction as responsible for Gaitskell's decision to oppose the British government's policy.[55] The party presented Bevan as the hero of the anti-war movement and described the demonstration as 'the most united', where 'Labour and Communist, trade unionist, Ministers of religion and students stood side by side'.[56] This unity reflected the CPGB's links with Labour left-wingers, especially with people such as Maurice Orbach and William Warbey. Prominent communists such as Idris Cox, Kay Beauchamp and Jack Woddis worked with Labour anti-colonialists in the MCF (Howe, 1993, pp. 262–5). Partly under the influence of the MCF, the Labour left began to support national liberation movements in the Third World, putting pressure on the leadership to pursue a more radical approach to foreign and colonial affairs (Kavanagh and Morris, 1989, p. 98). It was Labour members of the MCF, including Orbach, who protested against the war for anti-colonialist reasons, as did the CPGB.

There were also parallels between the CPGB's position and that of the Labour left in 1967. The CPGB's opposition to the government's pro-Israel orientation stemmed from its view that the war could not be understood outside the US neo-colonialist agenda in the Third World. It supported left-wing MPs such as James Dickens who opposed Israel's occupation of the territories.[57] Labour's left-wing dissenters from the party's pro-Israeli tradition similarly began to show some sympathy for the Arab countries because of their hostility towards US neo-colonialism. Having been influenced by the rise of Third World nationalism and new left politics, which centred on anti-colonialist politics, the Labour left started to see Israeli politics as helping to force through the US agenda in the Third World.

There were even stronger parallels in the 1980s, and these were twofold. First, in the early part of the decade Labour contained a small group of far left people such as Ted Knight who espoused anti-Zionist ideas, condemning Israel for being a racist, imperialist state and calling for its dissolution. Some of this anti-Zionism was anti-Semitic. The CPGB's traditionalist strand articulated identical themes, making links between Zionism and racism, comparing Zionism to Nazism and elaborating anti-Jewish themes. This faction differed from Labour's far left only insofar as it did not call for the abolition of Israel, in line with communist orthodoxy. Both the Labour far left's anti-Zionism and the CPGB's traditionalists reflected their unwillingness to adapt their basic ideological assumptions to changing situations. The orthodox communists were reluctant to depart from classical class analysis (see Callaghan, 1990b, p. 74). Labour's far left was unwilling to abandon conventional Trotskyist formulas.

The second similarity was between Labour's soft left and the CPGB reformers. By the late 1980s both of these factions had adopted an even-handed approach to the Palestinian–Israeli conflict, recognising Palestinian and Israeli nationalism. Both parties ended up in this position for similar reasons, including intra-party changes and the decision to make the parties more accountable to popular opinion. The entry of a younger generation of activists, influenced by the new left movements of the 1960s and anti-racist and anti-colonialist politics, resulted in Labour taking on board non-class issues such as national identity. This new current favoured the recognition of Palestinian as well as Israeli national rights. Moreover, under Neil Kinnock, Labour embarked on a policy review process designed to make the party more attractive by eradicating what the leadership saw as unpopular policies such as unilateralism. By the late 1980s this aim underpinned Kinnock's attempts to remove some of the more extreme aspects of the pro-Palestinian campaign, especially the far left's demands for the dissolution of Israel. The leadership wanted to rebuild the bridges that had collapsed in the late 1970s and early 1980s between Labour and the Jews.

Similarly, it was the rise of a younger generation of communists, people such as Martin Jacques, that forced the CPGB to take on board non-class issues such as gender and, ethnic and national identity, and to depart from communism's emphasis on class. This coincidence of ideas between the soft left and the (by now dominant), communist reformers reflected the links between these two groups. In the aftermath of Labour's 1983 election defeat, Neil Kinnock's supporters and the Labour Co-Ordinating Committee (LCC) worked with *Marxism Today* to push for policy changes (Callaghan, 1990a, p. 7) in order to combat Thatcherism. Like the Labour Party under Kinnock, the CPGB embarked on a policy review process, re-evaluating its position on questions such as public ownership and nuclear disarmament. Also like the new Labour leadership, the CPGB reformers began to purge their party of so-called Stalinists (Callaghan, 1990b, pp. 74–5) in order to rid the party of unpopular ideas. The CPGB's efforts to make the party into a more effective political force and to reconnect with socialist members of the Jewish community triggered this shift towards a more moderate approach to the Israeli–Palestinian conflict.

This review has shown that the CPGB's policies towards Israel and the Arab–Israeli conflict were more ideologically driven than those of Labour, although the party's subservience to the CPSU was largely responsible for its ideological stand. Communism's principled hostility towards Zionism frequently surfaced in the party's position on the various conflicts in the Middle East in the postwar period. This situation stemmed from the CPGB's subordination to the CPSU and its greater distance from the formal political system than was the case with Labour, leading it simply to repeat the Soviet line and ignore popular or Jewish opinion. However it is not the case that the party's stance was monolithic and unchanging. In this respect it is important to distinguish between the leadership and the activists. Until the 1980s there was far more stasis on the part of the leadership than among the activists. While Palme Dutt and Harry Pollitt were happy to conform to the communist line, party intellectuals and activists were not. People who were disillusioned with the party's refusal to be flexible over policies and its lack of internal democracy also challenged its automatic anti-Zionist stand. However the party's authoritarian structure made it very difficult for dissenters to influence its policy positions, especially at the height of the Cold War. The leadership's rigidity forced those who questioned communist anti-Zionism to take a highly oppositional position. This sometimes led opponents to go too far in the other direction and to ignore Arab nationalist feeling.

Nor is it the case that the CPGB's stance was unchanging and entirely unresponsive to external and internal developments. The rise of Eurocommunism and the introduction of Gramscian ideas into the party dovetailed with Labour's electoral defeat in 1979 and the rise of Thatcherism to introduce a whole new set of values into the CPGB. The reformers, or the Eurocommunists, were particularly willing to embrace the new social movements of the 1960s and 1970s and to take on board a range of issues, including feminism, environmentalism and ethnicity. After a bitter struggle with the party's traditionalists in the mid 1980s, the reformers gained control of the party (Callaghan, 1988, pp. 227–41). These developments produced significant changes in the revamped party's attitude towards the Israeli–Palestinian conflict. With the new times faction in the ascendant, the CPGB dropped its traditional hostility to Jewish nationalism, but without losing its commitment to Palestinian national rights.

Having considered the similarities and differences between the British Labour Party's and the British Communist Party's policy towards Israel, the next thing is to see how these parties' positions compared with the French left. To what extent did the French left reproduce these patterns of policy change? Did factors peculiar to French history and its political system produce different policy outcomes? In the following chapter I shall provide an account of the way in which the social democratic and communist left in France conceptualised the Israeli–Arab conflict in the postwar period.

7

The French Left and Israel: from the Creation of the Jewish State to the Invasion of Lebanon

The rival Jewish and Arab nationalist movements were a particular problem for French socialists because of France's history of colonialism in the Middle East and North Africa, combined with Germany's wartime occupation of France and its consequences for French Jews. The Suez War highlighted the problematic aspects of the Israeli–Arab conflict because it occurred when Arab nationalism was high on the French political agenda (Johnson, 1981, p. 42). The 1967 hostilities further tested the French left's commitment to anti-colonialist politics, and the 1982 war in Lebanon challenged the apparently pro-Israel government led by François Mitterrand. This chapter looks at the evolution of the French left's attitude towards Israel and how its approach compared with that of the British left. The first section considers changes in the Socialist Party's perceptions of Israel. The second section examines the PCF's attitude towards Israel and the third compares the French and British left.

The French Socialist Party

The French Socialist Party's attitude towards Israel and the Arab–Israeli conflict evolved in much the same way as that of Labour. In the 1940s the Section Français de l'Internationale Ouvrière (SFIO) was strongly committed to Zionist goals, supporting the establishment of a Jewish state in Palestine. Leon Blum, head of the 1936–38 Popular Front government and the party's leader until 1946, was generally on good terms with the British Labour leadership. However Blum's sympathy for Zionism put him at odds with Britain's postwar government (Birnbaum, 1992, p. 55). He regarded Bevin's Palestine policy as one of appeasement to 'pan-Arab fanaticism' and compared Arab nationalism to Spanish fascism.[1] Drawing on customary anti-Arab stereotypes, the SFIO thought that the Arabs should give up their 'feudalistic ways' in favour of solidarity with the Jews.[2] The SFIO leadership condemned Britain's restrictions on Jewish immigration as morally corrupt and explained the rise of Jewish terrorism in the activities of Irgun and the Stern Gang as a direct consequence of British policy.[3] In May 1948 Blum urged immediate recognition of the new state and opposed the UN's decision to put Jerusalem under international control (Birnbaum, 1992, p. 56). Under the leadership of Guy Mollet, Blum's successor, the party welcomed the establishment of Israel as an 'historic moment' and a symbol of the world's recognition of the Jews' right to live as a nation and not a minority.[4]

The SFIO's pro-Israel and anti-Arab stance was maintained during the Suez crisis. Whereas the British Labour Party campaigned vigorously against the war, the socialist-led government in France allied with Israel against Egypt. The party drew on traditional stereotypes of Arab nationalism, comparing it to fascism and Nazism, and depicted Nasser as a reactionary dictator intent on expansion. Mollet likened the Egyptian president to Hitler,[5] participating in the 'Munich syndrome', whereby politicians and journalists competed in pointing out similarities between Hitler and Nasser and between the 1930s and 1940s (Vaisse, 1989, p. 134). The government's policy attracted little internal dissent. The National Assembly and the Senate overwhelmingly supported Mollet's action. Despite the fact that a number of socialist deputies were concerned about breaches of international law and the conflict with the British Labour Party, few were willing to criticise the government, although a group of Paris socialists, including Robert Verdier, chair of the parliamentary party, showed some signs of dissent over the war.[6] The TUC equivalent, the Force-Ouvrière, was also reluctant to condemn the war because of its links with the party.[7] Pierre Mendès France, leader of the centre-left Radical Party and former prime minister, stood virtually alone in his condemnation of the government's stand. Although Jewish, Mendès France's attachment to Israel did not affect his policy position (Birnbaum, 1992, pp. 52–7). Known for having firm beliefs, Mendès France consistently maintained an anti-colonialist stance, having campaigned in favour of Algerian independence in the pre-1956 election campaign (Williams, 1970, pp. 30, 154).

During the 1967 Arab–Israeli War the SFIO's pro-Israel tradition remained strong. Immediately before the outbreak of the war, Mollet sent a telegram to Golda Meir expressing the SFIO's solidarity with Mapai. The socialist leader said that he would do his utmost at the 'heart of the Socialist International' to rally international support for Israel.[8] In the parliamentray debate on the Middle East in mid June, Mollet put forward the Israeli case, and at the SFIO national congress at the end of June all the key figures expressed their unswerving identification with Israel, including Mollet, Pineau and Gaston Deferre (Codding and Safran, 1979, p. 194). The Fédération de la Gauche Démocrate et Socialiste (FGDS) set up a 'Committee for Israel's right to exist', with the aim of mobilising support for Israel.[9] Formed in 1965 and headed by Mitterrand, the FGDS included the SFIO, the Radicals and the CIR (Convention des Institutions Républicains), but not the PCF (Safran, 1977, p. 88).

However the 1967 war did generate some dissent from the social democratic left's pro-Israel tradition. The PSU (Parti Socialiste Unifié) departed from the conventional approach to Israel by strongly criticising Israeli policy and adopting a pro-Arab stand (Codding and Safran, 1979, p. 193). Created in 1960, the party consisted of disillusioned members of the SFIO who felt that Mollet had become too right wing, as manifest in his Algerian policy and sanctioning of the torture of Algerian nationalists (Hazareesingh, 1994, p. 238) and his support for de Gaulle's new constitution in 1958 (Johnson, 1981, p. 53). The intellectual left also adopted a more pro-Arab position. *Le Nouvel Observateur* criticised Israel for engaging in expansionist policies and advocated a moderate postwar policy.[10] Whereas the SFIO paid little attention to the Palestinians, this journal carried articles on the Palestinian refugee crisis. Defending Israel's right to exist, it also argued in favour of Palestinian national rights.[11] In response to critical reactions to its coverage, the journal maintained that acknowledgement of Israel's right to exist implied recognition of the Palestinians' right to their country. It suggested that there was an urgent need to move beyond the extreme nationalist sentiment that expressed itself in racism on both sides: anti-Semitism on the one and anti-Arab racism on the other.[12]

The split in the social democratic left reflected the rise of the radical left. People such as Frantz Fanon and Regis Debray, whom Johnson described as 'prophets of Third World revolution', had captured the imagination of the younger generation of socialists (Johnson, 1981, p. ix), generating a sensitivity to Third World nationalist movements. The PSU consisted of activists who were alienated from both the SFIO and the Communist Party. Its outlook included opposition to the Algerian War, Gaullism and to the ideological stasis of the two left-wing parties, and it shared the ideals that informed the demonstrations of May 1968 (Hazareesingh, 1994, p. 238). The PSU's position reflected the younger generation of socialists' greater sensitivity towards the Third World. Its values made it more aware of the Palestinian crisis than of the wartime experiences of the Jews, and Israel's increasing identification with the United States reinforced the PSU's support for the Palestinian cause.

However it was not until the early 1980s that the socialists' pro-Israel tradition collapsed and gave way to a pro-Palestinian position. When the Parti Socialiste (PS) won its landslide victory in 1981 there were grounds for believing that the government would maintain France's pro-Israel stance. Mitterrand was sympathetic to Jewish concerns, encouraging Jewish ethnic and cultural projects and subsidising Jewish schools (Safran, 1985, pp. 52–3). He condemned the inadequate response to anti-Semitic attacks on the Jewish community, such as the explosion on the rue de Copernic in Paris in October 1981. The new president was personally committed to Israel, having connections with the Israeli Labour Party through the Socialist International, and, immediately after his election, being the first European head of state to visit Israel. The Hebrew University congratulated Mitterrand for his work on behalf of Jewish issues, including his involvement in the resistance and his recognition of Soviet Jewry's right to emigrate to Israel (Marrus, 1985, p. 227). However Israel's invasion of Lebanon in 1982 provoked a clear break from socialist tradition. Responding to a journalist's questions in Budapest, Mitterrand said that the Israeli military intervention reminded him of the Nazi massacre of over six hundred people in June 1944 at Oradour-sur-Glâne. This statement caused a deterioration in Franco-Israeli relations (Moïsi, 1981–2, p. 76), provoking public outrage in Israel and condemnation by the Israeli government.[13] Foreign Minister Claude Cheysson condemned Israel's entry into Beirut on 15 September as a violation of the Habib Plan[14] (which related to the evacuation of the PLO), saying that Israel had acted against international norms. Cheysson demanded Israel's immediate withdrawal from Beirut.[15]

France stood alone in Western Europe in the support it gave the PLO, providing the organisation with military protection for its departure from Beirut and constructing a peace plan with Egypt

based on the need to recognise Palestinian national rights and allow the PLO to participate directly in peace negotiations with Israel
(Moïsi, 1981–2, pp. 76–7). After the massacres at Sabra and Chatila,
Yasser Arafat asked Mitterrand for help.[16] In the European Community,
Mitterrand mobilised opposition to the 'annihilation of the Palestinian people'. Other key left-wing figures, such as the former Prime
Minister Mendès France, called for negotiations with the PLO (Marrus,
1985, pp. 227–8). France's identification with the Palestinians exacerbated the deterioration in its relations with Israel. Ariel Sharon,
Israel's defence Minister, accused Mitterrand of prolonging the war
by protecting the PLO and asked 'why, given the president's sympathy for Israel and the Jewish people, has Mitterrand done his
utmost to save the PLO, a terrorist and murderous organization?'[17]

The PSU was even more forthright in its support for the Palestinians and its condemnation of Israel's involvement in Lebanon. Along
with other left-wing organisations such as the PCF and the
Confédération Générale du Travail (CGT), the PSU participated in
mass demonstrations against the massacre of the refugees and demanded Israel's immediate withdrawal from Beirut.[18] In common
with the anti-Zionist left, the PSU drew on historical examples of
Israeli massacres of Palestinians. Huguette Bouchardeau, its national
secretary, said that: 'words cannot describe the horror and barbarity
of the Beirut massacres. After Deir Yassin, Black September, Tell-
el-Zaatar and the bombardments of Beirut, the Palestinian people
are once again the victims.'[19] She suggested that the massacres had
been carried out with the 'complicity of the Begin government'.[20]
Anti-racist groups such as the MRAP (Mouvement contre le Racisme
et pour l'Amitié entre les Peuples) also condemned the invasion
and called for a two-state solution to the conflict.[21]

Hence the 1980s saw the social democratic left break with its
traditional pro-Israeli stance. What accounted for the socialists' support
for the Jewish state throughout the 1940s, 1950s and 1960s and
then the breakdown in this support? Like the British left, French
socialism was not completely free from the legacy of colonialism,
despite its stated commitment to anti-colonialist politics. Traditionally,
the SFIO had a paternalistic attitude towards the colonies and
prioritised the maintenance of French interests abroad. Although
the SFIO opposed colonialism, it believed that the colonies' freedom
depended on France's lead (Shennan, 1989, pp. 159–64). Moreover
France's colonial presence in the Middle East and North Africa led
French politics as a whole to reflect a strong fear of Arab nationalism

as it might threaten French interests in Syria, Lebanon and North Africa. So despite its anti-colonialist principles, the social democratic left had little time for Arab nationalist aspirations. Prior to the Second World War the Blum government had objected to British policy initiatives that were perceived as appeasing the Arabs, including the Peel Commission's recommendation for partition (Abitbol, 1989, pp. 173, 277, note 22).

The SFIO's ambivalent attitude towards national independence movements informed the socialist government's attitude towards Nasser during the Suez conflict. The government's desire to protect French interests overrode its principled support for anti-colonialism. While the party defended movements for national self-determination that did not pose a great threat to France's economic and political interests, it refused to back movements that could endanger those interests. Mollet's aim to win the war against the Algerian Front de la Libération Nationale (FLN) and to punish Egypt for supporting the FLN was the principal motivation for his alliance with Israel and Britain (Codding and Safran, 1979, pp. 32, 140; Vaisse, 1989, p. 137). Christian Pineau, the Foreign Minister, believed that if France did not defeat Nasser then Europe's influence in and control of other parts of Africa would be jeopardised (Vaisse, 1989, p. 137). Mollet's decision to invade also arose out of his conviction that the closure of the Suez Canal would seriously affect France's supply of oil,[22] claiming that the economies of a number of countries in Europe and Asia depended upon free passage through the canal.[23]

During the 1967 Arab–Israeli hostilities, too, the perception that Arab nationalism posed a threaten remained entrenched. The socialists derided left-wing groups that equated the Arab cause with socialism (Codding and Safran, 1979, p. 194), comparing Nasser to Hitler and saying that the only socialism in Egypt was 'national socialism'.[24] In his discussion of 'Israel and the French tradition', Pineau spoke of Nasser's 'hatred' and 'envy' of Israel's achievements and asserted that 'civilization, culture and democracy are on Israel's side . . . we want nothing more than for Arab leaders to make an effort to achieve comparable results',[25] signalling his adherence to the traditional stereotype of Arabs as backward and reactionary.

In contrast the SFIO had a deeply rooted tradition of support for Zionism for ideological reasons, viewing it as a progressive and democratic nationalist movement. Leon Blum was actively pro-Zionist, being as committed to Zionism as he was to socialism (Birnbaum, 1992, p. 52). He supported Zionism because he thought it was a non-aggressive form of nationalism and that a Jewish Palestine would be a new democracy founded on the principle of social justice (Abitbol, 1989, pp. 94, 107). Like many social democratic socialists, Blum believed that Zionism could be 'reconciled with international socialism' because it was 'popular, just and humane' (Birnbaum, 1992, p. 55). The SFIO was particularly impressed by the socialist orientation of the Jewish community in Palestine and the Histadrut's role in developing the country.[26] The socialists thought that a Jewish state would facilitate cooperation between the Arabs and the Jewish workers and bring the Arabs out of 'feudalism' and into the modern world.[27]

The fact that Mapai (later the Israeli Labour Party) dominated Israel for decades after the state's formation further buoyed the left's perception of Israel as the only progressive democratic state in the Middle East. In 1956 government supporters of Israel viewed it as a major source of stability in an otherwise unstable region. They saw Egypt as a serious threat to Israel and wanted to arm the latter in preparation for war (Vaisse, 1989, pp. 133–5). During the 1967 Arab–Israeli War the SFIO referred to the connections between Israel and social democracy, appealing to the common traditions between France and Israel based on a shared attachment to 'civilisation, culture and democracy'.[28] Even when Israel invaded Lebanon in 1982 the PS referred to Israel's essentially democratic nature, with Prime Minister Pierre Mauroy claiming that France had not lost faith in the democratic values of the state of Israel and that it identified closely with progressive elements in that state.[29]

This perception of Zionism stemmed partly from linkages between the SFIO and the Zionist movement. As a result of the high degree of Jewish integration into French life, the Jewish community historically tended not to be attracted to Zionism and identified strongly with the French nation (Birnbaum, 1992, p. 52). Nevertheless a number of Zionist organisations of various political persuasions and with strong links with the Palestine Jewish community began to flourish after the First World War (Abitbol, 1989, pp. 147–8). Blum had been a member of the Comité France–Palestine since the 1920s (ibid., 108). Poale Zion, formed by Marc Jarblum (ibid., 1989, pp. 105–6, 23), was also a major influence on the SFIO. Blum enjoyed a close friendship with Jarblum and it was through him that he met Chaim Weizmann. Like Laski in Britain, Blum mediated between Weizmann and the French government on particular issues, for example the 1947 partition (Birnbaum, 1992, pp. 52–6). The

SFIO's support for Israel in the 1956 and 1967 wars reflected continuing links between the Socialist Party and the Israeli Labour Party. Both parties belonged to the Socialist International, which was an important arena for creating alliances between democratic socialist parties. Mollet was closely involved in the Socialist International (Codding and Safran, 1979, p. 124) and he was close to David Ben-Gurion in the 1950s, and later to Golda Meir.

A significant political link between Jews and the left was a further source of the SFIO's support for Israel. Although French Jews were politically heterogeneous, the popular conception of Jews as predominantly left wing was not totally unfounded (Cohen and Wall, 1985, pp. 84–5). In the 1920s France had opened its doors to immigrants from Russia, Poland, Romania and Lithuania, who tended to have sympathy for socialist politics and became involved in left-wing organisations (Cohen, 1987, p. 6). Germany's occupation of France and the deportation of French Jews meant that the Jewish community in France was relatively small during the war, standing at about three hundred thousand in 1940 (Rubinstein, 1982, p. 35). Nevertheless, as a member of the postwar government the SFIO could not ignore the fact that popular sympathy, especially in liberal circles, was with Jewish national aspirations.

France's Jewish community grew considerably from the early 1950s as a result of immigration from North Africa, and it eventually became one of the largest in Western Europe (ibid., p. 36). Studies of Jewish voting patterns in France have tended to conclude that there is no specifically Jewish vote because Jews vote according to their socioeconomic status. However French Jews have a specific interest in issues relating to their identity, including anti-Semitism and Israel (Schnapper and Strudel, 1983, p. 957). In the postwar period they continued to show a preference for socialist politicians (Safran, 1977, p. 32). Mollet's pro-Israeli stance in 1956 and his decision to invade Egypt could only have gone down well with the Jewish population. Moreover it did not risk alienating popular opinion generally because polls showed that 44 per cent of those questioned supported the invasion while 37 per cent opposed it (Codding and Safran, 1979, pp. 139–40).

Political considerations also played a part in the SFIO's pro-Israel stance in 1967. In the 1960s the party had suffered from a sharp decline in its membership and electoral base (Hazareesingh, 1994, p. 237). The Gaullists had won overall parliamentary majorities in the 1962 and 1967 elections. So out of government and powerless in the National Assembly, the SFIO decided to replace its 'constructive opposition' phase with outright opposition to de Gaulle's government (Johnson, 1981, pp. 54–6). In the post-Suez period de Gaulle adopted a policy of decolonisation as a way of strengthening France's influence in the Middle East (Vaisse, 1989, p. 343). This also informed his position on the Arab–Israeli hostilities, leading him explicitly to condemn Israel's postwar policies in the occupied territories and to sympathise with the Palestinians (Rondot, 1987, pp. 88–9). De Gaulle's contention that Jews were an 'elite and dominating people' created an uproar (Safran, 1986, p. 279). Although French Jews identified with France, they were interested in Israel and reacted negatively to the government's pro-Arab policy, especially as it resulted anti-Semitic incidents (Safran, 1977, p. 32). The SFIO knew that a pro-Israel position would go down well with French Jews.

National interest considerations also determined the SFIO's pro-Israel position. As a member of the tripartite government in the 1940s, the SFIO leadership had to assess the advantages to France of adopting a pro-Zionist stance. Eager to forge an alliance with the United States in order to attract postwar aid, the party's pro-Zionist position reflected this need. Under President Truman, the United States was one of the first countries to recognise the new state of Israel. Subsidised by the American Federation of Labour (AFL) (Johnson, 1981, pp. 32–4), *Le Populaire* consistently mirrored the United States' pro-Zionist stance. Blum's desire not to offend American public opinion was one of the reasons why he recommended immediate recognition of Israel (Birnbaum, 1992, p. 56).

In office again during the 1956 hostilities, the socialists adopted the Cold War consensus to the extent that anti-communism almost became its 'raison d'être' (Johnson, 1981, p. 40). Despite the party's pre-election commitment to decolonisation, Guy Mollet's government ended up opposing the Algerian nationalist movement (ibid., p. 42), displaying continuity with Antoine Pinay's former right-wing government, whose Middle East policy had aimed to undermine potential alliances between Egypt and the Soviet Union (Vaisse, 1989, p. 139). Despite the fact that Soviet influence in Egypt was negligible and Nasser had adopted a neutralist position (Hourani, 1989, pp. 400–1) the socialist leadership thought that the Egyptian president was pro-communist and compared him to Stalin.[30] The government's alliance with Israel was rooted in the fact that by the time of the war the latter had revealed its pro-Western orientation.

France's wartime experiences also significantly influenced the socialists' attitude towards Israel. The Nazis' anti-Jewish practices undermined anti-Semitic tendencies among the left. In the period of appeasement just before the Second World War, the SFIO and the communists alone opposed the Daladier government's restrictive refugee policies (Caron, 1985, pp. 165–7). The deportation of Jews from France during the Vichy regime critically affected the left's thinking on Zionism. Blum himself was incarcerated in Buchenwald concentration camp (Marrus and Paxton, 1981, p. 349), and although the socialist leader had been sympathetic to Zionist aims since the 1920s, the war sharpened his convictions. Blum was an assimilated Jew but he claimed that Hitler had made the Jews into a 'race' and believed that Israel should rescue Jews persecuted by Nazism (Colton, 1966, pp. 476–7). It was the 'collective memory' of Munich and the resistance that contributed to the SFIO's pro-Israel policy in 1956 (Vaisse, 1989, p. 134). Memories of the war and of France's withdrawal from Lebanon and Syria struck a chord with French politicians, motivating them to act against Egypt (Hourani, 1989, p. 393). The period between the Second World War and Suez was not enough for socialists to forget the persecution of the Jews. Reflecting on the government's policy, Foreign Minister Christian Pineau said that when confronted with the Israeli view that Egypt threatened the state's existence, the government remembered the horror of 'thousands of Jews who perished in the concentration camps' and wanted to avoid another Nazi 'pogrom'.[31]

French guilt about the past and ordinary citizens' complicity with Vichy policies did not start to diminish until the late 1970s (Safran, 1977, p. 11). In 1967 Sartre noted how the left experienced the Israeli–Arab war as a 'personal tragedy' because people old enough to have experienced the German occupation knew that the systematic extermination of French Jews had resulted from the French people's 'passive complicity' as much as Nazi policy.[32] The social democratic left's overwhelming support for Israel in 1967 sprang partly from this sense of guilt. The sight of hostile countries surrounding the Jewish state played on wartime memories. Pineau commented, in a way calculated to appeal to the older generation of party members, that 'when you have seen thousands of Jews die in concentration camps, victims of the most horrific genocide that history has known, you do not ... become an accomplice in a new form of Hitlerism'.[33]

The SFIO therefore remained committed to Israel during the various crises in most of the postwar period. There were a number of reasons for this stasis, including ideological ones such as the legacy of colonialism and a sense of shared purpose with the Zionist enterprise; political ones such as the linkages between the Zionist movement and the SFIO and appeals to popular and Jewish opinion; economic ones, including the view that French interests were best maintained by opposing Arab nationalism; and historical ones, mainly the effect of France's wartime experience. What, then, accounted for the breakdown in the socialists' pro-Israel consensus in the 1980s?

As happenend with the British Labour Party, in the early 1980s the PS shifted to the left, taking on board issues such as feminism, environmentalism and anti-racism as a result of the entry into the party of people who had identified with the 1968 students' and workers' movement (Hazareesingh, 1994, pp. 238–42). Under the PS's control from the mid 1970s, the PSU brought into the party a younger generation of socialists who had protested against the Algerian War, people such as Michel Rocard who had a radical perspective on Third World questions. This new current informed the Mitterrand government's efforts to improve relations with the Third World (Safran, 1985, p. 59). Mitterrand's outlook on foreign policy differed considerably from those of previous presidents. In particular he was highly critical of a whole series of Reaganite policies, protesting against the US support of El Salvador and the Contras in Nicaragua (Bell and Criddle, 1988, pp. 166–7). The foreign minister during the war in Lebanon, Claude Cheysson,[34] came from this background, being 'pro-Arab, pro-Third World, anti-American, pacifist', and he significantly influenced Mitterrand's attitude towards the Middle East (Howorth, 1993, pp. 169–70).

These changes in the party's approach to international affairs contrasted with converse developments in Israel. The PS's distaste for Reagan's policies towards the Third World coincided with Israel's strong identification, under Likud, with the United States. During the 1980s Israel helped to further the US agenda in the Third World by supplying arms and counter-insurgency skills to countries such as El Salvador and Guatemala, as well as arms to the South African apartheid regime (Pieterse, 1985, p. 10). The party's response to the invasion of Lebanon reflected its growing disillusionment with the policies of the right-wing government in Israel. The French socialists' past support for Israel had been linked to the fact that the Israeli Labour Party had dominated Israel for decades, so the PS viewed the political changes in Israel and the country's links with the United States as a departure from its social democratic tradition. The socialists' break from their pro-Israeli tradition also sprang from the government's need to take account of the rise of ethnic politics within the Maghrebi community. During the 1980s the socialists embarked on a series of policy initiatives designed to accommodate ethnic sentiment in the face of increased ethnic diversity following the entry of Muslims and Jews from North Africa (Safran, 1985, pp. 41–64). At the same time the Maghrebi population began to organise itself into a significant pressure group. In particular a 'shared Arab identity' arose and resulted in a demand for mosques, the emergence of a 'Beur vote' and collective action that centred on Islam. Organisations such as SOS Racisme took up the goals of this new force in French politics (Feldblum, 1993, pp. 58–60). France's Muslim minorities were key protesters against the Israeli invasion of Lebanon. The Convention Nationale des Français Musulmans called for a break in diplomatic relations between France and Israel, while the Association France–Palestine wanted the government to recall the French ambassador from Israel and pressed for an international tribunal to 'judge those guilty of the horrific crime' committed against the Palestinian refugees.[35]

This new activism countered the history of Jewish political activism in the shape of organisations like CRIF (Conseil Représentatif des Institutions Juives de France), a key political representative of French Jewry centring principally on questions relating to Israel (Schnapper, 1987, p. 167). In 1982 it condemned prominent left-wing Jews such as Mendès France for calling for peace negotiations between Israel and the PLO, saying that the PLO was the enemy of peace. L'Alliance France–Israel also opposed Mitterrand's and Cheysson's calls for a Palestinian state.[36] Some Jewish groups called the president an assassin when six people were killed on the rue de Rosiers in August 1982 (Marrus, 1985, pp. 228–9). Moreover some Zionist groups tried to sabotage peaceful Jewish protests against the invasion.[37]

The war in Lebanon split French Jews in an unprecedented way. In the past French Jewry had believed that Israel was fighting for its survival, but in 1982 a significant section believed that the war was not legitimate because Israel's survival was not at risk.[38] A number of left-wing and liberal Jewish organisations demonstrated against the massacre of the Palestinians. In September the Association des Juifs de Gauche, Hashomer Hatzir, Identité et Dialogue and the

Mouvement des Juifs Progressistes demanded a commission of inquiry into the massacres and the resignation of Begin and Sharon. They chose a demonstration date to coincide with a 'Peace Now' protest in Israel to show that a number of Jewish groups rejected a military solution to a political problem that they believed jeopardised the original values of the Jewish state.[39] This made the government's decision to ally itself with the Palestinians much easier in terms of domestic political considerations, because it did not risk alienating Jewish opinion to the extent that de Gaulle had done in 1967.

Finally, the constraints of office influenced the government's policy, forcing Mitterrand to end his series of pro-Israel gestures. As president, Mitterrand had considerable control over foreign policy, but political and diplomatic factors or external contingencies, such as France's world interests, bound policy options (Howorth, 1993, pp. 150–1). France's membership of the European Community influenced the PS's position on Israel. Mitterrand was fully committed to Europe, saying that 'France is my country, but Europe is my future' (Howorth, 1990, p. 211). In the 1980s the EC tried to accommodate Palestinian national aspirations, putting the question of Palestinian self-determination at the centre of its Middle East policy as a result of a series of negotiations between Arab countries and the EC. Various international organisations such as UNESCO, numerous NGOs and the Socialist International itself did likewise (Said, 1992, p. xx). These developments both affected and reflected the government's attitude, especially as Claude Cheysson himself had been EC commissioner for external affairs.

Moreover Mitterrand wanted to restore France's political, economic and strategic interests in the Arab countries, and did so by adopting a pro-Palestinian policy after the first year of his presidency (Moïsi, 1981–2, p. 75). France had previously been a major arms supplier to Israel (Kyle, 1989, p. 105), but Mitterrand decided not to sell arms to Israel and contributed French troops to the international peacekeeping force in Lebanon (Wright, 1992, p. 56). The socialist government's policy towards the Israel–Palestinian conflict in the 1980s was part of a wider approach to foreign policy that, in a contradictory way, combined a progressive attitude towards human rights issues and Third World nationalism with an instrumental attitude based on furthering French interests (Howorth, 1990, p. 212).

The socialists' pro-Israeli tradition therefore collapsed in the early

1980s, giving way to a pro-Palestinian position. Again, a combination of external and internal factors contributed to this situation, including the rise of a younger generation of socialists with a radical, pro-Third World outlook; national interest considerations; and political considerations. How did the PCF's position compare with that of the socialists?

The French Communist Party

As a member of the international communist movement, the PCF's (Parti Communiste Français) internationalism was more sharply defined than that of the socialists. This ideological orientation shaped the party's stand on Zionism. Like other members of the international communist movement, the PCF was ideologically opposed to Jewish nationalism, favouring assimilation and portraying Zionism as a divisive and reactionary movement. Nevertheless, in the immediate postwar period the communists joined the socialists in supporting the new Jewish state and the party urged the Arabs to join the Jews in the struggle against imperialism.[40] In the National Assembly, communist deputies stated that the West's aim was to secure oil resources and military bases in the Middle East,[41] and that Bevin's Palestine policy was part of this goal.[42] Towards the end of the British mandate, French communists protested against British policy, opposing restrictions on Jewish immigration into Palestine. In July 1947 the PCF and the CGT (Confédération Générale du Travail) joined various Jewish organisations in Marseilles to protest against the British treatment of Jewish immigrants.[43] Upon Israel's establishment the party's central committee offered the new state its 'warmest greetings'.[44]

The agreement between the socialists and the communists over Palestine, whereby both parties favoured Zionist aims, collapsed in 1956 when the PCF adopted an overtly pro-Arab position, supporting Nasser's nationalisation of the Suez Canal. At the start of the crisis, four hundred and twenty-two members of the National Assembly supported a vote that called for France to react firmly against Egypt and one hundred and fifty communist members opposed it.[45] The party argued that France and Britain were engaged in an imperialist struggle, designed to secure oil reserves for Western capitalism. It described measures to protect the right of passage through the canal as a breach of Egyptian sovereignty. The communists attacked the Mollet government for engaging in anti-socialist behaviour and for allying with 'international capitalism's exploitation of the Egyptian people'.[46] They condemned Mollet and Pineau for putting national interests before socialist principles, which demanded recognition of Egypt's rights over the canal.[47]

The SFIO retaliated by criticising Thorez for supporting a dictator and acting as the Soviet Union's lackey.[48] The party accused Nasser and Khrushchev of confusing 'independence' with 'sovereignty', arguing that although it supported independence, defined as a nation's right to develop freely inside its borders, Egypt's nationalisation of the canal was not a quest for independence.[49] In response the PCF restated the communist line on nationalism, with Thorez claiming that

> Marxist–Leninists have been . . . well aware of the fact that the progressive nature of a national movement does not necessarily imply that this movement will have a progressive programme. When the Egyptian bourgeoisie were fighting for independence . . . it was a bourgeois nationalist movement, and yet it objectively favoured the overthrow of imperialist forces and the progress of socialism throughout the world.[50]

With respect to Israel's part in the war, the Communist Party was relatively silent.[51] Whenever the communists did mention Israel, it was in a fairly uncritical way. They argued that although Israel was guilty of aggression, it was far less responsible for the war than France and Britain. Communist theorists contended that Israel could be criticised for providing Britain and France with a pretext for the war, but that both the Israeli government and the Israeli people bitterly regretted the episode. The party stated that France and Britain had used the Jewish state for their purposes and that peace in the Middle East and Israel's survival depended upon negotiation between Israel and the Arab countries.[52] This moderate tone on Israel contrasted sharply with the anti-Zionist campaign of the early 1950s.[53] Then, at the height of the Cold War, the PCF had joined the Soviet anti-Zionist campaign, bringing out Jewish members such as Annie Kriegel to defend its record on anti-Semitism. It was difficult for Jews to get promotion in the PCF (Cohen and Wall, 1985, pp. 92–4).

The divisions over Suez reflected the political gulf between the two parties. The relationship between the SFIO (and later the PS) and the PCF was historically characterised by bitter rivalry and conflict, with each party struggling to maintain a distinctive identity,

even when ostensibly forging political alliances (Wright, 1992, p. 215).
In the 1950s the socialists' hostility towards the communists was
so great that they would rather accept political obscurity than take
advantage of opportunities for unity. Between 1951 and 1956 the
SFIO used its time in opposition to compete with the PCF, which
had won almost twice as many votes as the socialists at the 1951
election (Johnson, 1981, p. 410). In the Cold War period the two
parties fought principally over foreign policy questions, with the
communists supporting the Soviet Union's 'anti-imperialist camp'
and the SFIO adopting an unyieldingly pro-US and anti-communist
position (Adereth, 1984, p. 149).

During the 1967 hostilities the PCF's anti-Israel, pro-Arab policy
remained in place. The communists maintained that Israel was a pawn
for US imperialism and that the United States was using Israel
for strategic purposes. They claimed that the West viewed the rise
of Arab nationalism as a threat to its oil supply.[54] At the start of
the war, Waldeck Rochet, the party's general secretary, blamed
Israel for initiating the hostilities, arguing that the country's attack
on Syria violated the armistice agreements and proved that Israel's
leaders were the instruments of US imperialism. He drew a parallel
with Vietnam, maintaining that US imperialists were behind both wars,
the only difference being that whereas US nationals were actively
engaged in Vietnam, the United States was using Israelis to do
its work for it in the Middle East.[55] The PCF also drew attention
to the Palestinian refugee crisis, claiming that peace in the area
depended upon finding a solution to the Palestinian question.[56]

The party's press returned to the extreme anti-Zionism of the
early Cold War period, lapsing into anti-Semitism with a conspiracy
theory of Zionism. It maintained that '"Zionist agents" had orches-
trated the anti-Arab campaign along with the most reactionary forces,
including fanatical anti-Semites and the most relentless supporters
of American imperialism'.[57] In an article entitled 'An American Agent',
the PCF contended that General Dayan had acted as a US agent in
the war against Vietnam.[58] *L'Humanité*'s depiction of the Rothschilds
at the Wailing Wall after the war was highly insensitive: 'The presence of certain personalities of high finance conferred on the event
another meaning than religious fervor. . . . The spectacle made one
think that, as in Faust, it was the Devil who was "leading the ball"'
(quoted in Cohen and Wall, 1985, p. 95), thus drawing on customary
anti-Jewish themes including the association of Jews with finance
and the anti-Christ.

The war again highlighted the differences between the socialists and the communists and threatened the parties' attempts at unity. Former Minister Pineau derided the communists for assuming that any ally of the Soviet Union was left wing and suggesting that far from being a socialist, Nasser was a reactionary racist.[59] Pineau further commented that 'we are back to the time when . . . one could correctly describe the PCF as a mere branch of the Soviet Communist party'. The anti-communist Deferre held the same view and Mollet began to doubt the potential for unity. Aware of the damage the different attitudes could do to the left-wing alliance, the PCF showed some restraint in the parliamentary debates on the Middle East and both parties refrained from discussing the issue for some time (Codding and Safran, 1979, pp. 193–4). The Arab–Israeli war revealed the fragility of the social democratic–communist alliance, drawing attention to the parties' different allegiances and the PCF's loyalty to the Soviet Union.

During Israel's invasion of Lebanon in 1982, the PCF adopted an anti-Israel and pro-Palestinian stance, attacking the Begin government for using Lebanon to bolster the 'greater Israel' movement and stating that: 'too many Palestinians, Lebanese, Syrians and Israelis have been sacrificed in the name of an archaic colonialism supported militarily, economically and financially by the USA'.[60] George Marchais, the party's leader, emphasised his 'complete agreement' with Mitterrand on the question of imposing an international UN force in Lebanon.[61] After the massacres the PCF's political bureau criticised the Americans, the Italians and the French for leaving Beirut without first bringing about the withdrawal of the Israeli forces, and stated that Israel was 'fundamentally responsible' for the 'pogrom' against the refugees.[62] The party's press carried articles on Palestinians in the occupied territories and Israel's repressive policies, especially forms of collective punishment such as the demolition of houses.[63] René Andrieu, deputy editor of *L'Humanité*, and Pierre Juquin, a member of the communist party's political bureau, refused to take part in a press conference given by Ariel Sharon, saying that to interview Sharon when the victims of the massacre had yet to be taken from Beirut was 'obscene and dangerous'.[64] Nevertheless the PCF's previously extreme anti-Zionism was largely absent, with the party confining its hostility to the Begin government and distinguishing between the Israeli government's policies and the Jewish people's views.

For most of the postwar period the PCF's position on Israel reflected its loyalty to the CPSU. After being forced out of Ramadier's (SFIO) cabinet in 1947, this subordination increased. Repaying Stalin's patronage with undivided loyalty, Thorez, the party's leader from 1930 to 1964, earned the reputation of being 'the best Stalinist in France' (Johnson, 1981, pp. 43–4). At the start of the Cold War the CPSU jettisoned its anti-Zionist policy and spoke in favour of the creation of a Jewish state in its effort to undermine Britain's role in the Middle East. The French party, like the other national CPs, followed suit, arguing that Western economic and strategic interests had caused the first Arab–Israeli War and attacking Bevin's Palestine policy as imperialistic. The PCF's shift to a pro-Arab policy in 1956 also reflected developments in the Soviet Union's foreign policy. In the Cold War period the West and the Soviet Union competed for influence in the Middle East. Distracted by Hungary and lacking strong relations with countries such as Egypt, Moscow did not play an active part in the crisis (Hourani, 1989, p. 403) but it did express support for Nasser, and the PCF did likewise.

By the time of the 1967 Arab–Israeli War the PCF had dropped its simple loyalty to the CPSU, with Waldeck Rochet, Thorez's successor, initiating liberalisation initiatives (Wright, 1992, p. 234). Yet despite its greater independence from the Soviet Union, the party's language reflected its inability to break free from orthodox communist themes. The PCF's resort to a conspiracy theory of Zionism indicated its unwillingness to move away from a deeply held belief system. The 1967 hostilities sparked off an aggressive anti-Zionist campaign in the Soviet Union (Wistrich, 1979b, p. 288) and the PCF's extremist views reflected this development. Under Marchais the party dropped its Stalinist image. However its short-lived Eurocommunist spell in the late 1970s gave way to a new alignment with Soviet policy, most obviously when it sanctioned the Soviet Union's invasion of Afghanistan in 1980 (Hazareesingh, 1994, p. 308). This identification between the PCF and the Soviet Union was evident in its treatment of the Palestinian–Israeli conflict in 1982, when it repeated commonplace communist formulas and put forward a traditional class analysis of the hostilities. Moreover the PCF identified with the Palestinian Communist Party, believing that its revival in the early 1980s expressed the Palestinian working class's increasing influence in the nationalist movement. It called for an alliance between the Palestinian and Jewish working class.[65]

However, to understand the party's attitude towards Israel and the Arab–Israeli conflict, it is not enough simply to trace it back to Soviet policy. While the party had to heed the CPSU's line, it also had to take account of the domestic situation because of its institutionalisation in the political system (Tarrow, 1975, pp. 579–95). As a member of the tripartite government from 1944 to 1947, the PCF was subject to domestic circumstances and internal pressures such as public opinion. The PCF enjoyed close ties with Jews of East European origin, presenting itself as the 'natural defender' of the Jewish workers, to the extent that Poale Zion and Marc Jarblum were worried about Jewish support for communism (Abitbol, 1989, pp. 206–8). Although the Soviet Union's entry into the war precipitated the party's resistance activities (Wingeate Pike, 1993, pp. 465–85), ordinary activists were genuinely moved by the Jews' situation.[66] After the war there was a good deal of popular support for Zionist goals, and as a member of the government the PCF was responsive to this.

In 1956 the PCF refrained from the anti-Zionist sloganising of the early 1950s, and its uncritical attitude towards Israel reflected the contradictions facing the communists. The furore in France that resulted from the anti-Zionist campaigns in 1953 had left its mark. Moreover, when Jewish communists returned from the Soviet Union with evidence of widespread anti-Semitism under Stalin after the Khrushchev revelations, Jewish membership of the party dropped (Caute, 1964, p. 205). This happened when the other political parties had marginalised the PCF and it was outside government (see Johnson, 1981, pp. 40–3). Israel enjoyed considerable popular support and the PCF could not afford to alienate public opinion too greatly. These political factors forced the communists to adopt a more moderate stance on politically sensitive issues such as the Israeli–Arab conflict.

The 1967 war occurred when the rival left-wing parties were trying to undermine de Gaulle's dominance through political alliance. De Gaulle's overwhelming electoral victories in the 1960s forced the SFIO and the PCF towards a new phase of left-wing unity (ibid., p. 54). Starting in 1962, this unity was later expressed during the 1965 presidential elections, when both the SFIO and the communists supported Mitterrand, and again during the 1967 and 1968 legislative elections, when the two parties entered into a second-ballot electoral agreement (Wright, 1992, p. 215). In this context the PCF was forced to tone down its anti-Israel comments in the National Assembly debates and the two parties agreed not to debate the war openly, ending up with Mitterrand commenting that 'we have passed the Mideast crisis with the requisite serenity' (Codding and Safran, 1977, p. 194).

The PCF further moderated its anti-Zionist stance during its brief Eurocommunist phase in 1976–77, making a series of gestures towards specifically Jewish interests. These included an appeal to the Jewish vote in 1978 and a celebration of the forty-fifth anniversary of the Paris Yiddish communist newspaper, *Naie Presse*, in 1979. The party also made joint declarations with the Israeli Communist Party, claiming that its position on Jewish nationalism had been misread and stating that the PCF accepted a Jewish community and culture based on shared history. It even sent a delegation to demonstrate against anti-Semitism in response to the bombing of the synagogue in the rue Copernic in 1981. Kriegel believed that Jews played a greater part in the party during its Eurocommunist phase, which was initiated by the Jewish Jean Kanapa (Cohen and Wall, 1985, pp. 97–100).

The party's moderate position on the Israeli invasion of Lebanon, the absence of the anti-Zionist sloganising of earlier periods and its agreement with the Mitterrand policy also stemmed from internal political considerations. By the early 1980s the communist party had suffered a massive electoral decline, with Marchais winning about 15 per cent of the votes in the presidential election and the party obtaining around 16 per cent of the votes in the legislative election in 1981 (Wright, 1992, p. 241). This meant that the party had lost two thirds of its postwar electorate (Bell and Criddle, 1989, p. 516). Even so the new Mitterrand government contained four communist ministers, entering government for the first time since 1947. As an unpopular party it could not use well-worn and outmoded communist formulas, and as a minority member of the government it had to cooperate with the president's policies.

In 1982, then, the two left-wing parties converged in their attitude towards the Israeli–Palestinian conflict, both protesting against Israel's invasion of Lebanon and both promoting the recognition of Palestinian national rights. The PCF's position was a continuation of with its former pro-Arab stance but differed from past policy in the absence of extreme anti-Zionism. The PS's policy represented a sharp break with the past. The left's pro-Palestinian stand in 1982 generated accusations of left-wing anti-Semitism. Alain de Rothschild, president of the CRIF, complained about political commentaries holding Israel responsible for the massacres before the results of an inquiry were published, and argued that statements about Israel's role in the massacres were dangerous and would produce a climate of anti-Semitism and racism.[67] Was the French left's stand a new form of anti-Jewish hostility? Mitterrand's comments about Oradour were insensitive and offensive to Jews, but the remark was not necessarily anti-Semitic. The PCF's characterisation of the massacre of the Palestinians as a pogrom could have upset Jews. However as Marrus has commented, the 'misuse of Nazi references' reflects the way in which major historical reference points are used to encapsulate feeling about significant contemporary events and is not necessarily anti-Jewish (Marrus, 1986, p. 174). The PCF defended itself rigorously against accusations of anti-Semitism, arguing that it had never faltered in its efforts to combat anti-Semitism. This defence was spurious since the party had used anti-Jewish stereotypes in its treatment of the Arab–Israeli conflict. For instance in the early 1950s the PCF had drawn heavily on the dual loyalty theme, arguing that according to Zionist ideology. 'A French Jew would not be French. He would be, by right, Israeli, that is a citizen of another state . . . the French Jew would be a stranger in his own country. Just like Marras, leading Zionists say to the Jews "Go to Palestine! You are not welcome here.'[68] Moreover the party's treatment of the 1967 war had included the use of anti-Jewish themes, including the association between Jews and usury and making connections between Jews and the devil.

In the following section I shall look at how the French left's views compared with those of the British left.

Conclusion: comparing the British and French left

There were important similarities between British and French left-wing attitudes towards Israel in the postwar period. The social democratic parties in the two countries moved from a consensus of support for Israel in the 1940s to a consensus of support for the Palestinians in the 1980s, maintaining (with the exception of Bevin's Palestine policy) a more or less pro-Israel stance in the intervening period. In both cases the history of colonialism led the parties to underestimate the strength of Arab nationalist sentiment, and to believe that the modernising potential of a Jewish state would eradicate nationalist tensions. Both parties had strong connections with the socialist Zionist movement, and later with the Israeli Labour Party. The networking between Zionist and Israeli political groups

and the British Labour Party and the French Socialist Party, especially through the Socialist International, helped to create a strong
sense of mutual identity. Moreover both Britain and France contained politically articulate Jewish communities that identified closely
with the social democratic left until the 1970s, and in this context
the two parties believed that it was politically advantageous to identify
with Israel. Finally, the Holocaust led Labour and the SFIO to exonerate Israel for policies that anti-colonialist parties would normally
condemn, such as Israel's role in the 1956 Arab–Israeli War and its
occupation of Arab territories in 1967.

The breakdown in this consensus of support for Israel within Labour
and the PS also stemmed from a similar set of dynamics. In the
1980s both parties came under the influence of a younger generation of left-wing activists who introduced a radical perspective on
international affairs. Israel's shift to the right and its close relationship with the United States, alienated the social democratic left in
Britain and France, which by the 1980s was opposed to US neo-
colonialism. Moreover Western Jewry's move to the political right
and the left's new interest in other ethnic minorities, including
Afro Caribbeans and Asians in Britain and the Maghrebi community in France, also played a part in the parties' adoption of a
pro-Palestinian policy. Finally, the rise of the PLO and its impact
on international organisations such as the UN and organisations
closer to home such as the EC, affected the outlook of both Labour
and the PS.

Nevertheless there were differences between the British and French
democratic left. The SFIO and Labour governments came into conflict
over Palestine in the 1940s. Whereas Labour could not maintain
its pro-Zionist policy once in government because it believed that
to do so would threaten British interests, the SFIO was free to continue
with tradition because, first, it did not have direct links with Palestine
and, second, by the time of Israel's creation France had withdrawn
from Syria and Lebanon. There were differences in 1956 too. Mollet's
policy isolated the SFIO from democratic socialist parties in the
rest of Europe.[69] The French socialists took a more anti-Arab line
than Labour, despite Gaitskell's hostility towards Nasser. The Labour
left in Britain condemned Mollet for engaging in war against Egypt
in order to create a 'second front in the war against Algerian
freedom'.[70] The SFIO's more explicit pro-Israel, anti-Arab line was
linked to the fact that France's continuing role in Algeria served to
maintain a deeply rooted fear of Arab nationalism even in the left.

Moreover the socialist government had directly to deal with the Algerian crisis and to balance French people's views against the national liberation movement, whereas in Britain, Labour was in opposition and its priority was to oppose the government's policy. Furthermore its leadership was subject to pressure from the Labour left whereas in France the major left-wing force, the PCF, was discredited at the time of the crisis.

Although the SFIO and Labour both adopted a pro-Israel stand in 1967, there were differences between them. The French party was again more overtly pro-Israel, and anti-Arab than the Labour government. Whereas the Labour leadership tried to appear neutral in order to sustain Britain's status in the Arab countries and to avoid negative economic repercussions, the SFIO was out of office and trying to win public favour by distinguishing its Middle East policy from that of de Gaulle. The apparent similarities in the 1980s also obscured significant differences. The principal factor behind Labour's pro-Palestinian stand was the rise of the Labour left. While such intra-party dynamics also played a part in Mitterrand's pro-Palestinian policy, the leadership's interest in enhancing France's image in the Middle East was more important. Moreover, unlike Labour, Mitterrand had to appease internal Muslim opinion, which in the 1980s became politicised, centring on the idea of an Arab identity.

The British and French communist parties' attitudes towords Israel also evolved in a similar way. Both parties jettisoned their anti-Zionist ideology in the 1940s in order to oppose Bevin's Palestine policy and support the formation of a Jewish state. Both parties reverted to a pro-Arab stance in the 1950s and maintained this during the 1967 hostilities. While recognising Palestinian national rights in the 1980s, both parties moderated their criticism of Israel and refrained from using anti-Zionist slogans. This similarity between the British and French communists' position reflected their subordination to Soviet policy, which for most of the period in question was considerable. However there were differences. The PCF's attitude towards Israel in 1956 was more exonerating than that of the CPGB. Furthermore the PCF attempted to moderate their criticism of Israel in 1967 whereas the CPGB did not. These differences stemmed from the fact that the PCF was a more significant political force in France than the CPGB was in Britain, attracting a substantial part of the electorate until its decline in the 1980s and periodically engaging in political alliances with the Socialist Party. Whereas these political factors sometimes forced the French communists to moderate their views on Israel, the British communists' marginal role in mainstream politics allowed them freely to articulate unpopular themes. Moreover the rise of Eurocommunist politics, translated into the new times current, led the CPGB to drop its anti-Zionist orthodoxy in the 1980s. In contrast the French communists' moderation during the Lebanon war reflected the fact that it was eager to enhance its public image in a period of unprecedented unpopularity. Furthermore the party's participation in the Mitterrand government imposed some constraint on its views and obliged it to cooperate with the president's policy on the conflict.

There was, then, a clear pattern of policy change associated with the social democratic and communist left in Britain and France, with the former moving from a general consensus of support for Zionism to a pro-Palestinian position in the 1980s, and the latter jettisoning its orthodox anti-Zionism in favour of a more accommodating approach to Jewish nationalism. These similarities do not mean that the dynamics underpinning the parties' shifting policies were the same in the two countries. Historical and political factors unique to France, including its continuing links with North Africa, the presence of a significant Maghrebi population and the nature of its political system, which allowed the PCF to have a mainstream role, did not operate in the British case. Nevertheless there are sufficient continuities to make qualified generalisations about the policy changes. In the following chapter I shall consider some possibilities for theorising these changes.

8
Conclusion

What does this examination of Labour's and the other parties' changing position on Israel say about the general question of policy change and internal democracy? Bearing in mind the limitations of a single case study approach that relies primarily on the use of documentary sources, the study does shed some light on this process. As I showed at the start of the book, there are two key ways of understanding party policy change: the first emphasises the importance of parties adapting to their external environment, and the second stresses that parties may act independently and internal party changes are the main impetus. I suggest here that the two processes of change are continuously at work and interact closely to bring about a policy shift.

Policy change: internal and external factors

The internal model of policy change explains changes in terms of internal party dynamics and bargaining between contending factions. The approach to political parties that analyses them in terms of their organisational dynamics makes an important contribution here. It jettisons the idea of the party as a unitary actor and instead sees it as made up of competing factions and groups, whereby coalitions and their disintegration underpin party life. Proponents of this position show that strategies of conflict management pervade parties' internal life. The outcome of party platforms reflect the distribution of power between contending factions, and battles over programmes have less to do with the content of policy than with the question of who controls the party because leaders are motivated primarily by the desire to stay in control (Mulé, 1997, pp. 501–2).

It would be impossible to understand Labour's adoption of the Palestinian cause in the early 1980s without reference to some of the internal changes that took place at the time, namely the campaign for greater intra-party democracy and the rise of the Labour left throughout the party's structures. Although the campaign for Palestinian national rights was not confined to the left, this faction tended to dominate it. Many of the pro-Palestinian campaigners belonged to groups such as the Campaign Group, the Tribune Group and the Labour Co-ordinating Committee in Scotland, and in the PLP the, supporters of pro-Palestinian motions tended to come from the left.

However these internal developments were not the sole movers. The external model of policy change suggests that position developments come about in response to environmental influences, particularly electoral pressures. The internal developments in Labour interacted with a series of external developments, both domestic and international, to produce a policy change. The shift to the left introduced a strong anti-colonialist current into the party, producing an ideological climate that favoured identification with Third World nationalism. Such an outlook reacted negatively to political developments inside Israel such as the rise of the Likud right and its adoption of a hard-line approach to the Palestinians, as well as Israel's increasingly close relationship with the United States and its promotion of the US agenda in the Third World. Moreover Labour's unilateralists were disenchanted by the development of Israel's nuclear capacity.

The policy change has also to be understood in terms of changes in the domestic political situation and the collapse of consensus politics. The British political system is basically a stable two-party system, although it has gone through various phases when this has either been enhanced or diminished: there was even some speculation that Britain was turning into a dominant party system during Margaret Thatcher's era (Norris and Lovenduski, 1993, pp. 36–7). Labour's adoption of the Palestinian cause took place during this period. When Thatcher came to power she rejected consensus politics. As the Conservatives moved to the right, Labour moved to the left (Kavanagh and Morris, 1989, p. 2).

In this context of heightened inter-party competition, Labour adapted to other pressures that had a bearing on its position on Israel, namely issues relating to ethnic minorities. In Britain the two main parties differed in their attitudes towards ethnic minorities, with the Conservatives (especially under Thatcher) taking a hard-line approach and Labour seeking to accommodate minority views (see Messina, 1989). This development had a bearing on the party's policy towards Israel because Labour's traditional ethnic constituency, the Jewish community, had moved to the right. In an unprecedented way, the Conservative Party under Thatcher's leadership began to strengthen its standing with the Jewish community. The political alliance between Labour and the Jews had given way to one between Labour and other ethnic minorities, especially the Afro-Caribbean and South Asian communities in inner London. Even though these minorities' interests were mainly domestic, they contained anti-Israeli elements.

The change of tactics on the part of the PLO and related groups was another source of external pressure for change. The PLO had a base in London and Palestinian activists lobbied the main political parties to gain support for their cause. From the 1970s in particular, Palestinian activists targeted the Labour Party, holding fringe meetings at the annual conference and getting involved in constituency party activities. They also worked with Labour MPs and the trade union movement through the formation of TUFP. Given the unions' block vote at the time, this strategy was critical to the party's policy change. Later they made contact with Gerald Kaufman, then the Labour front-bench spokesperson on foreign affairs.

An interplay between internal and external factors also produced the policy retreat in the late 1980s. Kinnock's effort to reverse the left's dominance and his desire to make the party viable again played a part in the abandonment of some of the more controversial aspects of the party's Middle East policy. The leader's awareness of possible damage to the party's standing made him sensitive to criticism of Labour's support for the Palestinians, in contrast to Michael Foot. Kinnock took on board the complaints about the party's anti-Israel elements and attempts by parts of the Jewish community to publicise Labour's policy in both local elections and the general election. During the 1987 general election some Labour candidates in Jewish constituencies explicitly distanced themselves from the left's views on Israel, winning Poale Zion's support. Even Ken Livingstone made an effort to be more conciliatory, distancing himself from the anti-Zionist left.

According to the perspective that emphasises internal dynamics, conflict and divisions are a normal part of party life, as are strategies of conflict management (Mulé, 1997, p. 501). Labour's retreat to a more moderate stance in the late 1980s resulted partly from the leadership's attempt to manage divisions within the party. Members of the leadership made a definite effort to prevent a repeat of the heated debate about Israel that had taken place at the 1982 annual conference. Moreover Kinnock appointed Gerald Kaufman and Tony Clarke to revise the party's Middle East policy as part of the wider review process. Kaufman had links with the Jewish community, but he was also critical of trends in Israel in the 1980s and willing to forge links with Palestinian representatives in Britain.

The policy outcome in the late 1980s also demonstrated the left's fallibility, resulting from its own lack of unity. The division between the soft and the hard left played itself out on the Israel question, with the former continuing to support Israel's existence while the latter objected to it. The presence of hard left activists such as Knight in the pro-Palestinian campaign was damaging. Clare Short, for example, became concerned that some elements in the campaign were exploiting a conspiracy theory of Zionism. Even Palestinians linked to the party saw the hard left's stance as alienating. It was the blurring of boundaries between these two that caused the leadership to take out policies that might otherwise have been regarded as acceptable, such as recognition of the PLO. While the new leadership could not ignore the groundswell of opinion in favour of Palestinian national rights (both inside and outside the party), the presence of the hard left in the pro-Palestinian campaign had a decided effect on a leadership that was dedicated to removing far left groups and extreme policies from the party.

These internal developments were made all the more possible by external changes in the Israeli–Palestinian conflict itself. The 1982 events in Lebanon had provided the impetus for an Israeli peace movement and key Israeli Labour figures began to move towards a settlement with the Palestinians. The PLO simultaneously jettisoned its long-held opposition to Israel's existence and moved towards a solution that involved the formation of a separate Palestinian state. Labour's new moderate policy therefore fitted in quite well with developments in the Middle East itself and made the anti-Zionist elements seem out of touch not only with Labour feeling but also with the Palestinian nationalist movement.

Nor is it possible to understand the French socialists' policy shift without reference to internal organisational changes. Like Labour, the PS moved leftwards as a result of the entry of a younger generation of socialists who had identified with the events of the late 1960s. The incorporation into the party of the PSU brought in a younger generation of socialists who had a radical perspective on international affairs. They introduced into the party an ideological opposition to neo-colonialism and US intervention in the Third World, which also provided a climate for opposition to Israel and support for the Palestinians. At the time of the 1982 war in Lebanon, Claude Cheysson, who encapsulated this way of thinking, was foreign minister.

This trend inside the party dovetailed with various external political pressures to create a shift towards sympathy for Palestinian nationalism. The particular factors in play in the French case differed from those operating in the British case because of its particular political and historical imperatives. As with the Labour Party, the PLO's tactics also influenced socialist party policy. However most important in this respect was the PLO's involvement in the EEC and the shift in thinking within the EEC towards a Middle East peace process based on a two-state solution. This development had a direct bearing on a government that was so closely involved in European politics.

Other significant environmental factors included the rise of social movements that focused on issues such as gender, the environment and immigration and acted as 'ginger groups' by bringing new issues on to the political agenda and mobilising support for specific policies (Hall, 1990, pp. 89–90). One of the most important movements in relation to the PS's position on ethnic conflicts was SOS-Racisme, which was formed in 1980 with the aim of combating the Front Nationale's increasing popularity. Mitterrand actively tried to build links with this organisation, which had widespread support from all ethnic minorities but especially the beurs (North African immigrants' children with French citizenship), many of whom had been pro-socialist before 1981 (Machin, 1993, p. 141).

Domestic ethnic politics were probably an even more important consideration in France than in Britain. In the early 1980s the French right started to appeal to racist popular feeling as a way of undercutting the growing support for the far right. In direct contrast the socialists embarked on a series of policy initiatives designed to accommodate ethnic sentiment in the face of the increased ethnic diversity that had resulted from the entry of Muslims and Jews from North Africa (Safran, 1985, pp. 41–64). Inter-party competition was important here because, by identifying with the beurs, Mitterrand aimed to split the right (Machin, 1993, p. 142).

Minorities of North African origin had begun to engage in collective action centred on Islam and forging a political identity based on the demand for mosques and the beur vote (Feldblum, 1993, pp. 58–60). During the Israeli invasion of Lebanon, France's Muslim minorities were at the forefront of the protest against the war. Their new activism was targeted at the Socialist Party and acted as a counterbalance to well-established Jewish organisations' activities. It was important for the socialist government to prevent the protests from becoming excessively volatile, and its position on Lebanon pacified the minorities of North African origin.

The government's pro-PLO stand did alienate some sections of the Jewish community, elements of which wanted the president to be more favourable towards Israel. However Mitterrand was able to deflect this criticism to some extent by introducing policies that were sensitive to Jewish feeling. For example the academic who played down the Holocaust was dismissed for his views (see Safran, 1985, p. 53). Moreover it was significant that many of the protesters against the war in Lebanon were Jewish. They formed part of a growing movement for peace amongst Jews in the diaspora and Israel.

Unlike Labour, Mitterrand and his party had just enjoyed a massive electoral victory. The PS had gained an absolute majority in the 1981 legislative elections and it held office almost continuously throughout the decade (Hazareesingh, 1994, p. 239). Being in office, the socialist government had to take account of national interest considerations in its stand on international affairs. The government's support for the PLO was at least in part rooted in the potential damage that could be done to the country's economic and strategic interests in the Arab countries by failing to oppose Israel (see Moïsi, 1981–2, p. 75). It just happened that the policy that best protected France's economic interests in the Maghreb also fitted in with a socialist outlook on international affairs, enabling Mitterrand to adopt a policy that was both pragmatic and principled.

The evolution of the communist parties' stand differed from that of the social democratic left insofar as forces for change pushed in an opposite direction. Despite the two parties' support for the formation of Israel, they basically adopted a pro-Arab, anti-Israel position throughout most of the postwar period, condemning Zionism as a reactionary movement that divided the working class and supporting Arab nationalism on anti-imperialist grounds. Unlike the social democratic left, the communist parties' support for Palestinian national rights in the 1980s was a continuation of their previous pro-Arab policies. The innovative aspect was that they combined this position with a less hostile attitude towards Israeli nationalism, abandoning the extreme anti-Zionism that was characteristic of communist orthodoxy.

Authors stressing the organisational approach to parties have suggested that the tighter the organisation of a party's internal decision-making structure, the less responsive it is to external developments (Guadagnini, 1993, p. 181). To some extent this seems to capture the situation with respect to the communist left, whose position on Israel throughout most of the postwar period flew in the face of popular opinion and the position of other left-wing political parties. Yet despite this relative stasis, there were developments in communist policy, some of which were surprising, such as the PCF's appeal to the Jewish vote in the late 1970s.

Again, an interaction between intra-party factors and environmental influences lay behind the CPGB's shift to a more moderate outlook on Israel. The reformists' rise to dominance was vital. Challenging the indiscriminate use of class analysis, the revisionists argued for recognition of a multitude of identities, including ethnic and national ones, enabling it to recognise the legitimacy of both Israeli and Palestinian nationalist identities. Seeking to enhance its political viability but unable to compete electorally with Labour, the party's reformers forged links with Labour's soft left. It became irrational to hold on to past orthodoxies such as anti-Zionism even if, paradoxically, other left-wing groups had begun to adopt this stand. Acknowledging that the party's anti-Zionist perspective had alienated the Jews, it tried to appeal again to Jewish opinion by rejecting anti-Zionist slogans.

These organisational changes themselves resulted from external pressures. The CPGB's rejection of orthodox anti-Zionism also has to be understood in terms of the wider Eurocommunist movement. Under the influence of this trend, the revisionists refused to follow blindly the Soviet line, rejecting the traditionalists' emphasis on class and embarking on a major revision of communist policy (see Callaghan, 1990 b, p. 75). The decline of the national communist parties made it irrational for them simply to follow the CPSU line. In Britain, both communist MPs lost their seats in 1950 and from that point the party's electoral fortunes never recovered, either nationally or locally. During the 1950s and 1960s the party's membership also dropped, and by the 1980s its influence in the trade union movement had collapsed, partly because of the decline of its industrial base and partly because of internal divisions over ideology (ibid., p. 74). The reformists gained ground as a result of recruiting from new social movement political activists such as students and feminists. More importantly, Thatcher's victory in 1979 and 1983 strengthened the reformist strand.

In France, similar developments took place in the PCF. Maintaining its basic pro-Arab position in the early 1980s, the PCF condemned Israel's invasion of Lebanon as an expansionist policy and supported the PLO. Marchais, the party's leader, generally supported Mitterrand's policy, his only criticism being that France, together with other Western countries, had failed to secure an Israeli withdrawal. However, as in the British case, the party's previous anti-Zionism was largely absent, with the communist leadership seeking to distinguish Begin's policy from Israeli and Jewish opinion. Moreover it condemned anti-Semitic and terrorist attacks on Jews and even started to court the Jewish vote.

Intra-party factors underpinned this shift too. The abandonment of anti-Zionist slogans in the early 1980s stemmed partly from the rise of the reformist faction, which had grown in the aftermath of the party's failure in the 1978 legislative elections and formed the basis of a challenge to the party's organisational structure. Prominent left-wing intellectuals such as Louis Althusser joined the dissenters in demanding the demise of centralism and greater internal democracy with regard to policy formulation. Despite Marchais' success in stemming dissent, he was clearly on the defensive in the context of increasingly poor electoral fortunes, a drop in membership and an increasingly hostile public (Raymond, 1990, pp. 45–7).

Its more moderate stance also stemmed from external political pressures that differed from those in the British party. Although the party did go through a brief Eurocommunist phase, this affected it less than its immediate electoral problems and participation in government. By the 1980s the PCF had suffered a major blow to its electoral position, having lost out to the PS in the 1978 legislative elections, it failed to stem a drop in membership rates and failed to prevent a collapse in its popular image (see ibid., pp. 43–4). This electoral and membership decline meant that it could no longer ignore the fact that the public had become alienated from the traditional communist positions. Moreover its new position in the early 1980s made it untenable simply to repeat customary formulas. The PCF leadership allied with the PS in 1981 in the belief that its participation in government would prevent further marginalisation. As a result of Mitterrand's victory in 1981, the party entered government for the first time in thirty-four years and Pierre Mauroy's second government included four communist ministers (ibid., pp. 42–60). Given its previous pro-Palestinian orientation, it was natural for the party to agree with Mitterrand. Nevertheless it diluted its previous anti-Zionist rhetoric to fit in with its new status as part of the government.

Intra-party democracy

Turning now to the question of intra-party democracy, what does this account of the evolution of the parties' policy towards Israel say about this issue? Labour's structure and voting procedures predispose it towards openness and debate (Seyd, 1987, pp. 3–4). However some authors maintain that Labour's constitution, which 'asserts the sovereignty of conference and is self-consciously democratic', obscures the organisation's centralising nature, and that even since the democratisation measures in the 1970s mechanisms have been put in place that secure the leadership's dominance (Webb, 1994, p. 122). The question really hinges on whether the party activists can move the leadership towards a policy that it has not previously supported.

For much of the postwar period the matter of internal democracy did not really arise over the question of Israel because the extra-parliamentary party's opinion did not significantly differ from that of the leadership. However dissent from the prevailing consensus did emerge after 1956 and gained ground in the 1960s and 1970s. Previously the dissenters had been very much a disorganised minority, but after the 1967 Arab–Israeli hostilities the pressure mounted and a small group in the PLP and some members of the Labour left refused to exonerate Israel for its actions after the war. This time the dissenters started to organise themselves, with both right-wingers and left-wingers joining together to form LMEC with the explicit aim of trying to change policy.

In the 1970s the pro-Palestinian campaign gained ground in the constituency party section and the rest of the extra-parliamentary party. In 1973 the growing split between the leadership's position and that of the party's grass-roots became apparent, with around twice as many CLPs now opposing Israel. This trend continued throughout the 1970s, and in response the Callaghan leadership oversaw the formation of MESC as a way of exploring the Israeli–Arab conflict in more depth. Its concession to the emergent feeling was evident in the co-option of people such as Fred Halliday and Christopher Hitchens to the committee. The pressure accelerated in the early 1980s when pro-Palestinian feeling became widespread in the constituency parties, the trade unions, local Labour councils and even the PLP. Led by the constituency parties and the local councils, especially in London and Scotland, this movement went on to influence all sections of the party, including the PLP.

Until then the successive leaderships, especially Gaitskell and Wilson, had been very reluctant to recognise dissenters' views. They resisted attempts by pro-Arab party members to get their agenda incorporated into policy, repeatedly refusing to allow LMEC to affiliate. Mayhew went on to resign from Labour and join the Liberal Party, which during the 1970s contained a significant pro-Arab, anti-Israel current. McKay's involvement in the Arab cause was detrimental to her career prospects because it resulted in her constituency party seeking to deselect her. Nor was it politically rewarding for Andrew Faulds to take up the Arab cause because he lost his front bench position under Wilson's leadership for describing Jewish MPs as having dual loyalty. There were only minor changes under Callaghan's leadership. Although he oversaw the formation of MESC, he prohibited his parliamentary private secretary from joining a pro-Palestinian organisation. These examples illustrate the centralising tendencies that were characteristic of the Wilson era and beyond.

As in the British case, pressure for change in the French Socialist Party came from the bottom up. A small minority began to challenge the leadership's position during the Suez War. The challenge to the party's pro-Israel tradition grew in the post-1967 period, with the left playing a significant part in this through the PSU. Although the PSU was not formally linked to the SFIO at this stage, it was closely associated with it. In contrast most of the postwar leadership, including Blum, Mollet and Pineau, as well as the FGDS, remained resolutely pro-Israel. Moreover for most of the postwar period the SFIO leadership had no time at all for the PCF's anti-Israel position. It was only under Mitterrand's leadership that there were signals of a new approach to the Israeli–Palestinian conflict.

In the CPGB too it was the activists and dissidents who first pressed for a policy change. As early as 1956, in response to revelations about Soviet anti-Semitism, leading Jewish members of the pro-democracy movement began to challenge anti-Zionism, arguing for a re-evaluation of communism's approach to Jewish nationalism. The 1967 hostilities provoked a second wave of dissent, with some Jewish members questioning the communists' automatic anti-Israel, pro-Arab line. However those who dissented from the anti-Zionist orthodoxy had no effect on party policy until the 1980s as the leadership had no time for these views. For most of the postwar period, democratic centralism was deeply entrenched and was responsible for the leadership's refusal to give in to internal pressure for the party to reconsider its position on Zionism. The British Communist Party did not contain overt rivalries like those in Labour because its priority was to present a united front and the leadership dealt harshly with dissent (Samuel, 1986, pp. 63–5). This lack of internal democracy led Palme Dutt to denounce calls for a re-evaluation of the Communist Party's attitude towards Israel and its decision to reorganise the NJC, forcing it to put forward an anti-Zionist line. In 1967, too, the leadership repressed demands for a more sympathetic approach to Jewish nationalism.

The impetus for change in the PCF also came from the bottom up. Jewish members such as Annie Kriegel began early on to question the party's position, and even people such as Maxime Rodinson started to re-evaluate the party's traditional policy towards Zionism. In the French case too, specific personalities played a part in getting the PCF to take a more sympathetic attitude towards Jewish interests. The Jewish Eurocommunist, Jean Kanapa, significantly influenced Marchais' views on the Israeli–Palestinian question. In the PCF's case too, the leadership had no patience with people who challenged its views on Zionism and for most of the postwar period the dissidents' only option was to leave the party. The PCF leadership mainly refused to moderate its stand until the late 1970s and early 1980s.

There is, then, evidence that the grass roots played a part in policy change in all of these parties. At the very least this supports Whiteley's contention (made in relation to the Labour Party) that although activists have no effect on policy implementation, they play a significant part in setting the agenda of debate and setting priorities once they are on the agenda (Whiteley, 1983, p. 8). The trend in the French Socialist Party also lends support to Mitterrand's reputation for taking the party's views more into account than his predecessors had (Machin, 1993, p. 137). Moreover the move away from orthodox anti-Zionism in the communist left supports the modernisation thesis. However, greater openness and tolerance of ideas was more characteristic of social democrats than the communist left.

Even so it is interesting to note that, in the case of the Labour Party, the campaign's success to some extent depended on those supporting a policy change taking control of the centre: the NEC, the International Department and the parliamentary leadership. It was only when the left started to dominate these bodies and a left-wing leader (Michael Foot) was in place that support of the PLO was incorporated into official policy statements. Moreover it should not be forgotten that in the end it was the activists who acquiesced to the leadership's position rather than controlled it. They included clauses explicitly stating their support for Israel's existence in their conference motions. The leadership also overturned the 1988 and 1989 resolutions despite the fact that they had won the two-thirds majority needed to become policy. In the end, too, the activists were compelled to accept a policy that refused to include an explicit reference to Palestinian statehood, preferring to use the more neutral sounding concept of self-determination without specifying its content.

Moreover in France the presidential system of the Fifth Republic enhanced the leadership's dominance, and there can be no doubt that Mitterrand was a very dominant leader (Bell and Criddle, 1988 p. 236). Despite Mitterand's reputation for listening to his party, some socialist deputies complained that the presidency was dictatorial and that many decisions were taken behind closed doors (Machin, 1990, p. 37). In this particular case, moreover, the dominance was sharpened by the fact that French presidents have traditionally had a lot of say in foreign affairs. According to Howorth, this area of presidential supremacy stems from a number of factors, including the personalised nature of foreign relations and the effects of a long term of office (Howorth, 1990, pp. 201–2). Although the influence of left-wing figures, notably Claude Cheysson, was evident in Mitterrand's attitude towards the Middle East hostilities, the president's say over foreign policy was as 'watertight' as that of de Gaulle and Pompidou (ibid., pp. 201–2). Nor should it be forgotten that in his first year as president, Mitterrand bucked the trend by seeking to strengthen relations with Israel.

It is also worth noting that, in the CPGB's case, once the reformists had gained control of the party in some respects they behaved in as authoritarian a way as their predecessors. The reformers' rise was by no means smooth and uncontested. Rather it was strongly contested by traditionalists and groups seeking closer links with the Soviet Union. However the reformists did not try to absorb these elements or negotiate with them. Rather they set about marginalising and eventually expelling them. As Callaghan has noted, it was ironic that the Eurocommunist democrats conducted a purge of the party's traditionalists, and that in the 1980s the party lost thousands of members either through their own decision or by being removed (Callaghan, 1988, pp. 240–1).

In the PCF, however, the reformers failed to make a dramatic impact on the party, which only briefly accommodated Euro-communism and held out against this wider trend. Moreover in 1984 the party decided to leave the government in order to take an oppositional stand on socialist policies. This showed that the leadership was unwilling to take on board the seriousness of its electoral decline and the warnings coming from the reformist strand (Courtois and Peschanski, 1988, p. 67).

The question of internal democracy is therefore contingent and open-ended. There is evidence that activists in the Labour Party and the French Socialist Party were important in changing their parties' position on Israel in so far as they set the agendas for de-bate through campaigning. However, the leaderships seemed to have the final say, in particular, they controlled the detail of the policy outcomes. Nevertheless, opportunities for activists influencing de-velopments in policy were more evident in the social democratic parties than in the communist parties. For most of the postwar period, members whose views differed from those of the commu-nist leaderships had either to leave their parties voluntarily or they were expelled. Both the PCF and the CPBG were highly centralised and their leaderships generally unresponsive to shifts in opinion within the memberships.

Turning back to the question of how programmatic change takes place and abstracting a little further, there is evidence from this study to support the conception of parties as instrumental rather than principled and essentially vote maximisers (Downs, 1957, p. 96; see also Demker, 1997). The four discussed here all suffered some kind of electoral setback in the period preceding their policy shifts and adopted positions designed to attract ethnic votes at various stages. However, it would be difficult to show the weight of this factor over others and it looks likely that greater understanding is achieved through adopting an approach that takes account of the various environmental influences apart from electoral considerations as well as intra-party dynamics. With respect to the question of the effect of internal versus external pressures on party policy, this study confirms the view that the two interact so closely that the one cannot be prioritised over the other (Harmel and Janda, 1994, pp. 263–5). However, it should be noted that I have not tried to provide definitive answers to the theoretical issues in this book. My aim has been more moderate, namely, to offer some insights into the questions of policy change and internal party life through an in-depth examination of a single case study. The hope is that it will stimulate further empirical studies that might be even more illuminating.

Appendix 1: Sources

Newspapers and Journals

*Cahiers du Communisme**
*Comment**
*Daily Herald**
*Daily Mail**
Daily Worker
*France Nouvelle**
*The Guardian**
*Horizons**
L'Humanité
*Israel Labour News**
Jewish Chronicle
*Jewish Clarion**
*Jewish Vanguard** (Poale Zion)
*Labour Herald**
*Labour Israel**
*Labour Leader**
*Labour Monthly**
*Labour Woman**
*LFI News**
Marxism Today
*Le Matin**
Le Monde
Morning Star
*New Socialist**
*New Statesman (and Nation)**
*La Nouvelle Critique**
*Le Nouvel Observateur**
*Paris-Presse**
*La Pensée**
Le Populaire
*Quotidien de Paris**
*The Spectator**
The Times
*Les Temps Modernes**
Tribune
*Twentieth Century**
*Vanguard** (Poale Zion)
*World News (and Views)**
*Zionist Review**

---

* = occasional.

Labour Party Published Documents

Agenda for the Annual Conference
Labour Party Annual Conference Report (LPACR)
Agenda for the National Conference of Labour Women (NCLW)
NCLW Reports
Resolutions
TUC Reports
Problems of Foreign Policy (1952 Labour Party discussion document)
Labour Party Foreign Affairs, 1946/47
Labour's Foreign Policy (1958 LPAC)
Britain in the Modern World (1959 Labour Party discussion document)
Notes for Speakers (1974, Foreign Policy)
A Socialist Foreign Policy (1981 Labour Party discussion document)

Parliamentary Documents

Early Day Motions (EDMs)
Parliamentary Reports (Hansard)

Labour Party Internal Documents

NEC
International Department/Committee
Middle East Sub-Committee (MESC)
Parliamentary Group, LFI

Communist Party of Great Britain Internal Documents

International Department

Private Papers

Hugh Dalton (British Library of Political and Economic Science)

Pamphlets

Labour Looks at Israel, 1967–1971, LFI
The EEC Initiative on the Middle East, 1980, LFI conference literature
30 Years of LFI (1957–1987)
Palestine: An End To The Silence, 1988/89, Labour Middle East Council
A Cry for Justice, 1990/91, National Union Briefing for Trade Unionists, NUCPS
European Jewry and the Palestine Problem, 1946, CPGB
A Land With People, May 1982, *Morning Star*
Manifesto for New Times, 1988, CPGB

Interviews

Michael Foot, Labour MP
Ian Mikardo, Labour MP
Ernie Ross, Labour MP
Richard Clements, *Tribune*
Phil Kelly, *Tribune*

Jack Elliot, LFI
Peter Grunberger, LFI
Yousef Allen (Medical Aid for Palestine)
Bridget Gilchrist, LMEC
John Gee, CAABU
Solly Kaye, CPGB
Phil Piratin, CPGB

Appendix 2: Pro-Israel Labour MPs,* 1956

Edward Short (Newcastle Upon Tyne, Central)
Marcus Lipton (Lambeth, Brixton)
J. Dickson Mabon (Labour and Co-op, Greenock)
Barnett Janner (Leicester, North West)
Mark Hewitson (Kingston Upon Hull, West)
William Owen (Northumberland, Morpeth)
John McKay (Wallsend)
Alice Bacon (Leeds, South East)
Horace Holmes (Yorkshire, W.R., Hemsworth)
R. J. Mellish (Bermondsey)
Arthur Lewis (West Ham, North)
William Reid (Glasgow, Provan)
James Hutchinson Hoy (Edinburgh, Leith)
Charles Frederick Grey (Durham, Durham)
Roy Mason (Barnsley)
William Reid Blyton (Durham, Houghton le-Spring)
Leslie Lever (Manchester, Ardwick)
David Rhys Grenfell (Glamorgan, Gower)
Arthur Moody (Gateshead, East)
John Ainsley (Durham, North West)
Arthur Blenkinsop (Newcastle Upon Tyne, East)
George Jeger (Yorkshire W.R., Goole)
Emanuel Shinwell (Durham, Easington)
Alfred Broughton (Batley and Morley)
Alice Cullen (Glasgow, Gorbals)
Frank Anderson (Cumberland, Whitehaven)
William Stones (Durham, Consett)
Charles Simmons (Staffordshire, Brierley Hill)
Benjamin Parkin (Paddington, North)
Lynn Ungoed-Thomas (Leicester, North East)
Albert Roberts (Yorkshire W.R., Normanton)
Simon Mahon (Bootle)
Elizabeth Braddock (Liverpool, Exchange)
Harold Neal (Derbyshire, Bolsover)
Percy Daines (Labour and Co-op, East Ham, North)
Morgan Philips Price (Gloucestershire, West)
Eric Fletcher (Islington, East)
Stephen Davies (Merthyr Tydfil)

---

* This list is based on signatories to the pro-Israel EDM.

David Logan (Liverpool, Scotland)
Thomas Oswald (Edinburgh, Central)
John Paton (Norwich, North)
David Jones (The Hartlepools)
Elwyn Jones (West Ham, South)
Harold Finch (Monmouthshire, Bedwellty)
Percy Morris (Swansea, West)
Eustace George (Edinburgh, East)
Hector Hughes (Aberdeen, North)
Lena Jeger (Holborn and St. Pancras)
Cyril Bence (Dunbartonshire, East)
John Edwards (Brighouse and Spenborough)
David Weitzman (Stoke Newington and Hackney North)
Frederick Willey (Sunderland, North)
Maurice Orbach (Willesden, East)
Michael Stewart (Fulham)
Samuel Philip Viant (Willesden, West)
Joseph Reeves (Greenwich)
Henry Usborne (Birmingham, Yardley)
Thomas Hubbard (Kirkcaldy)
Ernest Davies (Enfield, East)
Leslie Plummer (Deptford)
Roy Jenkins (Birmingham, Stechford)
Julius Silverman (Birmingham, Aston)
George Alfred Isaacs (Southwark)
Edward Redhead (Walthamstow, West)
George Darling (Labour and Co-op, Sheffield, Hillsborough)
M. K. MacMillan (Western Isles)
Norman Dodds (Erith and Crayford)
J. Harrison (Nottingham, North)
Daniel Granville West (Monmouthshire, Pontypool)
John Forman (Labour and Co-op, Glasgow, Springburn)
Charles Hobson (Keighley)
Stephen Swingler (Newcastle Under Lyme)
George Albert Pargiter (Southall)
G. R. Chetwynd (Stockton-On-Tees)
Bernard Taylor (Nottinghamshire, Mansfield)
George Craddock (Bradford, South)
Charles Royle (Salford, West)
W. J. Edwards (Stepney)
M. Herbison (Lanarkshire, North)
Hugh Dalton (Bishop Auckland)
Frank Allaun (Salford, East)

Appendix 3: Pro-Israel Labour MPs,* 1967

David Weitzman (Stoke Newington and Hackney North)
John Dunwoody (Falmouth and Camborne)
Ian Mikardo (Poplar)
Sydney Silverman (Nelson and Colne)
Mr. Winterbottom (Sheffield, Brightside)
Renee Short (Wolverhampton, North East)
James Tinn (Cleveland)
E. M. Braddock (Liverpool, Exchange)
Donald Chapman (Birmingham, Northfield)
Robert Sheldon (Ashton-Under-Lyne)
David Winnick (Croydon, South)
Maurice Miller (Glasgow, Kelvingrove)
William Hamling (Woolwich, West)
Edward Lyons (Bradford, East)
John Lee (Reading)
Eric Moonman (Billericay)
Elystan Morgan (Cardigan)
Arthur Davidson (Accrington)
Alfred Morris (Manchester, Wythenshawe)
Raphael Tuck (Watford)
Maurice Orbach (Stockport, South)
Archie Manuel (Ayrshire and Bute, Central Ayrshire)
Arnold Shaw (Ilford, South)
Hector Hughes (Aberdeen, North)
Hugh Gray (Norfolk, Yarmouth)
Peter Jackson (Derbyshire, High Peak)
Raymond Fletcher (Derbyshire, Ilkeston)
Arthur Lewis (West Ham, North)
Joel Barnett (Lancashire, Heywood and Royton)
Edwin Brooks (Bebington)
William S. Hilton (Bethnal Green)
Edward Rowlands (Cardiff, North)
Bert Hazell (Norfolk, North)
William Hamilton (Fife, West)
James Griffiths (Carmarthenshire, Llanelly)
G. R. Strauss (Lambeth, Vauxhall)
Paul Rose (Manchester, Blackley)
Dennis Hobden (Brighton, Kemp Town)

---

* This list is based on signatories to the pro-Israel EDM.

Eric Varley (Chesterfield)
David Ginsburg (Dewsbury)
David Kerr (Wandsworth, Central)
William Price (Warwickshire, Rugby)
Roland Moyle (Lewisham, North)
Arnold Gregory (Stockport, North)
Desmond Donnelly (Pembroke)
John Rankin (Labour and Co-op, Glasgow, Govan)
Ben Whitaker (Hampstead)
Denis Walter Coe (Lancashire, Middleton and Prestwich)
John Parker (Dagenham)
Alan Lee Williams (Hornchurch)
Robert Maxwell (Buckinghamshire, Buckingham)
George Rogers (Kensington, North)
Stanley Henig (Lancashire, Lancaster)
George Henry Perry (Nottingham, South)
Herbert Butler (Hackney, Central)
Leo Abse (Monmouthshire, Pontypool)
Gwilym Roberts (Bedfordshire South)
Will Owen (Labour and Co-op, Northumberland, Morpeth)
Tony Gardner (Nottingham, Rushcliffe)
Robert Woof (Durham, Blaydon)
Hugh Delargy (Essex, Thurrock)
Richard Crawshaw (Liverpool, Toxteth)
James Dempsey (Coatbridge and Airdrie)
Julius Silverman (Birmingham, Aston)
Cyril Bence (Dunbartonshire, East)
James Johnson (Kingston-Upon-Hull)
Peter Archer (Rowley Regis and Tipton)
Edward Stanley Bishop (Nottingham, Newark)
Laurence Pavitt (Labour and Co-op, West Willesden)
Roy Roebuck (Harrow, East)
Gwyneth Dunwoody (Exeter)
Leslie Lever (Manchester, Ardwick)
Lena Jeger (Holborn and St. Pancras, South)
Simon Mahon (Bootle)
Alice Cullen (Glasgow, Gorbals)
Michael Barnes (Brentford and Chiswick)
Ivor Richard (Barons Court)
Edwin Wainwright (Yorkshire W. R., Dearne Valley)
Albert Roberts (Yorkshire W. R., Normanton)
Arthur Pearson (Glamorganshire, Pontypridd)
Daniel Jones (Burnley)
Alistair Macdonald (Kent, Chislehurst)
James A. Dunn (Liverpool, Kirkdale)
Eric Ogden (Liverpool, West Derby)
Thomas Steele (Dunbartonshire, West)
William Wilson (Coventry, South)
Neil Carmichael (Glasgow, Woodside)

Leslie Huckfield (Nuneaton)
Peter Mahon (Preston, South)
Arthur Probert (Aberdare)
Arthur Palmer (Labour and Co-op, Bristol, Central)
James Hamilton (Lanarkshire, Bothwell)
Samuel Charles Silkin (Camberwell, Dulwich)
Idwal Jones (Denbighshire, Wrexham)
Maurice Edelman (Coventry, North)
John Binns (Keighley)
John Forrester (Stoke-on-Trent, North)
John Horner (Oldbury and Halesowen)
Geoffrey Rhodes (Labour and Co-op, Newcastle, East)
Charles Mapp (Oldham, East)
Malcolm MacMillan (Western Isles)
John Ellis (Bristol, North-West)
Robert Edwards (Bilston)
John Robertson (Paisley)
Shirley Summersill (Halifax)

Appendix 4: Pro-Arab Labour MPs,* 1967

Margaret McKay (Wandsworth, Clapham)
Derek Page (Norfold, Kings Lynn)
John Ryan (Middlesex, Uxbridge)
Will Owen† (Labour and Co-op, Northumberland, Morpeth)
William Molloy† (Ealing, North)
James Dickens (Lewisham, West)
Christopher Mayhew (Woolwich, East)
David Watkins (Durham, Consett)
George Lawson (Lanarkshire, Motherwell)
Alan Beaney (Hemsworth, Yorks)
Evan Luard (Oxford)
Thomas Urwin (Durham, Houghton-le-Spring)
Sydney Bidwell (Southall)
Michael McGuire (Lancashire, Ince)
Roy Hughes (Newport)
Andrew Faulds (Smethwick)
Will Griffiths (Manchester, Exchange)
Brian Parkyn (Bedfordshire, Bedford)

---

* This list is based on signatories to a top-scoring pro-Arab EDM.
† MPs who signed both pro-Israel and pro-Arab EDMs

Appendix 5: Pro-Palestinian Labour MPs,* 1982

Michael Foot (Gwent, Ebbw Vale)
Denis Healey (Leeds, East)
John Silkin (Lewisham, Deptford)
Royland Moyle (Lewisham, East)
Jack Dormand (Durham, Easington)
Ioan Evans (Labour and Co-op, Aberdare)
Alexander Lyon (York)
Dennis Skinner (Derbyshire, Bolsover)
Tony Benn (Bristol, South East)
Frank Haynes (Ashfield)
A. W. Stallard (Camden, St. Pancras North)
Peter Snape (West Bromwich, East)
David Stoddart (Swindon)
Ray Powell (Ogmore)
Robin F. Cook (Edinburgh, Central)
Frank Dobson (Holborn and St. Pancras South)
Don Dixon (Jarrow)
Robert C. Brown (Newcastle Upon Tyne)
John Home Robertson (Berwick and East Lothian)
Laurence Pavitt (Labour and Co-op, Brent South)
Stanley Newens (Labour and Co-op, Harlow)
David Watkins (Durham, Consett)
Lewis Carter-Jones (Eccles)
Roger Stott (Westhoughton)
David Winnick (Walsall, North)
Frank Hooley (Sheffield, Heeley)
Neil Carmichael (Glasgow, Kelvingrove)
Neil Kinnock (Bedwellty)
Allan Roberts (Bootle)
Ernie Roberts (Hackney North and Stoke Newington)
Ken Woolmer (Batley and Morley)
John Maxton (Glasgow, Cathcart)
Stanley Orme (Salford, West)
Roy Hughes (Newport)
Allen McKay (Yorkshire, W. R., Penistone)
Joan Maynard (Sheffield, Brightside)
Bruce Millan (Glasgow, Craigton)
Ted Fletcher (Darlington)

---

* This list is based on signatories to the top-scoring pro-Palestinian EDM.

Ernie Ross (Dundee, West)
Norman Hogg (Dunbartonshire, East)
Robert Parry (Liverpool, Scotland Exchange)
William McKelvey (Kilmarnock)
Harold Walker (Doncaster)
Guy Barnett (Greenwich)
George Morton (Manchester, Moss Side)
Martin O'Neil (Clackmannan and East Stirlingshire)
Stan Thorne (Preston, South)
John Sever (Birmingham, Ladywood)
Reg Race (Haringey, Wood Green)
J. D. Concannon (Nottinghamshire, Mansfield)
David Ennals (Norwich, North)
Clive Soley (Hammersmith North)
Dick Douglas (Dunfermline)
Sheila Wright (Birmingham, Handsworth)
Andrew Faulds (Warley, East)
J. W. Rooker (Birmingham, Perry Bar)
Martin Flannery (Sheffield, Hillsborough)
Tom Urwin (Durham, Houghton-le-Spring)
Terry Davis (Birmingham, Stechford)
Roger Thomas (Carmarthen)
George Park (Coventry, North East)
Hugh McCartney (Dunbartonshire, Central)

Appendix 6: Pro-Palestinian Labour Activists,* 1982

Albert Booth (Barrow-in-Furness)
Dale Campbell-Savours (Workington)
J. D. Concannon (Nottinghamshire, Mansfield)
Andrew Faulds (Warley, East)
Martin Flannery (Sheffield, Hillsborough)
Norman Hogg (Dunbartonshire, East)
John Home Robertson (Berwich and East Lothian)
Roy Hughes (Newport)
David Lambie (Ayrshire, Central)
Joan Maynard (Sheffield, Brightside)
Hugh McCartney (Dunbartonshire, Central)
William McKelvey (Kilmarnock)
Robert McTaggart (Glasgow, Central)
Stanley Newens (Labour and Co-op., Harlow)
Martin O'Neil (Clackmannan and East Stirlingshire)
Robert Parry (Liverpool, Scotland Exchange)
Allan Roberts (Bootle)
Leslie Spriggs (St. Helens)
Roger Stott (Westhoughton)
Roger Thomas (Carmarthen)
James Tinn (Teesside, Redcar)
Stan Thorne (Preston, South)
Tom Urwin (Durham, Houghton-le-Spring)
David Watkins (Durham, Consett)
Ken Weetch (Ipswich)

---

* I have defined as activists those Labour MPs who signed two or more
EDMs which were critical of Israel and pro-Palestinian in orientation.

Notes and References

1 Introduction

1 An EDM is a parliamentary member's motion for which no date has been fixed but in most cases is debated. Its function is to record members' opinions and to canvass support from other members (Fact Sheet No. 30, Early Day Motions, Public Information Office).
2 See Appendix 1.

2 The Labour Party and the Establishment of the State of Israel

1 Interview with Michael Foot.
2 Colonial Secretary, 1946–50.
3 *The Labour Woman*, September 1937, pp. 136–7.
4 *Tribune*, 17 November 1944, pp. 1–2; see also *Tribune*, 9 April 1943, p. 10.
5 *Jewish Chronicle*, 11 May 1945, p. 10.
6 *Zionist Review*, 30 April 1943.
7 Jewish Telegraphic Agency, London, 15 September 1943.
8 Jewish Telegraphic Agency, London, 22 November 1943.
9 Correspondence, Hugh Dalton to Herbert Morrison, 28 October 1944. Hugh Dalton's Private Papers, File 8/1.
10 'Economic Approach to the Palestine Problem', International Department, No. 276A (Labour Party discussion document October 1944).
11 'Foreign Affairs' (Labour Party policy statement) 1946–1947, p. 9.
12 *Tribune*, 25 May 1945, p. 8.
13 Ibid., p. 8.
14 *Tribune*, 31 July 1942, p. 8.
15 The Revisionist Party was formed in 1925 in opposition to Chaim Weizmann's and Labour Zionism's practical approach to the establishment of a Jewish state (Lucas, 1974, p. 131).
16 Interview with Ian Mikardo.
17 Interview with Richard Clements.
18 *Jewish Chronicle*, 29 June 1945, p. 1.
19 Ibid.
20 Ibid.
21 *Jewish Chronicle*, 18 May 1945, p. 1.
22 *Jewish Chronicle*, 15 June 1945, p. 7.
23 *Jewish Chronicle*, 8 June 1945, p. 12.
24 *Jewish Chronicle*, 25 May 1945, p. 8.
25 *Guardian*, 8 September 1994, p. 22.
26 *Tribune*, 10 December 1943, p. 11.
27 *Tribune*, 31 July 1942, p. 8.
28 Labour Party Annual Conference Report (LPACR) (1944), pp. 4–9, 140.

29 The Labour government's Palestine policy has been thoroughly documented (see Bullock, 1983; Gorny, 1983; Louis, 1984; Morgan, 1989). I shall therefore provide only a brief account of it here.
30 *The Times*, 22 February 1946, p. 7, 1 May 1946, p. 1.
31 *Jewish Chronicle*, 5 December 1947, p. 1.
32 'Foreign Affairs' (Labour Party discussion document, 1946–1947) p. 6.
33 *Jewish Chronicle*, 23 May 1947, p. 5, emphasis added.
34 *Jewish Chronicle*, 1 August 1947, p. 1, 8 August 1947, p. 5.
35 *The Times*, 2 July 1946, p. 4.
36 TUC Report, 1947, p. 205.
37 *The Times*, 13 June 1946; *Jewish Chronicle*, 14 June 1946, p. 1.
38 *Jewish Chronicle*, 6 June 1947.
39 *Labour Woman*, May 1946, p. 109.
40 *Labour Woman*, 15 August 1946, p. 181.
41 *Jewish Chronicle*, 9 November 1945, p. 5; *The Times*, 8 July 1946, p. 8.
42 *Jewish Chronicle*, 12 October 1945, p. 12.
43 *Jewish Chronicle*, 19 October 1945, p. 12.
44 'Resolutions' (Labour Party 1947), p. 28.
45 LPACR (1946), pp. 155, 169; *The Times*, 13 June 1946, p. 2; *Jewish Chronicle*, 14 June 1946, p. 1.
46 Keep Left also included Ian Mikardo, Geoffrey Bing, Donald Bruce, Harold Davies, Leslie Hale, Fred Lee, Benn Levy, Ronald MacKay, J. P. W. Mallalieu, E. R. Millington and Stephen Swingler (Jackson, 1968, pp. 62–3).
47 *The Times*, 2 July 1946, pp. 1–2.
48 Ibid., p. 2.
49 Ibid., pp. 1–2; *Jewish Chronicle*, 5 July 1946, pp. 5–6.
50 Published by Victor Gollancz in 1946.
51 Notices of Motions, House of Commons Vote Bundle: The Stationery Office vol. 1, 1948–49, p. 626.
52 *Tribune*, 7 February 1947, p. 2.
53 Ibid.
54 *The Times*, 11 June 1946, p. 2; *Jewish Chronicle*, 14 June 1946, p. 1, emphasis added.
55 The Portsmouth Treaty (15 January 1948) between Britain and Iraq was designed to replace the Anglo-Iraqi Treaty of 1930 with the aim of forging an equal relationship between the two countries. British air bases were to be handed to Iraq and strategic interests considered by a joint defence board. Demonstrations against the treaty in Iraq led to its retraction (Ovendale, 1992, p. 205).
56 *Tribune*, 13 February 1948, p. 9.
57 *The Times*, 11 January 1949, p. 4.
58 *The Times*, 19 January 1949, p. 4.
59 Report of the Delegation to Israel (29 December 1949 to 13 January 1950), January 1950.
60 *Labour Israel*, 27 January 1950, p. 1.
61 *The Times*, 27 January 1949, p. 4.
62 *Tribune*, 28 May 1948, p. 7; *The Times*, 20 May 1948, p. 2; *Jewish Chronicle*, 21 May 1948, p. 11.

3 Labour, Suez and Israel

1 Alderman, 1983, p. 133.
2 Labour Party Annual Conference Report (LPACR) (1951), pp. 9–10, (1954), pp. 74–5, (1955), pp. 178–9, (1956), pp. 70–8.
3 TUC Report (1951), pp. 218–19; TUC Report (1956), p. 436.
4 See for example, *Tribune*, 8 April 1955, pp. 1, 8, 4 November 1955, p. 4, 13 January 1956, p. 1.
5 National Conference of Labour Women Report (NCLWR) (1954), p. 15, (1956), pp. 44–5.
6 In his chapter on 'cross-pressure' Epstein focuses principally on the way in which Jewish Labour MPs dealt with the pressures arising out of Israel's role in the war (see Epstein, 1964, pp. 173–98).
7 Parliamentary Debates, Commons, vol. 560, 1956–7, col. 32.
8 Parliamentary Debates, Commons, vol. 561, 1956–7, col. 1296.
9 Parliamentary Debates, Commons, vol. 570, 1956–7, cols 472–3.
10 NEC, 28 November 1956, pp. 1–2.
11 *Tribune*, 14 December 1956, p. 1.
12 Press release issued by Transport House, 15 February 1957.
13 This account draws heavily on Epstein (1964), pp. 189–95 and Alderman (1983), pp. 131–2.
14 *Jewish Chronicle*, 7 December 1956, p. 1.
15 These were Austen Albu, Frank Allaun, Maurice Edelman, George Jeger, Harold Lever, Leslie Lever, Marcus Lipton, Ian Mikardo, Maurice Orbach, Emanuel Shinwell, Julius Silverman, Sydney Silverman, George Strauss, Barnet Stross, Moss Turner-Samuels and David Weitzman (Epstein, 1964, p. 185).
16 The other Jewish MPs who abstained from this vote were Austin Albu, Leslie Lever, Moss Turner-Samuels and David Weitzman (Alderman, 1983, p. 199, note 26) Shinwell and Harold Lever.
17 *Jewish Chronicle*, 17 August 1956, p. 8.
18 *Tribune*, 2 November 1956, p. 2.
19 Parliamentary Debates, Commons, vol. 570, 1956–7, cols 608–9.
20 LPACR (1956), pp. 70–5.
21 TUC Report (1956), pp. 436–40.
22 NCLWR (1956), p. 44.
23 NCLWR (1957), pp. 42–3.
24 Parliamentary Debates, Commons, vol. 561, 1956–7, col. 1294.
25 Reggie Paget represented Northampton from 1945 to 1974. Frank Tomney was the MP for North Hammersmith from 1950–79. Jack Jones was a junior minister from 1947–50, MP for Bolton from 1945–50 and MP for Rotherham from 1950–62 (Williams, 1983, p. 349, note 17, p. 366, note 4, p. 569, note 21).
26 *The Times*, 1 September 1956, p. 6.
27 Former minister and Labour MP for Sheffield Attercliffe from 1944–70.
28 *Jewish Chronicle*, 9 November 1956, p. 8.
29 Labour MP for Smethwick.
30 *The Times*, 2 October 1956, p. 11.
31 TUC Report (1956), p. 434.
32 *Tribune*, 10 August 1956, p. 12.

33 *The Times*, 10 August 1956, p. 2.
34 Poale Zion press release, 7 October 1955.
35 Parliamentary Debates, Commons, vol. 561, 1956–7, col. 1299.
36 Parliamentary Debates, Commons, vol. 566, 1956–7, cols 1418–19.
37 *Tribune*, 2 November 1956, p. 12.
38 *Tribune*, 3 August 1956, p. 1
39 Parliamentary Debates, Commons, vol. 566, 1956–7, col. 1420.
40 Parliamentary Debates, Commons, vol. 570, 1956–7, col. 420.
41 *The Times*, 9 August 1956, p. 5.
42 Labour MP for Dundee West.
43 *The Times*, 3 September 1956, p. 5.
44 *Tribune*, 10 August 1956, p. 12.
45 Parliamentary Debates, Commons, vol. 561, 1956–7, col. 1295.
46 *Tribune*, 9 March 1956, p. 4.
47 *Tribune*, 24 August 1956, p. 2; TUC report, 1956, p. 440.
48 Interview with Ian Mikardo.
49 See TUC Report, 1950, pp. 201–2; LPACR, 1951, pp. 9–10.
50 See NCLWR (1954), p. 15.
51 Middle East Visit, 12–26 August 1959, Int/1958–9/34, p. 1.
52 Telegram from Mapai, 8 November 1956.
53 LPACR (1956), pp. 72–3.
54 LFI leaflet, '30 Years of LFI' (1957–1987).
55 Parliamentary Debates, Commons, vol. 570, 1956–7, col. 609.
56 *Jewish Chronicle*, 17 August 1956, p. 8, 31 August 1956, p. 14.
57 Orbach returned to parliament in 1964 as MP for Stockport South.
58 *The Times*, 15 August 1956, p. 6.
59 *Tribune*, 2 November 1956, p. 1.
60 This account derives from Howe (1993), pp. 231–49, 265, 272, note 14.
61 *Tribune*, 19 October 1956, p. 1.
62 *Tribune*, 21 September 1956, p. 5.
63 *Tribune*, 21 September 1956, p. 5.
64 *Tribune*, 2 November 1956, p. 1.
65 Interview with Michael Foot.
66 Correspondence from Tony Benn to John Hatch, 4 November 1957.
67 Correspondence from John Clarke to Tony Benn, 20 November 1957.
68 The Middle East, ID, November 1957, p. 1.
69 Int/ME/1958–9/3.
70 Correspondence from David Ennals to Leslie Carver, Deputy Director of UNRWA, 21 July 1959.
71 Report of Middle East Visit, 12–26 August 1959, Int/1958–59/34, p. 1.
72 Ibid., p. 3.
73 Unpublished article by David Ennals, 31 August 1959, p. 1.

4 The 1967 War

1 Kingsley Martin, 'Dual Sympathies on the Left', *Jewish Chronicle*, 20 October 1967.
2 *The Times*, 6 June 1967, p. 1.
3 *The Times*, 6 June 1967, p. 7.
4 *The Times*, 22 June 1967, p. 4.

5 *Jewish Chronicle*, 7 July 1967, p. 7.
6 *Jewish Chronicle*, 4 August 1967, p. 16.
7 *Jewish Chronicle*, 7 July 1967, p. 7.
8 Notices of Motions, House of Commons Vote Bundle: The Stationery Office, 5 June–6 July 1967, p. 11389.
9 Parliamentary Debates, Commons, vol. 749, 1966–7, cols 2059–60.
10 *The Times*, 28 June 1967, p. 6.
11 *The Times*, 29 July 1967, p. 11.
12 *Jewish Chronicle*, 13 October 1967, p. 26.
13 *The Jewish Year Book* (Jerusalem: Rubin Mass 1967), pp. 257–8.
14 Parliamentary Debates, Commons, vol. 749, 1966–7, cols 2044–51.
15 Ibid., cols 2084–90.
16 *Jewish Chronicle*, 9 June 1967, p. 5.
17 'The Middle East War – the Aftermath' (Labour Party Overseas Sub-Committee, 1967).
18 For the full text of the resolution, see Djonovich (1989), p. 8.
19 *Jewish Chronicle*, 2 October 1970, p. 40.
20 'Resolutions from CLPs and Trade Unions', NEC Overseas Department, OV/1966–67, p. 61.
21 See 'Resolutions' (Labour Party 1967), pp. 58–61.
22 'Resolutions' (Labour Party 1968), pp. 50–3.
23 LPACR (1970), pp. 200–5, 327.
24 TUC report (1967), pp. 489–92; *Jewish Chronicle*, 8 September 1967, p. 1.
25 NCLW (1968), p. 40.
26 NAD/W/80/7/70; OV/1969–70/78 (Labour Party internal documents).
27 TUC report (1967), pp. 489–91.
28 See 'Labour Looks at Israel' (LFI, 1971).
29 *The Times*, 22 June 1967, p. 4.
30 See for example Parliamentary Debates, Commons, vol. 749, cols 2046–7, 2059, 2089–90.
31 LPACR (1970), p. 327.
32 See 'Labour Looks At Israel' (LFI, 1971), p. 31.
33 Ibid., p. 30.
34 *Jewish Chronicle*, 7 July 1967, p. 7.
35 TUC Report (1964), p. 477; TUC Report (1965), p. 251; TUC Report (1966), p. 264; TUC Report (1967), p. 266.
36 NCLW (1968).
37 *Jewish Chronicle*, 10 November 1967, p. 19.
38 *Jewish Chronicle*, 7 July 1967, p. 7.
39 *Jewish Chronicle*, 9 June 1967, p. 26.
40 *Jewish Chronicle*, 14 July 1967, p. 16.
41 *The Times*, 6 June 1967, p. 1.
42 Correspondence from Sidney Goldberg to Gwyn Morgan, Overseas Department; see also *Jewish Chronicle*, 14 July 1967, p. 7.
43 *Jewish Chronicle*, 9 June 1967, p. 6.
44 *The Times*, 8 June 1967, p. 7.
45 *Jewish Chronicle*, 21 July 1967, p. 17, 3 November 1967, p. 18.
46 Telegram, 22 June 1967.

47 *Jewish Chronicle*, 4 August 1967, p. 1.
48 *Jewish Chronicle*, 7 July 1967, p. 7.
49 MPs for Woolwich East, Clapham, Smethwick and Durham Consett respectively.
50 Notices of Motions, House of Commons Vote Bundle: The Stationery Office, 7 July 1967–27 October 1967, p. 12811.
51 Parliamentary Debates, Commons, vol. 749, 1966–7, col. 2047.
52 Parliamentary Debates, Commons, vol. 749, 1966–7, cols 2098–9.
53 *The Times*, 7 June 1967, p. 5.
54 Parliamentary Debates, Commons, vol. 749, 1966–7, cols 2096–7.
55 Council for the Advancement of Arab-British Understanding (CAABU) leaflet.
56 *Jewish Chronicle*, 13 October 1967, p. 26.
57 Minutes of the meeting of the Organisation Committee, Org/9, 10 July 1972; NEC 26 July 1972 (Labour Party internal documents).
58 Parliamentary Debates, Commons, vol. 747, 1966–7, cols 142–53.
59 Notices of Motions, House of Commons Vote Bundle: The Stationery Office, 5 June 1967–6 July 1967, p. 12122.
60 *Tribune*, 16 June 1967, p. 1, 30 June 1967, p. 2.
61 *Tribune*, 7 July 1967, p. 3.
62 *Tribune*, 9 June 1967, p. 1.
63 *Tribune*, 30 December 1967, p. 2.
64 Interview with John Gee, information officer, CAABU.
65 *Jewish Chronicle*, 7 July 1967, p. 7.
66 *Who's Who* (London: Black 1993).
67 Interview with Michael Foot.
68 *Tribune*, 30 June 1967, p. 2.
69 See *New Left Review*, no. 44 (1967), pp. 30–45.
70 Parliamentary Debates, Commons, vol. 747, 1966–7, cols 143–4.
71 *Who's Who* (London: Black 1992).
72 *Tribune*, 2 June 1967, p. 7, 9 June 1967, p. 1, *Tribune*, 16 June 1967, p. 7.
73 Correspondence, David Ennals to Patrick Gordon Walker, 11 March 1963.
74 Interview with Michael Foot.
75 Interview with Richard Clements.
76 Parliamentary Debates, Commons, vol. 749, 1966–7, cols 2049–50.
77 *Jewish Chronicle*, 16 June 1967, p. 23; Crossman (1976), p. 364.
78 *The Times*, 13 June 1967, p. 4.
79 *Tribune*, 2 June 1967, p. 6.
80 *Tribune*, 16 June 1967, p. 6.
81 Interview with Michael Foot.
82 See Parliamentary Debates, Commons, vol. 747, 1966–7, col. 170; Mayhew in *Twentieth Century*, vol. 1066 (1971), p. 4.
83 *The Times*, 7 June 1967, p. 5.
84 *Tribune*, 9 June 1967, p. 1.
85 See LPACR (1970), pp. 200–5, 327, 334.
86 *Jewish Chronicle*, 9 October 1970, p. 16.

5   Israel in Lebanon

1   Sources include the Agenda of the Labour Party Annual Conference Report (LPACA) (1982); the LPACR (1982); the *Jewish Chronicle* and an interview with Ernie Ross MP. The list of pro-Palestinian parties is not exhaustive.

2   Interview with Yousef Allen.

3   Interview with Ernie Ross.

4   *Jewish Chronicle*, 17 September 1982, p. 6.

5   Interview with Peter Grunberger, Director of LFI.

6   It should be noted that Jewish groups also benefited from EMU funding, including the ultra-orthodox Agudas Israel (Alderman, 1989, pp. 130–4).

7   *Jewish Chronicle*, 16 July 1982, p. 6.

8   *The Times*, 10 September 1982, p. 4; TUC Report (1982), p. 615.

9   *The Times*, 25 September 1982, p. 6.

10   See 'A Cry For Justice: Trade unions and life in the occupied territories of Palestine', NUCPS (1990), pp. 25–6.

11   Interview with Yousef Allen.

12   LPACR (1988), p. 134; LPACR (1989), p. 156.

13   LMEC membership list, 1991.

14   Agenda of the National Conference of Labour Women (NCLWA) (1984), p. 55; NCLWA (1986), p. 110.

15   Notices of Motions, House of Commons Vote Bundle: The Stationery Office, vol. VIII, 1981–82, p. 7214.

16   *Jewish Chronicle*, 11 June 1982, p. 44.

17   LPACR (1982), pp. 136–7.

18   *Jewish Chronicle*, 4 December 1981, p. 21.

19   *New Socialist*, September/October 1982, pp. 40–1.

20   *The Times*, 9 August 1982, p. 1.

21   Interview with Yousef Allen.

22   Interview with Ernie Ross MP.

23   *Jewish Chronicle*, 20 September 1988, p. 44.

24   Int/9, 12 November 1974; NEC, 26 November 1974 (Labour Party internal documents). As chair of the international committee, Ian Mikardo had opposed the Socialist International's decision to make these links.

25   *New Socialist*, September/October 1982, p. 40.

26   1981–86.

27   TUFP information sheet, 1980.

28   *Jewish Chronicle*, 4 June 1982, p. 6.

29   Minutes of the Parliamentary Group (LFI, 1 July 1980).

30   TUC Report (1983), pp. 555–8.

31   Pro-Palestinian activists include Labour MPs who signed two or more EDMs in 1982 that were critical of Israel and supportive of Palestinian national rights. Pro-Israel activists include Labour MPs who signed critical amendments to pro-Palestinian EDMs. I have discounted members who signed both pro-Palestinian motions and critical amendments.

32   Interview with Ernie Ross.

33   *Guardian*, G2T, p. 18.

34 LPACR (1982), p. 148.
35 Ibid., p. 133.
36 *Jewish Chronicle*, 3 October 1986, p. 52.
37 *Jewish Chronicle*, 3 September 1982, London Extra, p. 1.
38 *Labour Leader*, September 1982, pp. 6–7.
39 Agenda for the NCLW (1984), p. 55.
40 Agenda for the NCLW (1986), p. 110.
41 *Labour Leader*, September 1982, pp. 6–7.
42 LPACR (1982), p. 133.
43 Interview with Ernie Ross.
44 *Jewish Chronicle*, 3 October 1986, p. 52.
45 LPACR (1982), p. 137.
46 The principle of a two-state solution was advocated by Short at a talk given at the LSE on the Gulf War on 25 February 1991. Before talking about the conflict, Short criticised the Trotskyist element of the party.
47 Interview with Yousef Allen.
48 Interview with Ian Mikardo.
49 Mikardo chaired the International Committee between 1973 and 1979.
50 Int/9, 12 November 1974; NEC, 26 November 1974.
51 Minutes of the meeting of the Parliamentary Branch of LFI, 20 July 1982.
52 LPACR (1982), p. 134.
53 *Jewish Chronicle*, 11 June 1982, p. 8.
54 Joseph Finklestone, diplomatic editor of the *Jewish Chronicle*, made this point (*Guardian*, 27 March 1992, p. 23).
55 *Jewish Chronicle*, 7 May 1982, p. 14.
56 *Jewish Chronicle*, 25 June 1982, p. 9.
57 *Jewish Chronicle*, 3 June 1983, p. 1.
58 *Jewish Chronicle*, 7 October 1988, p. 1.
59 *Jewish Chronicle*, 4 June 1982, p. 6.
60 LPACR (1983), p. 167.
61 Interview with Peter Grunberger, director of the LFI.
62 *Jewish Chronicle*, 5 June 1987, p. 8
63 *Jewish Chronicle*, 12 June 1987, London Extra, p. 4.
64 *Jewish Chronicle*, 12 June 1987, London Extra, p. 4.
65 Interview with Bridget Gilchrist, LMEC.
66 *Jewish Chronicle*, 14 October 1988, p. 6.
67 LPACR (1989), p. 156.
68 LPACR (1988), p. 180; LPACR (1989), p. 156.
69 *Jewish Chronicle*, 12 October 1990, p. 6.
70 *Guardian*, 31 January 1991, p. 4.
71 *Jewish Chronicle*, 14 October 1988, p. 6.
72 *Guardian*, 6 February 1991, p. 19.
73 *Jewish Chronicle*, 5 June 1987, p. 8.
74 See 'Palestine, An End To The Silence' (LMEC, 1987), p. 13.

6 The British Communist Party and Israel

1 'European Jewry and the Palestine Problem' (CPGB, 1946), pp. 14–15.
2 *Daily Worker*, 15 May 1948, p. 1.
3 *Daily Worker*, 18 May 1948, p. 1.
4 Notices of Motions, House of Commons Vote Bundle: The Stationery Office, vol. 4, 1947–48, pp. 3217, 3242.
5 *Daily Worker*, 22 May 1948, p. 1.
6 *Daily Worker*, 22 May 1948, p. 1.
7 The Slansky trials took place in Prague in 1952 when 14 Czech politicians, 11 of whom were Jews, were accused of taking part in a 'world-wide Jewish nationalist–Zionist imperialist' conspiracy against Czechoslovakia. Under torture, the deputy premier Rudolf Slansky, confessed to being a Zionist and a US agent. The so-called 'Doctors' Plot' took place in 1953: nine Russian doctors, seven of whom were Jewish, were accused of collaborating with the Western intelligence services (Caute, 1964, p. 202; Gitelman, 1990, pp. 19–21).
8 *World News and Views*, no. 50 (1953), p. 591.
9 *Daily Worker*, 31 July 1956, p. 1.
10 *Daily Worker*, 1 September 1956, p. 1.
11 *Labour Monthly*, December 1956, p. 560.
12 *World News*, 22 December 1956, pp. 815–19.
13 *Marxism Today*, January 1959, p. 24.
14 *World News*, 27 October 1956, p. 687.
15 *Marxism Today*, March 1959, p. 96.
16 Interview with Solly Kaye.
17 *World News*, 8 March 1958, p. 156.
18 Undated document (CPGB).
19 Memorandum from Idris Cox to the Political Committee (CPGB, 7 November 1956).
20 Minutes of a meeting of 'Jewish comrades' (CPGB, 11 September 1957).
21 Policy statement on the Jewish Question (CPGB, September 1958).
22 NJC policy statement (CPGB, September 1958).
23 *Morning Star*, 10 June 1967, p. 2.
24 *Morning Star*, 6 June 1967, p. 1
25 *Morning Star*, 14 June 1967, p. 2.
26 Untitled document signed by A. Lewish and D. Jacobs from the Prestwich branch and D. Nesbitt and J. Garman from the Crumpsall branch.
27 Correspondence from Idris Cox to Tom McWhinnie (CPGB, 16 December 1968).
28 Correspondence from Idris Cox to Maurice Lichtig (CPGB, 13 January 1969).
29 See *Comment*, 25 February 1967, p. 117.
30 Report of the 36th National Conference of the CPGB (1979), p. 7.
31 *Morning Star*, 8 June 1982, p. 1.
32 *Marxism Today*, August 1982, pp. 6–7.
33 *Morning Star*, 11 October 1982, p. 3.
34 *Morning Star*, 8 June 1982, p. 1.
35 *Morning Star*, 3 April 1982, p. 3.
36 *Morning Star*, 8 June 1982, p. 1.

37 *Morning Star*, 9 October 1982, p. 3.
38 *Morning Star*, 9 October 1982, p. 3.
39 'A Land With People' (CPGB, May 1982), p. 30.
40 *Marxism Today*, April 1983, pp. 14–17. The Kach Party was founded by Rabbi Meir Kahane in 1977. Kahane became a member of the Knesset in 1984 but the Israeli High Court stopped him from seeking a return to the Israeli parliament in 1988 on the ground that he was racist and undemocratic for advocating the expulsion of Palestinians from Israel and the occupied territories (Ovendale, 1992, p. 285).
41 *Marxism Today*, August 1982, p. 11.
42 *Marxism Today*, April 1983, p. 14.
43 *Marxism Today*, May 1987, p. 47.
44 'Soviet Opinion in the Middle East and the Adventures of International Zionism' (Moscow: Novosti Press Agency Publishing House, 1970), pp. 48–50.
45 For a full discussion of anti-Zionism in Poland, see Ciolkosz (1979), pp. 137–52.
46 *Jewish Chronicle*, 23 January 1953.
47 *Morning Star*, 11 June 1982, p. 1, 13 June 1982, p. 3.
48 Interview with Solly Kaye.
49 Weekly letter of the CPGB Executive Committee, 5 October 1945; *Jewish Clarion*, December 1945, pp. 1, 4.
50 Manifesto For New Times (CPGB, 1988), p. 13.
51 US Secretary of State George Marshall's plan for the economic reconstruction of Europe. The Soviet Union opposed the plan because it viewed it as a US attempt to undermine its influence in Europe.
52 *Labour Monthly*, December 1956, p. 564.
53 *Morning Star*, 16 June 1967, p. 1.
54 *Daily Worker*, 17 September 1956, p. 1.
55 *World News*, 25 August 1956, p. 534.
56 *Daily Worker*, 5 November 1956, p. 1.
57 *Morning Star*, 13 June 1967, p. 1.

7 The French Left and Israel

1 *Le Populaire*, 6 July 1946.
2 *Le Populaire*, 2 May 1947, p. 4.
3 *Le Populaire*, 6 July 1946, 18 March 1947, p. 4.
4 *Le Populaire*, 15 May 1948, p. 1.
5 See *Le Populaire*, 27 November 1956.
6 *Tribune*, 16 November 1956, p. 3.
7 *Tribune*, 9 November 1956, p. 3.
8 *Le Populaire*, 1–2 June 1967, p. 1.
9 *Le Populaire*, 3–4 June 1967.
10 *Le Nouvel Observateur*, 4 October 1967.
11 *Le Nouvel Observateur*, 28 June 1967.
12 *Le Nouvel Observateur*, 1 June 1967.
13 *Le Monde*, 13 July 1982.
14 Philip Charles Habib, special US presidential envoy to the Middle East, 1981–83 (Ovendale, 1992, p. 163).

15 *Le Monde*, 21 September 1982.
16 *Le Matin*, 20 September 1982, p. 14.
17 *Le Monde*, 1 October 1982.
18 *Le Monde*, 21 September 1982.
19 *Le Monde*, 23 September 1982.
20 *Le Monde*, 23 September 1982.
21 *Le Monde*, 11–12 July 1982.
22 *Le Populaire*, 6 November 1956.
23 *Le Populaire*, 13 September 1956, p. 1.
24 *Le Populaire*, 13 June 1967.
25 *Le Populaire*, 1–2 June 1967, p. 4.
26 *Le Populaire*, 7 May 1947, p. 4.
27 *Le Populaire*, 2 May 1947, p. 4.
28 *Le Populaire*, 1–2 June 1967, p. 4.
29 *Le Monde*, 23 September 1982.
30 *Le Populaire*, 27 November 1956.
31 *Le Monde*, 4 November 1966, p. 4; *Quotidien de Paris*, 13 October 1976.
32 *Le Nouvel Observateur*, 15 June 1967.
33 *Le Populaire*, 1–2 June 1967, p. 4.
34 Foreign minister from 1981 to 1984.
35 *Le Monde*, 21 September 1982.
36 *Le Monde*, 7 July 1982.
37 *Le Monde*, 23 September 1982.
38 *Le Monde*, 3 July 1982.
39 *Le Monde*, 24 September 1982.
40 *L'Humanité*, 15 May 1948, p. 3.
41 *L'Humanité*, 28 April 1948, p. 1.
42 *L'Humanité*, 15 May 1948, p. 3.
43 *Daily Mail*, 1 August 1947.
44 *L'Humanité*, 19 May 1948, p. 1.
45 *Paris-Presse*, 4 August 1956.
46 *L'Humanité*, 17 September 1956.
47 *L'Humanité*, 10 September 1956, 13 September 1956.
48 *Le Populaire*, 27 November 1956.
49 *Le Populaire*, 21 September 1956.
50 *L'Humanité*, 10 September 1956.
51 See *Horizons*, July–August 1956, pp. 13–18; *La Pensée*, September–October 1956, pp. 3–9, November–December 1956, pp. 9–31.
52 *Horizons*, December 1956, pp. 3–4.
53 See *La Nouvelle Critique*, no. 44 (March 1953), pp. 3–31.
54 *L'Humanité*, 7 June 1967.
55 *L'Humanité*, 13 June 1967.
56 *L'Humanité*, 5 June 1967, 11 July 1967.
57 *Cahiers du Communisme*, July–August 1967, p. 6.
58 *L'Humanité*, 6 June 1967.
59 *Le Monde*, 13 June 1967.
60 *L'Humanité*, 7 June 1982.
61 *Le Monde*, 22 September 1982.
62 *Le Monde*, 21 September 1982.

63 *L'Humanité*, 7 January 1982, p. 1; *La Pensée*, July–August 1982, pp. 11–12.
64 *Le Monde*, 24 September 1982.
65 *La Pensée*, July–August 1982, p. 11.
66 I got this impression from a conversation with a long-time member of the PCF.
67 *Le Monde*, 23 September 1982.
68 *La Nouvelle Critique*, March 1953, p. 21.
69 *Le Monde*, 21 September 1956.
70 *Tribune*, 7 September 1956, p. 1.

Bibliography

Abitbol, M. (1989) *Les Deux Terres Promises, Les Juifs de France et le Sionisme, 1897–1945*, Paris: Olivier Orban.

Abrams, P. (1980) 'History, Sociology, Historical Sociology', *Past and Present*, vol. 87, pp. 3–16.

Adams, J. (1992) *Tony Benn: A Biography*, London: Jonathan Cape.

Adams, M. and Mayhew, C. (1975) *Publish it Not... The Middle East Cover-Up*, London: Longman.

Adereth, M. (1984) *The French Communist Party, a Critical History (1920–84)*, Manchester: Manchester University Press.

Ahmed, Akbar S. (1992) *Postmodernism and Islam, Predicament and Promise*, London and New York: Routledge.

Ajami, F. (1983) *The Arab Predicament*, Cambridge: Cambridge University Press.

Alderman, G. (1983) *The Jewish Community in British Politics*, Oxford: Oxford University Press.

Alderman, G. (1989) *London Jewry and London Politics, 1889–1986*, London: Routledge.

Alderman, G. (1992) *Modern British Jewry*, Oxford: Clarendon Press.

Allen, J. (1987) *Perdition*, London: Ithaca.

Al-Mani, S. and Al-Shaikhly, S. (1983) *The Euro-Arab Dialogue, A Study in Diplomacy*, London: Frances Pinter.

Anwar, M. (1986) *Race and Politics*, London: Tavistock.

Avineri, S. (1982) 'Antisemitism Today: A Symposium', *Patterns of Prejudice*, vol. 16, pp. 4–5.

Avineri, S. (1992) 'Marxism and Nationalism', in J. Reinharz and G. L. Mosse (eds), *The Impact of Western Nationalisms*, London: Sage, pp. 283–304.

Ayubi, N. (1994) 'Pan-Arabism', in M. Foley, (ed.), *Ideas That Shape Politics*, Manchester: Manchester University Press, pp. 162–71.

Bell, C. and Newby, H. (eds) (1977) *Doing Sociological Research*, London: George Allen & Unwin.

Bell, David S. and Criddle, B. (1988) *The French Socialist Party, Resurgency and Victory*, Oxford: Clarendon Press.

Bell, David S. and Criddle, B. (1989) 'Review Article: The Decline of the French Communist Party', *British Journal of Political Science*, vol. 19, pp. 515–36.

Benn, T. (1987) *Out of the Wilderness, Diaries, 1963–1967*, London: Hutchinson.

Benn, T. (1992) *The End of an Era, Diaries, 1980–90*, ed. R. Winstone, London: Hutchinson.

Benner, Erica L. (1988) 'Marx and Engels on Nationalism and National Identity: A Reappraisal', *Millennium*, vol. 17, pp. 1–23.

Berrington, H. (1973) *Backbench Opinion in the House of Commons, 1945–55*, Oxford: Pergamon Press.

Berrington, H. (1982) 'The Labour Left in Parliament: Maintenance, Erosion and Renewal', in D. Kavanagh, (ed.), *The Politics of the Labour Party*, London: Allen & Unwin.

Billig, M. (1984a) 'Anti-Jewish Themes and the British Far Left – I', *Patterns of Prejudice*, vol. 18, pp. 3–17.

Billig, M. (1984b) 'Anti-Jewish Themes and the British Far Left – II', *Patterns of Prejudice*, vol. 18, pp. 28–34.

Billig, M. (1995) *Banal Nationalism*, London: Sage.

Birnbaum, P. (1992) *Anti-Semitism in France, A Political History from Leon Blum to the Present*, Oxford UK and Cambridge, Mass.: Blackwell.

Bourne, J. (1987) 'Homelands of the mind: Jewish feminism and identity', *Race and Class*, vol. 29, pp. 5–24.

Bowie, Robert R. (1989) 'Eisenhower, Dulles and the Suez Crisis', in W. R. Louis and R. Owen (eds), *Suez 1956*, Oxford: Clarendon Press, pp. 189–214.

Brand, Carl F. (1974) *The British Labour Party*, Stanford, CA: Hoover Institution Press.

Brenner, L. (1983) *Zionism in the Age of the Dictators*, London: Croom Helm.

Brod, P. (1979) 'Soviet–Israeli Relations 1948–56: from Courtship to Crisis', in Robert S. Wistrich (ed.), *The Left Against Zion, Communism, Israel and the Middle East*, London: Vallentine, Mitchell, pp. 50–70.

Brown, G. (1971) *In My Way*, London: Gollancz.

Budge, I. and Keman, H. (1990) *Parties and Democracy*, Oxford: Oxford University Press.

Bullock, A. (1983) *Ernest Bevin, Foreign Secretary, 1945–1951*, London and Basingstoke: Heinemann.

Bulmer, M. (1974) 'Review Article: Sociology and History: Some Recent Trends', *Sociology*, vol. 8, pp. 137–150.

Bulmer, M. (ed.) (1977) *Sociological Research Methods*, London: Macmillan.

Burns, John W. (1997) 'Party Policy Change: The Case of the Democrats and Taxes, 1956–68', *Party Politics*, vol. 3, pp. 513–32.

Butler, D. and Kavanagh, D., (1992) *The British General Election of 1992*, Basingstoke: Macmillan, St Martin's Press.

Butler, D. and Pinto-Duschinsky, M. (1971) *The British General Election of 1970*, London and Basingstoke: Macmillan, St Martin's Press.

Byrd, P. (1987) 'Great Britain: Parties in a Changing System', in A. Ware (ed.), *Political Parties, Electoral Change and Structural Response*, Oxford: Basil Blackwell, pp. 205–24.

Callaghan, J. (1988) 'The British Road to Eurocommunism: The Communist Party of Great Britain', in M. Waller and M. Fennema (eds), *Communist Parties in Western Europe, Decline or Adaptation?*, Oxford: Basil Blackwell, pp. 224–43.

Callaghan, J. (1990a) *Socialism in Britain*, Oxford: Basil Blackwell.

Callaghan, J. (1990b) 'The Left Since 1964', in A. Seldon (ed.), *U.K. Political Parties Since 1945*, New York and London: Philip Allan, pp. 63–78.

Callaghan, J. (1993) 'In Search of Eldorado: Labour's Colonial Economic Policy', in J. Fyrth (ed.), *Labour's High Noon, the Government and the Economy 1945–51*, London: Lawrence & Wishart, pp. 115–34.

Campbell, J. (1987) *Nye Bevan and the Mirage of British Socialism*, London: Weidenfeld and Nicolson.

Campbell, John C. (1989) 'The Soviet Union, the United States, and the Twin Crises of Hungary and Suez', in W. R. Louis and R. Owen (eds), *Suez 1956*, Oxford: Clarendon Press, pp. 233–56.

Carlebach, J. (1985) 'Review of That's Funny, You Don't Look Anti-Semitic', *The Jewish Journal of Sociology*, vol. 27, pp. 38–41.

Carlton, D. (1988) *Britain and the Suez Crisis*, Oxford: Basil Blackwell.

Caron, V. (1985) 'Prelude to Vichy: France and the Jewish Refugees in the Era of Appeasement', *Journal of Contemporary History*, vol. 20, pp. 157–76.

Castle, B. (1984) *The Castle Diaries 1964–70*, London: Weidenfeld and Nicolson.

Castle, B. (1993) *Fighting All The Way*, London: Pan.

Caute, D. (1964) *Communism and the French Intellectuals, 1914–1960*, London: Andre Deutsch.

Caute, D. (1973) *The Fellow-Travellers*, London: Weidenfeld and Nicolson.

Caute, D. (1988) *Sixty-Eight, The Year of the Barricades*, London: Paladin.

Cesarani, D. (1987) 'The Perdition Affair', *The Jewish Quarterly*, vol. 34, pp. 6–9.

Cesarani, D. (1990) 'The Perdition Affair', in R. S. Wistrich (ed.), *Anti-Zionism and Antisemitism in the Contemporary World*, London: Macmillan in association with the Institute of Jewish Affairs, pp. 53–60.

Charlot, M. (1985) 'The Ethnic Minorities' Vote', in A. Ranney (ed.), *Britain at the Polls 1983*, American Enterprise Institute, Duke University Press, pp. 139–54.

Cheyette, B. (1983) 'Pathological anti-Zionism and the "revisionism" of the left', *Patterns of Prejudice*, vol. 17, pp. 49–51.

Chomsky, N. (1986) 'Middle East terrorism and the American ideological system', *Race & Class*, vol. 28, pp. 1–27.

Chomsky, N. (1987) *The Chomsky Reader*, ed. J. Peck, London: The Serpent's Tail.

Ciolkosz, A. (1979) '"Anti-Zionism" in Polish Communist Party Politics', in Robert S. Wistrich (ed.), *The Left Against Zion*, London: Vallentine, Mitchell, pp. 137–52.

Coates, D. (1975) *The Labour Party and the Struggle for Socialism*, Cambridge: Cambridge University Press.

Codding, G. A. and Safran, W. (1979) *Ideology and Politics: The Socialist Party of France*, Boulder, CO: Westview Press.

Cohen, Percy S. (1980) *Jewish Radicals and Radical Jews*, London: Academic Press.

Cohen, Richard I. (1987) *The Burden of Conscience, French Jewish Leadership during the Holocaust*, Bloomington and Indianapolis: Indiana University Press.

Cohen, S. (1984) *That's Funny You Don't Look Anti-Semitic*, Leeds: Beyond the Pale Collective.

Cohen, W. B. and Wall, I. M. (1985) 'French Communism and the Jews', in F. Malino and B. Wasserstein (eds), *The Jews in Modern France*, Hanover and London: Brandeis University Press, pp. 81–102.

Colton, J. (1966) *Leon Blum, Humanist in Politics*, New York: Alfred A. Knopf.

Connor, W. (1984) *The National Question in Marxist–Leninist Theory and Strategy*, Princeton, NJ: Princeton University Press.

Connor, W. (1993) 'Beyond reason: the nature of the ethnonational bond', *Ethnic and Racial Studies*, vol. 16, pp. 373–89.

Coopey, R., Fielding, S. and Tiratsoo, N. (eds) (1993) *The Wilson Governments 1964–1970*, London and New York: Pinter.
Courtois, S. and Peschanski, D. (1988) 'From Decline to Marginalization, the PCF Breaks with French Society', in M. Waller and M. Fennema (eds), *Communist Parties in Western Europe, Decline or Adaptation?*, Oxford: Basil Blackwell, pp. 47–68.
Crick, B. (1982) *George Orwell, a life*, Harmondsworth: Penguin.
Crick, M. (1986) *The March of Militant*, London: Faber and Faber.
Criddle, B. (1987) 'France: Parties in a Presidential System', in A. Ware (ed.), *Political Parties, Electoral Change and Structural Response*, Oxford: Basil Blackwell, pp. 137–57.
Crossman, R. H. S. (1946) *Palestine Mission*, London: Hamish Hamilton.
Crossman, R. H. S. (1960) *A Nation Reborn*, London: Hamish Hamilton.
Crossman, R. H. S. (1976) *Diaries of a Cabinet Minister, Volume Two, 1966–68*, London: Hamish Hamilton and Jonathan Cape.
Crossman, R. H. S. (1981) *The Backbench Diaries of Richard Crossman*, ed. J. Morgan, London: Hamish Hamilton and Jonathan Cape.
Crossman, R. H. S. and Foot, M. (1946) *A Palestine Munich?*, London: Victor Gollancz.
Dalton, H. (1957) *The Fateful Years, Memoirs 1931–1945*, London: Frederick Muller.
Dalton, H. (1962) *High Tide and After*, London: Frederick Muller.
Davis, H. B. (1965) 'Nations, Colonies and Social Classes: The Position of Marx and Engels', *Science & Society*, vol. 29, pp. 26–43.
Davis, U., Mack A. and Yuval-Davis, N. (eds) (1975) *Israel and the Palestinians*, London: Ithaca.
Debray, R. (1977) 'Marxism and the National Question', *New Left Review*, vol. 105, pp. 25–41.
Demker, M. (1997) 'Changing Party Ideology: Gaullist Parties Facing Voters, Leaders and Competitors', *Party Politics*, vol. 3, pp. 407–26.
Denzin, N. K. (1970) *The Research Act in Sociology*, London: Butterworths.
Dessouki, Ali E. Hillal (1989) 'Nasser and the Struggle for Independence' in W. R. Louis and R. Owen (eds), *Suez 1956*, Oxford: Clarendon Press, pp. 31–42.
Deutscher, I. (1967) 'On the Israeli–Arab War', *New Left Review*, vol. 44, pp. 30–45.
Deutscher, I. (1968) *The Non Jewish Jew*, Oxford: Oxford University Press.
Djonovich, Dusan J. (ed.) (1989) *United Nations Resolutions Series II, Vol. VI 1966–67*, New York: Oceana.
Dobson, A. (1993) *Jean-Paul Sartre and the Politics of Reason*, Cambridge: Cambridge University Press.
Downs, A. (1957) *An Economic Theory of Democracy*, New York: Harper & Row.
Drucker, H. M. (1979) *Doctrine and Ethos in the Labour Party*, London: George Allen & Unwin.
Dunleavy, P. (1990) 'Reinterpreting The Westland Affair: Theories of the State and Core Executive', *Public Administration*, vol. 68, pp. 29–60.
Dunleavy, P. (1993) 'The Political Parties', in P. Dunleavy, A. Gamble, I. Holliday, G. Peele (eds), *Developments in British Politics 4*, London: Macmillan, pp. 123–53.

Duverger, M. (1964) *Political Parties, Their Organization and Activity in the Modern State*, London: Methuen.

Eban, Abba S. (1972) *My Country, The Story of Modern Israel*, Jerusalem: Weidenfeld and Nicolson.

Elazar, Daniel J. (1982) 'Religious Parties and Politics in the Begin Era', in R. O. Freedman (ed.), *Israel in the Begin Era*, New York: Praeger, pp. 102–20.

Elliot, G. (1993) *Labourism And The English Genius*, London and New York: Verso.

Epstein, Leon D. (1964) *British Politics and the Suez Crisis*, London and Dunmow: Pall Mall Press.

Esposito, John L. (1992) *The Islamic Threat, Myth or Reality?*, Oxford: Oxford University Press.

Ettinger, E. (1988) *Rosa Luxemburg: A Life*, London: Pandora Press.

Evans, M. (1991) 'The Left, Laïcité and Islam', *Modern & Contemporary France*, vol. 45, pp. 8–15.

Feldblum, M. (1993) 'Paradoxes of ethnic politics: the case of the Franco-Maghrebis in France', *Ethnic and Racial Studies*, vol. 16, pp. 52–74.

Finer, S. E., Berrington, H. B. and Bartholomew, D. J. (1961) *Backbench Opinion in the House of Commons, 1955–59*, New York and Oxford: Pergamon Press.

Foot, M. (1962) *Aneurin Bevan, A Biography, Volume One, 1897–1945*, London: MacGibbon & Kee.

Foot, M. (1973) *Aneurin Bevan, A Biography, Volume Two, 1945–1960*, London: Davis-Poynter.

Foot, M. and Jones, M. (1957) *Guilty Men*, London: Gollancz.

Foot, P. (1968) *The Politics of Harold Wilson*, Harmondsworth: Penguin.

Foote, G. (1986) *The Labour Party's Political Thought*, London: Croom Helm.

Freedman, R. O. (ed.) (1982) *Israel in the Begin Era*, New York: Praeger.

Gaffney, J. (1990) 'The Emergence of a Presidential Party: The Socialist Party', in A. Cole (ed.), *French Political Parties in Transition*, Aldershot: Dartmouth, pp. 61–90.

Gaitskell, H. (1983) *The Diary of Hugh Gaitskell, 1945–56*, ed. Philip M. Williams, London: Jonathan Cape.

Gewirtz, S. (1991) 'Anglo-Jewish Responses to Nazi Germany 1933–39: The Anti-Nazi Boycott and the Board of Deputies of British Jews', *Journal of Contemporary History*, vol. 26, pp. 255–76.

Gitelman, Z. (1990) 'The Evolution of Soviet Anti-Zionism: From Principle to Pragmatism', in R. S. Wistrich (ed.), *Anti-Zionism and Antisemitism in the Contemporary World*, London: Macmillan in association with the Institute of Jewish Affairs, pp. 11–25.

Glazer, N. (1982) 'Antisemitism Today: A Symposium', *Patterns of Prejudice*, vol. 16, pp. 23–4.

Golan, G. (1991) *Soviet Policies in the Middle East From World War II to Gorbachev*, Cambridge: Cambridge University Press.

Goldsworthy, D. (1971) *Colonial Issues in British Politics, 1945–1961*, Oxford: Clarendon Press.

Goldthorpe, J. H. (1991) 'The uses of history in sociology: reflections on some recent tendencies, *British Journal of Sociology*, vol. 42, pp. 211–30.

Gollancz, V. (1943) *Let My People Go*, London: Victor Gollancz.

Gollancz, V. (1945) *Nowhere To Lay Their Heads*, London: Victor Gollancz.

Gordon, M. R. (1969) *Conflict and Consensus in Labour's Foreign Policy, 1914–1965*, Stanford CA: Stanford University Press.

Gorny, J. (1983) *The British Labour Movement and Zionism 1917–1948*, London: Frank Cass.

Gourvish, T. and O'Day, A. (eds) (1991) *Britain Since 1945*, Basingstoke and London, Macmillan.

Graves, Pamela M. (1994) *Labour Women: Women in British Working Class Politics, 1918–1939*, Cambridge: Cambridge University Press.

Green, Nancy L. (1985) 'Socialist Anti-Semitism, Defense of a Bourgeois Jew and Discovery of the Jewish Proletariat', *International Review of Social History*, vol. 30, pp. 374–99.

Griffith, J. A. G. and Ryle, M. (1989) *Parliament, Functions, Practice and Procedure*, London: Sweet & Maxwell.

Guadagnini, M. (1993) 'A "Partitocrazia" Without Women: the Case of the Italian Party System', in J. Lovenduski and P. Norris (eds), *Gender and Party Politics*, London: Sage, pp. 168–204.

Gupta, P. S. (1975) *Imperialism and the British Labour Movement, 1914–1964*, London and Basingstoke: Macmillan.

Hall, Peter A. (1990) 'Pluralism and Pressure Politics', in P. Hall, J. Hayward and H. Machin (eds), *Developments in French Politics*, London: Macmillan, pp. 77–92.

Halliday, F. (1975) 'Inter-Imperialist Contradictions and Arab Nationalism', in Mack Davis, U. Davis, A. Mack and N. Yuval-Davis (eds), *Israel and the Palestinians*, London: Ithaca, pp. 160–71.

Halliday, F. (1979) *Arabia Without Sultans*, Harmondsworth: Penguin.

Halliday, F. and Alavi, H. (eds) (1988) *State Ideology in the Middle East and Pakistan*, London: Macmillan.

Halpern, B. (1961) *The Idea of a Jewish State*, Cambridge, Mass.: Harvard University Press.

Hanegbi, H. *et al.* (1971) 'The Class Nature of Israeli Society', *New Left Review*, vol. 65, pp. 3–11.

Harmel, R. and Janda, K. (1994) 'An Integrated Theory of Party Goals and Party Change', *Journal of Theoretical Politics*, vol. 6, pp. 259–87.

Harris, K. (1982) *Attlee*, London: Weidenfeld and Nicolson.

Harrison, R. (1991) 'Labour Party History: Approaches and Interpretations', *Labour History Review*, vol. 56, pp. 8–12.

Haseler, S. (1969) *The Gaitskellites, Revisionism in the British Labour Party 1951–64*, London: Macmillan.

Hazareesingh, S. (1994) *Political Traditions in Modern France*, Oxford: Oxford University Press.

Healey, D. (1989) *The Time of My Left*, London: Penguin.

Heffernan, R. and Marqusee, M. (1992) *Defeat From the Jaws of Victory*, London: Verso.

Hennessy, P. (1992) *Never Again, Britain 1945–1951*, London: Vintage.

Hirst, D. (1984) *The Gun and the Olive Branch*, London: Faber & Faber.

Hobsbawm, E. (1977a) *Revolutionaries*, London: Quartet Books.

Hobsbawm, E. (1977b) 'Some Reflections on the Break Up of Britain', *New Left Review*, vol. 105, pp. 3–23.

Hobsbawm, E. (1989) *Politics for a Rational Left*, London: Verso.

Hobsbawm E. and Ranger, T. (eds) (1983) *The Invention of Tradition*, Cambridge: Cambridge University Press.

Hodgson, G. (1981) *Labour At The Crossroads*, Oxford: Martin Robertson.

Holmes, C. (1979) *Antisemitism in British Society, 1876–1939*, London: Edward Arnold.

Hourani, A. (1989) 'Conclusion', in W. R. Louis and R. Owen (eds), *Suez 1956*, Oxford: Clarendon Press, pp. 393–410.

Howard, A. (1990) *Crossman*, London: Jonathan Cape.

Howe, S. (1993) *Anticolonialism in British Politics, The Left and the End of Empire 1918–1964*, Oxford: Clarendon Press.

Howorth, J. (1990) 'Foreign and Defence Policy: From Independence to Interdependence', in P. Hall, J. Hayward and H. Machin (eds), *Developments in French Politics*, Basingstoke: Macmillan, pp. 201–17.

Howorth, J. (1991) 'France and the Gulf War: From Pre-War Crisis to Post-War Crisis', *Modern & Contemporary France*, vol. 46, pp. 3–19.

Howorth, J. (1993) 'The President's Special Role in Foreign and Defence Policy', in J. Hayward (ed.), *De Gaulle to Mitterrand, Presidential Power in France*, London: Hurst, pp. 150–89.

Hunt, S. (1994) 'The "fringe" parties', in L. Robins, H. Blackmore and R. Pyper (eds), *Britain's Changing Party System*, London and New York: Leicester University Press, pp. 183–202.

Hunter, F. R. (1991) *The Palestinian Uprising: a War by Other Means*, Berkeley, CA: University of California Press.

Husbands, Christopher T. (1983) 'Race and Immigration', in T. Atkinson and J. Griffith *et al.*, *Socialism in a Cold Climate*, London: Unwin, pp. 161–83.

Husbands, Christopher T. (1986) 'Race and Gender', in H. Drucker, P. Dunleavy, A. Gamble and G. Peele (eds), *Developments in British Politics, 2*, Basingstoke: Macmillan, pp. 295–312.

Hyman, Paula E. (1985) 'French Jewish Historiography Since 1870', in F. Malino and B. Wasserstein, (eds), *The Jews in Modern France*, Hanover and London: University Press of New England, pp. 328–46.

Jackson, R. J. (1968) *Rebels and Whips*, London: Macmillan.

Jenkins, M. (1979) *Bevanism, Labour's High Tide*, Nottingham: Spokesman.

Johnson, R. W. (1981) *The Long March of the French Left*, London and Basingstoke: Macmillan.

Jones, M. (1970) 'Israel, Palestine and Socialism', *The Socialist Register*, London: The Merlin Press, pp. 63–87.

Judt, T. (1986) *Marxism and the French Left*, Oxford: Clarendon Press.

Katz, R. S. and Mair P. (1994) *How Parties Organize, Change and Adaptation in Party Organizations in Western Democracies*, London, Thousand Oaks, New Delhi: Sage Publications.

Kaufman, G. (1986) *Inside the Promised Land, A Personal View of Today's Israel*, Aldershot: Wildwood House.

Kavanagh, D. (ed.) (1982) *The Politics of the Labour Party* London: George Allen and Unwin.

Kavanagh, D. (1990) *Politics and Personalities*, London: Macmillan.

Kavanagh, D. and Morris, P. (1989) *Consensus Politics from Attlee to Thatcher*, Oxford: Basil Blackwell.

Kaye, S. (1971) *Zionism: A Socialist View*, London: CPGB.

Khalidi, R. (1989) 'Consequences of the Suez Crisis in the Arab World', in W. R. Louis and R. Owen (eds), *Suez 1956*, Oxford: Clarendon Press, pp. 377–92.

Kimche, J. (1960) *Both Sides of the Hill*, London: Secker & Warburg.

Knoke, D. (1990) *Political Networks, The Structural Perspective*, Cambridge: Cambridge University Press.

Knowles, C. (1979) 'Labour and anti-Semitism: An account of the political discourse surrounding the Labour Party's involvement with anti-Semitism in East London, 1934–6', in R. Miles and A. Phizacklea, *Racism and Political Action in Britain*, London: Routledge & Kegan Paul, pp. 50–71.

Koelble, Thomas A. (1987) 'Trade Unionists, Party Activists, and Politicians: The Struggle for Power over Party Rules in the British Labour Party and the West German Social Democratic Party', *Comparative Politics*, vol. 19, pp. 253–66.

Krammer, A. (1979) 'Prisoners in Prague: Israelis in the Slansky Trial', in R. S. Wistrich (ed.), *The Left Against Zion, Communism, Israel and the Middle East*, London: Vallentine, Mitchell, pp. 71–86.

Kramnick, I. and Sheerman, B. (1993) *Harold Laski, A Life on the Left*, London: Hamish Hamilton.

Kriegel, A. (1984) *Réflexion Sur Les Questions Juives*, Paris: Hachette.

Kushner, T. (1989) *The Persistence of Prejudice*, Manchester: Manchester University Press.

Kushner, T. (1990) 'Jewish Communists in twentieth-century Britain: the Zaidman Collection', *Labour History Review*, vol. 55, pp. 66–75.

Kyle, K. (1989) 'Britain and the Crisis, 1955–1956', in W. R. Louis and R. Owen (eds), *Suez 1956*, Oxford: Clarendon Press, pp. 103–30.

Kyle, K. (1991) *Suez*, London: Weidenfeld and Nicolson.

Lacouture, J. (1982) *Leon Blum*, New York and London, Holmes & Meier.

Lansley, S., Goss, S. and Wolmar, C. (1989) *Councils in Conflict: The Rise and Fall of the Municipal Left*, Basingstoke: Macmillan.

Laqueur, W. (1969) *The Struggle for the Middle East 1958–68*, London: Routledge & Kegan Paul.

Laqueur, W. (1971) 'Zionism and its Liberal Critics, 1896–1948', *Journal of Contemporary History*, vol. 6, pp. 161–82.

Laqueur, W. (1972) *A History of Zionism*, London: Weidenfeld and Nicolson.

Laqueur, W. and Rubin, B. (eds) (1984) *The Israel–Arab Reader*, Harmondsworth: Penguin.

Lawson, K. (ed.) (1980) *Political Parties & Linkage, A Comparative Perspective*, New Haven, CT, and London: Yale University Press.

Lawson, K. (1990) 'Political Parties: Inside and Out', *Comparative Politics*, vol. 23, pp. 105–19.

Lebzelter, G. C. (1978) *Political Antisemitism in England, 1918–1939*, London: Macmillan.

Leon, A. (1979) *The Jewish Question, A Marxist Interpretation*, New York and London: Pathfinder Press.

Lerman, A. (1990) 'Fictive Anti-Zionism: Third World, Arab and Muslim Variations', in R. S. Wistrich (ed.), *Anti-Zionism and Antisemitism in the Contemporary World*, London: Macmillan in association with the Institute of Jewish Affairs, pp. 121–38.

Lesch, A. M. and Tessler, M. (1989) *Israel, Egypt, and the Palestinians (From Camp David to Intifada)*, Bloomington and Indianapolis: Indiana University Press.

Leveau, R. and Schnapper, D. (1987) 'Religion et Politique: Juifs et Musulmans Maghrebins en France', *Revue Française de Science Politique*, vol. 37, pp. 855–85.

Levenberg, S. (1945) *The Jews and Palestine*, London: Poale Zion.

Levy, H. (1958) *Jews and the National Question*, London: Hillway.

Lewis, B. (1977) 'The Anti–Zionist Resolution', *Foreign Affairs*, vol. 55, pp. 54–64.

Lichtheim, G. (1968) 'Socialism and the Jews', *Dissent*, vol. 15, pp. 314–42.

Litvinoff, B. (1969) *A Peculiar People*, London: Weidenfeld and Nicolson.

Litvinoff, B. (ed.) (1984) *The Letters and Papers of Chaim Weizmann, Series B, Vol. II, December 1931–April 1952*, New Brunswick, NJ: Transaction Books and Rutgers University.

Lockman, Z. (1984) 'Review of J. Gorny, The British Labour Movement and Zionism, 1917–1948', *The Middle East Journal*, vol. 38, pp. 135–7.

Louis, W. R. (1984) *The British Empire in the Middle East, 1945–1951*, Oxford: Clarendon Press.

Louis, W. R. and R. Owen (1989) *Suez 1956*, Oxford: Clarendon Press.

Lovenduski, J. and Randall, V. (1993) *Contemporary Feminist Politics: Women and Power in Britain*, Oxford: Oxford University Press.

Lowdermilk, W. C. (1944) *Palestine, Land of Promise*, London: Victor Gollancz.

Lucas, N. (1974) *The Modern History of Zionism*, London: Weidenfeld and Nicolson.

Lustik, I. (1982) 'Israel's Arab Minority in the Begin Era', in R. O. Freedman (ed.), *Israel in the Begin Era*, New York: Praeger, pp. 121–50.

Machin, H. (1990) 'Changing Patterns of Party Competition' in Peter A. Hall, Jack Hayward, Howard Machin (eds), *Developments in French Politics*, Basingstoke: Macmillan.

Machin, H. (1993) 'The President, the Parties and Parliament', in J. Hayward (ed.), *De Gaulle to Mitterrand, Presidential Power in France*, London: Hurst; pp. 120–49.

Maidan, M. (1987) 'Marx on the Jewish Question: A Meta-Critical Analysis', *Studies in Soviet Thought*, vol. 33, pp. 27–41.

Mair, P. (ed.) (1990) *The West European Party System*, Oxford: Oxford University Press.

Malino, F. and Wasserstein, B. (eds) (1985) *The Jews in Modern France*, Hanover and London: University Press of New England.

Marrus, Michael R. (1985) 'Are the French Antisemitic? Evidence in the 1980s', in F. Malino and B. Wasserstein (eds), *The Jews in Modern France*, Hanover and London: University of New England Press, pp. 224–42.

Marrus, Michael R. (1986) 'Is There a New Antisemitism?', in M. Curtis (ed.), *Antisemitism in the Contemporary World*, Boulder, CO, and London: Westview Press, pp. 172–81.

Marrus, Michael R. and Paxton, Robert O. (1981) *Vichy France and the Jews*, New York: Basic Books.

Martin, K. (1953) *Harold Laski*, London and Southampton: Camelot.

Mayhew, C. (1975) 'A Personal Statement' in M. Adams and C. Mayhew, *Publish it not . . . The Middle East Cover-up*, London: Longman, pp. 16–26.

McKenzie, Robert T. (1963) *British Political Parties: the distribution of power within the Conservative and Labour Party*, London: Heinemann.

McLellan, D. (ed.) (1977) *Karl Marx, Selected Writings*, Oxford: Oxford University Press.

Medding, P. Y. (1972) *Mapai in Israel: Political Organisation and Government in a New Society*, Cambridge: Cambridge University Press.

Messina, Anthony M. (1989) *Race and Party Competition in Britain*, Oxford: Clarendon Press.

Michels, R. (1959) *Political Parties: A Sociological Study of the Oligarchical Tendencies of Modern Democracies*, New York: Dover.

Mikardo, I. (1988) *Back-Bencher*, London: Weidenfeld and Nicolson.

Miliband, R. (1976) 'Moving On', *Socialist Register*, London: The Merlin Press, pp. 128–40.

Miliband, R. (1985) 'The New Revisionism in Britain', *New Left Review*, vol. 150, pp. 5–28.

Minkin, L. (1980) *The Labour Party Conference: A Study in the Politics of Intra-Party Democracy*, Manchester: Manchester University Press.

Moïsi, D. (1981–2) 'France and the Middle East: A Balanced Policy is a Difficult Art', *Middle East Contemporary Survey*, vol. 6, pp. 75–8.

Morgan, J. (ed.) (1981) *The Backbench Diaries of Richard Crossman*, London: Hamish Hamilton and Jonathan Cape.

Morgan, Kenneth O. (1989) *Labour in Power, 1945–1951*, Oxford: Oxford University Press.

Morgan, Kenneth O. (1992) *Labour People*, Oxford: Oxford University Press.

Morgan, Kenneth O. (1994) 'Review of S. Howe, Anti-Colonialism in British Politics: The Left and the End of Empire, 1918–1964', *New Statesman and Society*, 18 February, pp. 40–1.

Morris, B. (1987) *The Birth of the Palestinian Refugee Problem, 1947–1949*, Cambridge: Cambridge University Press.

Mulé, R. (1997) 'Explaining The Party-Policy Link, Established Approaches and Theoretical Developments', *Party Politics*, vol. 3, pp. 493–512.

Nachmias, D. (1976) 'The Right-Wing Opposition in Israel', *Political Studies*, vol. 24, pp. 268–80.

Newton, K. (1969) *The Sociology of British Communism*, London: Penguin.

Norris, P. and Lovenduski, J. (1993) 'Gender and Party Politics in Britain', in J. Lovenduski and P. Norris (eds), *Gender and Party Politics*, London: Sage, pp. 35–59.

Norton, P. (1975) *Dissension in the House of Commons, 1945–1974*, London: Macmillan.

Norton, P. (1981) *The Commons in Perspective*, Oxford: Martin Robertson.

O'Hanlon, R. and Washbrook, D. (1992) 'After Orientalism: Culture, Criticism and Politics in the Third World', *Comparative Studies in Society and History*, vol. 34, pp. 141–67.

Oren, Michael B. (1990) 'Secret Egypt-Israel Peace Initiatives Prior to the Suez Campaign', *Middle Eastern Studies*, vol. 26, pp. 351–82.

Ovendale, R. (1979) 'The Palestine Policy of the British Labour Government, 1945–1946', *International Affairs*, vol. 55, pp. 409–31.

Ovendale, R. (1980) 'The Palestine Policy of the British Labour Government, 1947: The Decision to Withdraw', *International Affairs*, vol. 56, pp. 73–93.

Ovendale, R. (1984) *The Origins of the Arab-Israeli Wars*, London and New York: Longman.

Ovendale, R. (1989) *Britain, the United States and the End of the Palestine Mandate 1942–1948*, Woodbridge: Royal Historical Society and Boydell Press.

Ovendale, R. (1992) *The Middle East Since 1914*, London and New York: Longman.

Pappé, I. (1988) *Britain and the Arab-Israeli Conflict, 1948–1951*, London: Macmillan/St Antony's.

Pappé, I. (1990) 'Overt Conflict to Tacit Alliance: Anglo-Israeli Relations 1948–51', *Middle Eastern Studies*, vol. 26, pp. 561–81.

Peck, J. (ed.) (1987) *The Chomsky Reader*, London: The Serpent's Tail.

Peele, G. (1990) 'Parties, Pressure Groups and Parliament', in P. Dunleavy, A. Gamble, I. Holliday, G. Peele (eds), *Developments in British Politics 3*, London: Macmillan, pp. 69–95.

Pelling, H. (1975) *The British Communist Party, A Historical Profile*, London: Adam and Charles Black.

Pelling, H. (1991) *A Short History of the Labour Party*, London: Macmillan.

Peri, Y. (1983) *Between Battles and Ballots: Israeli Military in Politics*, Cambridge: Cambridge University Press.

Peters, J. (1994) 'Zionism', in M. Foley (ed.), *Ideas That Shape Politics*, Manchester and New York: Manchester University Press, pp. 155–61.

Pieterse, Jan N. (1985) 'Israel's role in the Third World: exporting West Bank expertise', *Race & Class*, vol. 26, pp. 9–30.

Pimlott, B. (1985) *Hugh Dalton*, London: Jonathan Cape.

Pimlott, B. (1986) *The Political Diary of Hugh Dalton, 1918–40, 1945–60*, London: Jonathan Cape.

Pitcairn, L. (1985) 'Crisis in British Communism: an Insider's View', *New Left Review*, vol. 153, pp. 102–20.

Platt, J. (1981a) 'Evidence and Proof in Documentary Research: I, Some Specific Problems of Documentary Research', *Sociological Review*, vol. 29, pp. 31–52.

Platt, J. (1981b) 'Evidence and Proof in Documentary Research: 2, Some Shared Problems of Documentary Research', *Sociological Review*, vol. 29, pp. 53–66.

Plummer, K. (1983) *Documents of Life, An Introduction to the Problems and Literature of a Humanistic Method*, London: George Allen & Unwin.

Polsby, Nelson W. (1984) *Political Innovation in America: The Politics of Policy Initiation*, New Haven, CT, and London: Yale University Press.

Pope, J. (1986) 'Anti-Racism, Anti-Zionism and Antisemitism – Debates in the British Women's Movement', *Patterns of Prejudice*, vol. 20, pp. 13–25.

Ramelson, B. (1967) *The Middle East, Crisis, Causes, Solution*, London: CPGB.

Rathbone, E. (1943) *Rescue The Perishing*, London: National Committee for Rescue from Nazi Terror.

Raymond, G. (1990) 'The Party of the Masses and its Marginalisation: The Communist Party', in A. Cole (ed.), *French Political Parties in Transition*, Aldershot: Dartmouth, pp. 42–60.

Reed, B. and Williams, G. (1971) *Denis Healey and the Policies of Power*, London: Sidgwick and Jackson.

Reinharz, J. and Mosse, George L. (eds) (1992) *The Impact of Western Nationalisms*, London: Sage.

Rennap, I. (1943) *Anti-Semitism And The Jewish Question*, London: Lawrence & Wishart.

Renzetti, Claire M. and Lee, Raymond L. (eds) (1993) *Researching Sensitive Topics*, London: Sage.

Rodinson, M. (1970) *Israel and the Arabs*, Harmondsworth: Penguin.

Rondot, P. (1987) 'France and Palestine: From Charles de Gaulle to Francois Mitterrand', *Journal of Palestine Studies*, vol. 16, pp. 87–100.

Rose, P. (1970) *Israel and the Left*, London: Labour Friends of Israel.

Rubinstein, W. D. (1982) *The Left, the Right and the Jews*, London: Croom Helm.

Safran, W. (1977) *The French Polity*, London and New York: Longman.

Safran, W. (1985) 'The Mitterrand Regime and its Policies of Ethnocultural Accommodation', *Comparative Politics*, vol. 18, pp. 41–64.

Safran, W. (1986) 'Problems of Perceiving and Reacting to Antisemitism: Reflections of a "Survivor"' in M. Curtis (ed.), *Antisemitism in the Contemporary World*, Boulder, CO, and London: Westview Press, pp. 273–87.

Said, Edward W. (1985) *Orientalism*, Harmondsworth: Penguin (first published in 1978).

Said, Edward W. (1980) *The Question of Palestine*, London and Henley: Routledge & Kegan Paul.

Said, Edward W. (1988) 'Spurious scholarship and the Palestinian question', *Race & Class*, vol. 29, pp. 23–39.

Said, Edward W. (1992) *The Question of Palestine*, London: Vintage.

Said, Edward W. and Hitchens, C. (1988) *Blaming The Victims*, London: Verso.

Samuel, R. (1986) 'Staying Power: The Lost World of British Communism, Part Two', *New Left Review*, vol. 156, pp. 63–113.

Sartre, J. P. (1965) *Anti-Semite and Jew* (New York: Schocken Books).

Saville, J. (1976) 'The Twentieth Congress and the Communist Party', *Socialist Register*, London: The Merlin Press, pp. 1–23.

Schnapper, D. (1987) 'The Jews and Political Modernity in France', in S. N. Eisenstadt (ed.), *Patterns of Modernity, Volume I: The West*, London: Frances Pinter, pp. 157–71.

Schnapper, D. and Strudel, S. (1983) 'Le "vote Juif" en France', *Revue Française de Science Politique*, vol. 33, pp. 933–61.

Schneer, J. (1988) *Labour's Conscience: The Labour Left 1945–51*, London: Unwin Hyman.

Schonfeld, William R. (1983) 'Review Article: Political Parties: The Functional Approach and the Structural Approach', *Comparative Politics*, vol. 15, pp. 477–500.

Seyd, P. (1987) *The Rise and Fall of the Labour Left*, Basingstoke: Macmillan.

Seyd, P. and Whiteley, P. (1992) *Labour's Grass Roots, The Politics of Party Membership*, Oxford: Clarendon Press.

Shamir, S. (1989) 'The Collapse of Project Alpha', in W. R. Louis and R. Owen (eds), *Suez 1956*, Oxford: Clarendon Press, pp. 73–102.

Shanin, T. (1988) 'The Zionisms of Israel', in F. Halliday and H. Alavi (eds), *State Ideology in the Middle East and Pakistan*, Basingstoke: Macmillan, pp. 222–55.

Sharabi, Hisham B. (1966) *Nationalism And Revolution In The Arab World*, Princeton, NJ, and New York: D. Van Nostrand.

Shaw, Eric (1994) *The Labour Party Since 1979: Crisis and Transformation*, London and New York: Routledge.

Shennan, A. (1989) *Rethinking France, Plans for Revewal 1940–1946*, Oxford: Oxford University Press.

Shlaim, A., Jones, P. and Sainsbury, K. (1977) *British Foreign Secretaries Since 1945*, Newton Abbot: David and Charles.

Sluglett, P. and M. Farouk-Sluglett (eds) (1991) *The Times Guide to the Middle East: the Arab World and its Neighbours*, London: Times Books.

Srebrnik, H. (1986) 'Communism and Pro-Soviet Feeling Among the Jews of East London, 1935–45', *Immigrants & Minorities*, vol. 5, pp. 287–304.

Szafran, M. (1990) *Les Juifs Dans La Politique Française: De 1945 a Nos Jours*, Paris: Flammarion.

Tarrow, S. (1975) 'Communism in Italy and France: Adaptation and Change', in Donald L. M. Blackmer and S. Tarrow (eds), *Communism in Italy and France*, Princeton, NJ: Princeton University Press, pp. 575–640.

Tessler, M. (1986) 'The Political Right in Israel: Its Origins, Growth, and Prospects', *Journal of Palestine Studies*, vol.15, pp. 12–55.

Vaisse, M. (1989) 'France and the Suez War', in W. R. Louis and R. Owen (eds), *Suez 1956*, Oxford: Clarendon Press, pp. 131–44.

Wainwright, H. (1987) *Labour: A Tale of Two Parties*, London: Hogarth Press.

Watkins, D. (1975) *Labour and Palestine*, London: LMEC.

Webb, C. (1979) *Eurocommunism and Foreign Policy*, London: Policy Studies Institute.

Webb, Paul D. (1994) 'Party Organizational Change in Britain: The Iron Law of Centralization?' in R. S. Katz and P. Mair (eds), *How Parties Organize. Change and Adaptation in Party Organizations in Western Democracies*, London, Thousand Oaks and New Delhi: Sage Publications, pp. 109–33.

Weiler, P. (1988) *British Labour and the Cold War*, Stanford, CA: Stanford University Press.

Weinstock, N. (1979) *Zionism: The False Messiah*, London: Ink Links.

Whiteley, P. (1983) *The Labour Party in Crisis*, London and New York: Methuen.

Wieviorka, M. (1991) *L'Espace du Racisme*, Paris: Editions Du Seuil.

Williams, Philip M. (1970) *French Politicians and Elections, 1951–1969*, Cambridge: Cambridge University Press.

Williams, Philip M. (1979) *Hugh Gaitskell, A Political Biography*, London: Jonathan Cape.

Williams, Philip M. (ed.) (1983) *The Diary of Hugh Gaitskell, 1945–1956*, London: Jonathan Cape.

Wilson, H. (1971) *The Labour Government, 1964–1970*, London: Weidenfeld and Nicolson.

Wilson, H. (1981) *The Chariot of Israel*, London: Weidenfeld and Nicolson and Michael Joseph.

Wingate Pike, D. (1993) 'Between the Junes: The French Communists from the collapse of France to the Invasion of Russia', *Journal of Contemporary History*, vol. 28, pp. 465–485.

Wistrich, Robert, S. (1975) 'The Marxist Concern With Judaism', *Patterns of Prejudice*, vol. 9, pp. 1–6.

Wistrich, Robert, S. (ed.) (1979a) 'Marxism and Jewish Nationalism: The theoretical roots of confrontation', in Robert S. Wistrich (ed.), *The Left Against Zion*, London: Vallentine, Mitchell, pp. 1–15.

Wistrich, Robert S. (1979b) 'Anti-Zionism in the USSR: From Lenin to the Soviet Black Hundreds', in Robert S. Wistrich, (ed.), *The Left Against Zion*, London: Vallentine, Mitchell, pp. 272–305.

Wistrich, Robert S. (1986) 'The "Jewish Question": Left-wing Anti-Zionism in Western Societies', in M. Curtis, (ed.), *Antisemitism in the Contemporary World*, Boulder, CO, and London: Westview Press, pp. 51–7.

Wistrich, Robert S. (ed.) (1990) *Anti-Zionism and Antisemitism in the Contemporary World*, Basingstoke and London: Macmillan in association with the Institute of Jewish Affairs.

Wright, V. (1992) *The Government and Politics of France*, London: Routledge.

Wrigley, C. (1993) 'Now you see it, now you don't: Harold Wilson and Labour's foreign policy', in R. Coopey, S. Fielding and N. Tiratsoo (eds), *The Wilson Governments, 1964–1970*, London and New York: Pinter, pp. 123–35.

Yuval-Davis, N. (1987) 'Marxism and Jewish Nationalism', *History Workshop*, vol. 24, pp. 82–110.

Ziegler, P. (1993) *Wilson, The Authorised Life*, London: HarperCollins.

Index

Abitbol, M. 139, 140, 152
Abramsky, Chimen 114, 115, 123, 126
Abse, Leo 69, 92
Acland, R. 36
Adams, J. 43, 52, 59
Adereth, M. 149
Afghanistan 122, 151
Afro-Asian Institute (Tel Aviv) 72
Ahmed, A. S. 26
Ajami, F. 25, 54, 71, 81
Alderman, G. 9, 20, 24, 29, 42, 43, 45, 46, 47, 48, 56, 58, 66, 69, 72, 76, 83, 87, 92, 94, 97, 99, 100, 102, 103, 104, 107, 112, 123, 124, 127
Algeria 9, 44, 60, 135, 139, 142
Allaun, Frank 59, 76
Allen, Jim 10
Allen, Yousef 87
Alliance France–Israel 145
Allon, Yigal 56, 72
Anderson, Evelyn 20
Andrieu, René, 150
Anglo-American Commission of Inquiry 28, 35, 112
anti-apartheid movement 81, 97, 98
anti-colonialism 19, 21, 26, 42, 53, 60, 64, 73–4, 138–9
anti-Semitism 9, 20–1
  anti-Zionism and 10, 83–4, 98–101
  in British Labour Party 28–30, 82–4
  Communist Party of Great Britain and 114
  in France 137
  Jewish terrorism and 31–2
  in Soviet Union 114–15, 120, 121, 148, 151
Anti-Slavery Society 26

Arab nationalism 19
  Communist Party of Great Britain and 112–13, 117–18, 129
  Foreign Office (UK) pro-Arab sentiments 36, 45
  in France 145, 162–3
  Labour Party (UK) and: creation of Israel and 25–7, 34; invasion of Lebanon (1982) and 87–106; Suez crisis and 48–51, 52–5, 59–62; war of 1967 and 70–1, 77–84
  socialism and 81–2
  Soviet support for 74, 120, 121
Arafat, Yasser 71, 106, 138
Argov, Shlomo 86, 89
Association France-Palestine 145
Attlee, Clement 6, 24, 128
  anti-Zionism 19, 30, 34
  Arab nationalism and 25
  creation of Israel and 38
  Jewish terrorism and 31–2
  Palestinian issue and 28
Austin, H. L. 36
Austria 57
Avineri, Uri 118
Ayrton-Gould, Barbara 34
Ayubi, N. 122

Ba'ath Party 25, 61, 62, 81
Bacon, Alice 36, 38, 47
Baghdad Pact 44
Baird, J. 36
Baker, Philip Noel 61
Balfour Declaration (1917) 19
Bandung conference 60
Barak, E. 5, 6
Barcai Zionist Party 24
Beauchamp, Kay 130
Begin, Menachem 11, 31, 90, 92, 99, 100, 107, 118
Bell, C. 15